Do We Need To Be So Screwed Up?!

A New Evolutionary Perspective on Happiness

Do We Need To Be So Screwed Up?!

A New Evolutionary Perspective on Happiness

Suki Pryce

BOOKS

Winchester, UK
Washington, USA

First published by O-Books, 2012
O-Books is an imprint of John Hunt Publishing Ltd., Laurel House, Station Approach,
Alresford, Hants, SO24 9JH, UK
office1@o-books.net
www.o-books.com

For distributor details and how to order please visit the 'Ordering' section on our website.

ISBN: 978 1 84694 663 9

A CIP catalogue record for this book is available from the British Library.

Design: Stuart Davies

Printed and bound by CPI Group (UK) Ltd, Croydon, CR0 4YY
Printed in the USA by Offset Paperback Mfrs, Inc

We operate a distinctive and ethical publishing philosophy in all areas of our business, from our global network of authors to production and worldwide distribution.

CONTENTS

Dedication:

To Hilary Alton, with gratitude and appreciation.

Foreword

by **Chris Knight**, author of *Blood Relations*

Nearly everyone assumes that the way we live in the Western world today is somehow 'natural'. It is supposedly natural for childcare to be such hard work, for women to be exploited within nuclear families, for kids to feel needy and insecure and for adults to suffer such extreme emotional pressures as to become mentally unbalanced or ill. Many today are unaware of the possibility of organising society in such a way that playfulness is a central value, childcare the most basic priority and free time the measure of our wealth. We have forgotten how to rear children so that they become spontaneously generous and caring.

This book by Suki Pryce surveys compelling evidence that for 90 per cent or more of our evolutionary history, humans have lived as egalitarian hunter-gatherers. The author reminds us that childcare throughout most of our evolution was co-operative, each child having several carers at all times. The effect was to produce emotionally balanced and joyous people. Anthropologist have long been aware of these facts, but this is the first book aimed at a general readership to break the conspiracy of silence on so much of our history. I do hope it is read widely and that its recommendations are taken up by all those who have ever asked themselves, "Isn't there a better way?"

Chris Knight is a political activist and professor of anthropology, best-known for his book *Blood Relations: Menstruation and the Origins of Culture.*

July, 2011

Chapter 1

Introduction

"There is a considerable industry in anthropology, and especially pop anthropology, to show the primitive as a Hobbesian being – with a life that is 'nasty, brutish and short'."
Lee, 1988

How This Book Came About

"History, such as it has hitherto been written, is almost entirely a description of the ways and means by which theocracy, military power, autocracy, and, later on, the richer classes' rule have been promoted, established and maintained… while, on the other side, the mutual-aid factor has been hitherto totally lost sight of; it was simply denied, or even scoffed at, by the writers of the present and past generation."
(Kropotkin, 1902)

"Tells me nothing that does not either vex or weary me"! I've always had an interest in simpler cultures – in hunter-gatherer and tribal peoples (for future reference, tribes are peoples who have domesticated plants and animals as opposed to hunter-gatherers who haven't); and from a young age read anything I could find on them. I also always had an instinctive disbelief in the sort of prehistory I was taught at school and in the popular stereotypes of cavemen; and an aversion to history generally as it was presented then. In fact, Jane Austen's character Catherine Morland in *Northanger Abbey* expresses my feelings very well:

"History, real solemn history, I cannot be interested in… I read it a little as a duty; but it tells me nothing that does not

> either vex or weary me. The quarrels of popes and kings, with wars and pestilences in every page; the men all so good for nothing, and hardly any women at all – it is very tiresome."!

As I got older, I increasingly tended to not subscribe to the agonic, 'nature red in tooth and claw' view of life – feeling that our culture consistently overemphasises the role that conflict, violence and so on has to play in animal and human societies.

One simple question. I have an academic background, but this book arose when I wasn't an academic any more. In my fifties, I had left my university career and was working in the world of contemporary crafts and arts. Always a keen and eclectic reader, some chance encounters with a few key thought-provoking books – notably Hugh Brody's *The Other Side of Eden*, and Terence McKenna's *Food of the Gods* – caused a little light bulb to switch on in my head. Many strands of thought which had been winding through my life for years came together in the one simple question: *"Do we humans actually need to be so screwed up?!"* At first I assumed that such an obvious and important question must have been tackled in at least one authoritative book or paper. But, as I started to contact authors, universities and other relevant institutions in the fields concerned, seeking mentors or colleagues, it gradually became clear that this wasn't the case. My interest in the subject therefore continued to grow; and what began as a research proposal gradually developed into a discussion paper, an article, and finally a book. And the more I investigated, the more evidence I found that, indeed, it seems we *don't* need to be so screwed up – that it's our genetic birthright, and our true nature to be *un*screwed up!

It has certainly been a great relief to me, as I've researched and written this book, to find masses of new research that confirms my own instinctive beliefs. A wide range of authors provide evidence which supports them; and it seems that a real sea-change is occurring among open-minded scholars across multiple disciplines from animal ethology to child psychology and neuroscience. In fact, I'm surprised that no one else wrote this book before me, as all the main bits of it already exist in other works. The key to putting everything together seems to me to hinge on distinguishing between *partnership* and *dominator* ways of living – something that most books don't do. These terms, coined by Riane Eisler in *The Chalice and the Blade* (1987), are used throughout the book, and can be defined as follows.

Partnership societies, which are exemplified by hunter-gatherer cultures, are strongly egalitarian and cooperative, mainly peaceful, and comprise largely happy and contented members. (The term *hunter-gatherers* is used in this book to cover various sorts of first or indigenous peoples, including those formerly denoted by the older term 'savages', most of whom have a largely hunter-gathering/foraging lifestyle. Occasionally the terms *foragers* or *indigenous peoples* are used in a similar way.)

This book is based on the premise that we evolved and lived in such societies from our prehuman beginnings maybe as much as two million years ago or even more, until the start of farming about 10,000 years ago. This ushered in the beginnings of dominator-style ways of life which have subsequently affected all cultures on earth to a greater or lesser extent, although partnership-style societies have continued to exist, and were widespread in historic times and into the twentieth century. And the point needs to be stressed that humans lived in this partnership-style way for *at least 90% of our time on earth,* and probably nearer 95% or more. This fact is widely agreed upon by authorities in the field (for example Hrdy, 2009).

Dominator societies, in contrast, are what we are used to and believe to be normal and inescapable. To a greater or lesser extent they are hierarchical, inequal, patriarchal, exploitative and materialistic, and tend to use manipulation, intimidation, coercion or force to achieve their ends, even if this is well hidden, as it tends to be in modern Western-style democracies. The result is usually social stratification, institutionalised unfairness or corruption, widespread popular resentment, and their negative consequences.

Mixtures of partnership and dominator ways. We also need to stress the point here that, although most societies have been largely dominator in nature for the past 10,000 years or so, partnership ways have always survived to some degree *within* them. For – if we are indeed designed by evolution and our genes (see the end of Chapter 3) to be partnership-type people, then dominator behaviour can only be an overlay on, or warping of, our fundamentally cooperative, egalitarian and cheerful natures. It may have been imposed on us by dominator upbringings and environment, but is a deviation from our innate temperaments – caused by nurture, not nature. So, if we look at everyday life, what we actually see is always a mixture of these two modes; and this point (which is touched upon again later in the book) needs to be borne in mind throughout the text. Nevertheless, much of what we experience in modern life is dominator-generated and driven; and this is discussed further in the last section of this chapter.

Sources

My academic and practical background is in amenity horticulture and landscape management – nothing to do with the subject of this book. So I'm not an anthropologist, archaeologist, sociobiologist, evolutionary psychologist, neuroscientist or expert in any of the fields used in making my case. However, it has been overseen by a professional anthropologist, which I trust ensures that it's free of any gross errors or omissions in that key area. Nor, in the writing of it, have I done any primary research in the relevant subjects or gone back to original papers. *Do We Need To Be So Screwed Up?!* is therefore based largely on other writers' reviews of information, and on key books which tie a lot of threads together or suggest new ways of looking at things.

Writing the book has also involved rediscovery – presenting the work of others in a new context, or reviving the message that forgotten classics still have to give us.

Esoteric/spiritual and popular culture sources. My main sources have been scientific and scholarly, but I've also used some esoteric and spiritual writings. Unfortunately, most professionals in the scientific community either don't believe in the actual reality of a spiritual dimension; or – if they do believe in it – usually don't feel free to admit this explicitly. So the importance of this aspect in, for example, the lives of hunter-gatherers or tribes is usually underplayed in professional accounts. Anthropologists have to acknowledge it, but they usually attempt to portray it 'objectively' in terms of beliefs, practices, rituals and so on ('non-utilitarian behaviours'), rather than entering sympathetically into the reality of the spiritual experiences themselves. And this lack of belief in alternative realities means that there must surely be a great gulf between the experienced reality of hunter-gatherers' actual lives, and what Western scientists describe? I have to break ranks with the scientific community here, as I *do* believe in the reality of a spiritual dimension, spiritual energies, and their effects – however, one wants to denote these; and am happy to talk about them directly. These matters are also relevant to this book's stance on its subject matter.

I've used quite a lot of sources and examples from popular culture too in order to illustrate ideas; and trust that strict rationalists or scholars will be tolerant of both the spiritual and the 'pop' material employed, for I want the book to accessible to open-minded everyday readers.

Below is a quick overview of the most important sources and their contribution to the lines of thought developed in *Do We Need To Be So Screwed Up?!*.

Conspiracies? However, first I'd like to explain something to lay readers who – like me – are naïve about anthropology and related disciplines such as sociobiology, evolutionary psychology, palaeontology, ethnography, ethology, neuroscience and so on. Be warned! Some of them are minefields of bias – riddled with hidden agenda and the skewing of information for ideological or political reasons. I was aware of some of the biases involved early on; but kept on being surprised and shocked by the extent to which valid information has been avoided, ignored, misread, belittled, dismissed, withheld, misinterpreted or explained away in the past, and even during the twentieth century and up to the present time. In his 1891 Preface to the Fourth Edition of *The Origin of the Family* (1884), Friedrich Engels described scholars as "attempting to kill" Karl Marx's *Capital* and Lewis H. Morgan's *Ancient Society*: "by silence"; and that the latter was "systematically suppressed". *Tout ca change,* one could say, as this is a process that has continued ever since.

Christopher Boehm (1999) highlights the fact that there are two opposing "philosophical folk traditions" about human origins and human nature in what he calls the Endless Debate; and that these are roughly aligned with the views of Rousseau ('noble savage') and Hobbes ('nasty, brutish and short'): "One tradition is hawkish and the other dovelike, and they lead many scholars to view humans as either essentially nice or essentially nasty." The biases I'm talking about mainly align with the hawkish, 'nasty' side, and are typically pro-dominator, pro-capitalist, pro-patriarchal, pro-nuclear-family, pro-Christian monogamy, pro-Protestant work ethic, and support a 'we are all selfish, competitive and warlike' nature-red-in-tooth-and-claw view of human nature. They are anti-feminist, anti-communism (in its true 'mutual aid' sense), and seek to hide or undervalue evidence for innate human egalitarianism, cooperativeness, altruism, kindness, peacefulness or other partnership-style traits. To what extent these biases are deliberate and to what extent unconscious let the conspiracy theorists among you decide! I just wish to alert readers to this issue, which runs through the disciplines above and has warped or limited much of what they have offered to date.

Thankfully, these biases have increasingly been challenged and redressed, particularly since the 1980s. For example, anthropologist Richard Lee tackled the egregious anti-communist agenda in his field head-on in his 1988 paper *Reflections on Primitive Communism*, wondering why: "If the evidence for primitive communism is so obvious and widespread, on what grounds do half the anthropologists in the world attempt to ignore it or explain it away?" Good publications have come out recently challenging the pro-nuclear-family, anti-matriliny agenda which has pervaded anthropology and its sister disciplines during the last hundred years (Knight, 2008; Alton, 2011). Recent research is also challenging unwarranted biases in fields such as ethology more and more; and new evidence is increasingly supporting the 'nice' point of view – a definite paradigm shift. This has encouraged me to believe that my own instincts about humans' innate unscrewed-upness, which initially got me writing this book, are valid. Opposing my views are many big-gun 'nasty' writers and schools of thought which oppose (vehemently, even) the stance of this book, and have amassed abundant contradictory evidence and reasoning to support their own, more dominator, views. We will look at both arguments throughout the book, and trust that this will give readers a fair basis on which to decide between them. Biases and suppression are discussed further in Chapter 8.

Main sources used. Clearly, in seeking sources, I've wanted to find authoritative, well-thought-of texts that broadly support my pro-partnership point of view regarding human origins and what's 'natural' to us. I've used four such books, all of which are discussed in much more detail Chapter 2. The first is *Wild Justice* (2009) by animal ethologist **Marc Bekoff** and his co-writer philosopher **Jessica Pierce**. This up-to-date book brings together the burgeoning scientific literature on animal prosocial behaviours and emotions such as cooperation, empathy, kindness, succourance, fairness, trust, and reciprocity; and makes a compelling case for common neural architecture and evolutionary continuity between social animals and humans. Bekoff is Professor Emeritus of Ecology and Evolutionary Biology at the University of Colorado. With Jane Goodall, he co-founded Ethologists for the Ethical Treatment of Animals, and is a patron of the Captive Animals Protection Society.

The other main sources comprise works by anthropologists.

Christopher Boehm is Professor of Anthropology and Director of the Jane Goodall Research Center at the University of Southern California. His *Hierarchy in the Forest: The Evolution of Egalitarian Behaviour* (1999) focuses on the 'puzzle' of egalitarianism and altruism in humans; and uses studies from primates and hunter-gatherers plus evolutionary theory to investigate how and why these might have arisen. (Altruistic behaviour is defined in social biology as reproductive donations to non-kin.)

Reader who, like me, are puzzled in turn as to why sharing and cooperation are 'puzzling', may be helped by this explanation:

> "Almost all evolutionary biologists assume that without sufficiently close genetic relatedness and an appropriate ratio of benefits to costs, caretaking and other cooperative propensities that do not directly increase the helper's own reproductive success would not have evolved."
>
> (Hrdy, 2009)

In other words, why do anything that doesn't directly aid the transmission of your own genes? This 'selfish gene' view is increasingly being challenged, and the issue is discussed further in later chapters of this book.

Also of great relevance here is London School of Economics-based British social anthropologist **James Woodburn**, particularly noted for his works on the nomadic Hadza hunter-gatherers of Africa, and his concepts of *immediate return* systems as opposed to *delayed return* systems. Woodburn adds an economist's penetrating analytical view, and unsentimental insights, to discussions of egalitarianism.

Sarah Blaffer Hrdy is Professor Emeritus of Anthropology at the University of California-Davis. Her *Mothers and Others: The Evolutionary Origins of Mutual Understanding* (2009) looks at the evolutionary basis for our striking "empathic responses to others and our eagerness to help and share with them" which make humans so unusual and different from other apes, and enabled us to develop shared parenting ('cooperative breeding') – a vital evolutionary gain.

Chris Knight was Professor of Anthropology at the University of East London from 2000 to 2010, and is a founding member of the Radical Anthropology Group. His ground-breaking *Blood Relations: Menstruation and the Origins of Culture* (1991) draws on anthropology, archaeology, primatology, human evolution and sociobiology; involves pre-capitalist economics, kinship, ritual and mythology; utilises Marxist theory, and is rooted in Engels' *The Origin of the Family, Private Property and the State*. Knight's radical and far-reaching theory is based on the idea of a 'sex strike' by women some time between 40,000 and 100,000 years ago bringing to an end prehuman ape-style behaviour, and instigating the great *Homo sapiens* social, sexual and cultural revolution.

These principal sources provide, I trust, sufficiently authoritative theoretical underpinnings to *Do We Need To Be So Screwed Up?!* In turn, their pro-partnership stance is a continuation of work done by others in the past – sometimes forgotten or misunderstood, but still of value. Writers and their works in this category that I've used include the following (in roughly chronological order).

Lewis Henry Morgan (1818–1881) was a pioneering American anthropologist and social theorist, "most readily, and justly, compared with those other giant intellects of his age, Charles Darwin and Herbert Spencer." (Fox, 2000, in Morgan, 2000 [1877]), and best known for his work on kinship and social structure, his theories of social evolution, and his ethnography of the Iroquois Native American peoples. He was excited to discover living matrilineal institutions among the Iroquois and other Native Americans; described comparable systems across much of the globe; and championed the historical priority of the matrilineal clan over patriliny and the nuclear family. He also championed the case for 'savages' having equal abilities to our own, in contrast to many of his contemporaries who viewed them as innately inferior; as "social fossils"; or as *cul-de-sac* "side branches of the main trunk of the evolutionary tree." (Fox in Morgan, 2000 [1877])

Friedrich Engels: *The Origin of the Family, Private Property, and the State: in the light of the researches of Lewis H. Morgan* (1884) is an anthropological classic – a discussion of 'Ancient Society' which describes the major stages of human development as they were commonly understood in Engels' time; and attempts to connect the transition into these stages with changes in the way that family is defined and the rules by which it is governed.

Peter Kropotkin was a zoologist, evolutionary theorist, geographer and anarcho-communist. *Mutual Aid: A Factor of Evolution* (1902) is his principal scientific work – an exhaustive scholarly and scientific investigation of collaborative, as opposed to competitive, behaviour in the plant, animal and human kingdoms. It provides a view of alternative life strategies to those of competition and hierarchy ('nature red in tooth and claw') proffered at the time by social Darwinists such as Francis Galton and Julian Huxley. Chris Knight describes Robert Briffault's 1927 *The Mothers* as an "encyclopaedic, magnificent, yet almost wholly ignored cross-cultural work"; and I feel that Kropotkin's *Mutual Aid* can be described in similarly glowing terms. Though aspects of it may be dated, or details have proved to be inaccurate, it is still an inspiring survey of its subject. Its overall message is as true now as it ever was; and some of Kropotkin's thoughts are decidedly prescient and are only lately being revealed as correct – for example, his belief in the extent of mutual aid among social animals, which is increasingly being confirmed by modern research and is reversing a long-standing pro-selfishness stance among scientists. And his overview of mutual aid in human history is, to my mind, a model of the way to teach history in schools – dealing with it as he does from the point of view of the long fall from, and battle for the mutual-aid way of life in the face of increasing dominator pressures. Largely unknown today, or ignored by scholars, I have found *Mutual Aid* to be a continuingly educational and inspirational work that has resoundingly survived the test of time. Bekoff and Pierce (2009) share this view, saying: "we might wonder what the intellectual history of evolution would look like had Kropotkin's ideas been taken more seriously."

Finally, of the older sources, **Robert Briffault**'s aforementioned 1927 *The Mothers* is a classic which has also shamefully fallen out of sight. Thankfully, however, it has been brought back into visibility through booklets prepared by Hilary Alton and published by the Radical Anthropology Group. Alton's 2011 *Matriarchy Really Did Exist*, which summarise Briffault's chapter on matrilocal marriage, is particularly relevant to this book. It also includes Briffault's *references*, which are omitted from most readily available copies of *The Mothers*.

Other scholars who have been important in the making of my case include Canadian anthropologist Professor **Richard B. Lee**, particularly famous for his work with hunter-gatherer societies. In 1966, Lee, with Irven DeVore, organised the seminal symposium (and subsequent 1968 book) *Man the Hunter* which aimed to bring together for the first time a comprehensive look at recent ethnographic research on hunter-gatherers. It marked a turning point in the way hunter-gatherers were viewed, ushering in an era where 'primitive' peoples began to be more widely recognised as the sophisticated and successfully adapted human beings that they are. Lee's ideas about primitive communism are particularly relevant to this book (Lee, 1988).

Because I'm not a professional anthropologist or archaeologist, I was helped to understand the field best by people who *are*, but who can also write readably for lay people like me. Such authors tend to reveal more about the kind of things relevant to this book (like fun, laughter and enjoyment of life, for example) than more scientific accounts do. An early inspiration for this book was anthropologist and activist **Hugh Brody**'s *The Other Side of Eden* (2001), which counterposes the nomadic yet psychologically-rooted and peaceful lives of hunter-gatherer peoples with the settled yet restless, expansionist, and potentially aggressive lifestyle of farmers. Like all the best anthropological writing for lay people it is observant, empathic, poetic and philosophical. British-American anthropologist **Colin Turnbull**'s classic *The Forest People* is a deservedly famous ethnographic study of the three years he spent with the Mbuti pygmies of the then-Belgian Congo in the late 1950s, in which he contrasts his forest-living subjects' lifestyle with that of nearby village-dwelling Africans, and compares the interactions of the two groups. The book became a best-seller when it appeared in 1961 – not surprisingly, as his style is accessible, and his observations are highly sympathetic and expressed in a most poetic way. **Daniel Everett**, US linguist and activist on behalf of indigenous peoples, is best known for his award-winning best-selling study of the Amazon Basin's Pirahã people and their language *Don't Sleep, There Are Snakes: Life and Language in the Amazonian Jungle* – a description of the decades that he and his family spent living with the Pirahã. This is another book that is both scientifically insightful, and sympathetic and readable. I also found **Annette Hamilton**'s in-depth analysis of the hunter-gatherer approach to childrearing in her excellent *Nature and Nurture* (1981; unfortunately not in print and expensive to obtain second-hand), based on her studies of Arnhem Land Aborigines in the late 1960s, invaluable. And well in advance of its time, too, is social worker **Hilary Alton**'s excellent 1984 unpublished paper, much inspired by Hamilton, on alternative approaches to childrearing and adoption.

More controversial authors who have been important to this book are **Riane Eisler** and **Marija Gimbutas**. Eisler is a social scientist, attorney and author whose work on cultural transformation has inspired scholars and social activists. Her best known book is *The Chalice and the Blade* (1987), which wove together evidence from art, archaeology, religion, social science, history and many other fields to tell a new story about humanity's cultural origins – painting a picture of peaceful, egalitarian, women-centred ancient societies which challenged patriarchal conceptions about our prehistoric past and our possible future. Eisler's invaluable concepts of partnership and dominator societies underlie the reasoning used in my book.

Eisler drew strongly on the works of **Gimbutas** – a Lithuanian-American archaeologist famous for her research into the Neolithic and Bronze Age cultures she termed "Old Europe". *The Civilization of the Goddess* (1991) set out what Gimbutas saw as the differences between the Old European system, which she considered peaceful, egalitarian, and goddess- and woman-centred ('matristic', 'gynocentric', or 'partnership' cultures in Eisler's terms), and the Bronze Age Indo-European patriarchal, male-centred (Eisler's 'androcratic' or 'dominator' cultures) societies which supplanted it. Unfortunately, both Gimbutas and Eisler are considered by many mainstream scholars to have unacceptably feminist, 'goddessy' or neopagan leanings, and tend to be distrusted for those reasons.

Also controversial is US author **Jean Liedloff**, whose tremendously insightful and lastingly influential *The Continuum Concept*

(1975) has been a key source for this book. As a young woman, she joined an expedition to Venezuela, and became fascinated by the indigenous Yequana people with whom she lived for two and a half years. *The Continuum Concept* documents her experience of the Yequana way of life, particularly their style of childrearing. Liedloff's prescient ideas relate to attachment theory; to Eisler's concept of a partnership way of life; and to this book's ideas about unscrewed-upness and its roots in undamaged childhoods, but she is definitely an outsider as far as mainstream academia goes. However, many scientists' work now backs up Liedloff's ideas – psychoanalytic psychotherapist **Sue Gerhardt**'s research in particular. Her highly-regarded 2004 book *Why Love Matters* (2004) proffers much the same message as Liedloff but reinforced with the accompanying underpinning biochemistry and neuroscience (see Chapters 6 and 7).

Another cogent critic of modern life and civilisation, and champion of the qualities of so-called primitive peoples, is anarcho-primitivist **John Zerzan** who brings what he calls a "Luddite/feminist/decentralized/anti-civilization" perspective to bear on modern life. As archaeologist Theresa Kintz puts it in her introduction to Zerzan's *Running on Emptiness* (2002):

> "The question of how we got from the Stone Age to the space age should be of interest to all inhabitants of planet earth. Zerzan argues that in understanding the primitive past we take the first step towards rejecting the pathological present and actualizing a future primitive."

Strangely parallel in attitude to Zerzan is **D.H. Lawrence**, whose *Lady Chatterley's Lover* (1928) expressed nearly identical views to Zerzan's three quarters of a century earlier!

My main spiritually-oriented sources include **Steve Taylor**'s *The Fall* (2005). This book has been important to me because its basic 'we don't need to be 'fallen'/screwed up' thesis is so similar to mine, although Taylor focuses on different aspects of the subject. *The Fall* has been criticised for its lack of academic rigour, and I disagree with some of its contentions; but its passionately-made case for the qualities of unfallen societies, for the ills of dominator society, and for the possibility of new, unfallen modes of life are very sympathetic to the theme of my book.

More classic spiritual writings which I've found helpful throughout my life as well as in the writing of this book are those of the early twentieth century practical visionary **Rudolph Steiner** (Wilkinson, 1993); and of the extraordinary Sufi-based teacher **George Gurdjieff** (Ouspensky, 1950). I've found both men proffer thought-provoking questions about, and satisfying answers to, many of life's big questions.

I've also felt I had to include **Marlo Morgan**'s *Mutant Message Down Under* (1991). I understand that this book is controversial, particularly in Australia, where it is set, because of its evident lack of authenticity and misrepresentation of Aboriginal life. However, if one takes it, as I do, simply as a sort of imaginative exploration of how human beings (Morgan's 'Real People') might once have existed – physically living in the simplest foraging way, but emotionally living in the most fully prosocial way, complete with extended spiritual abilities (telepathy, healing, ESP and so on) – I find it extraordinarily interesting and full of spiritual wisdom and inspiring ideas.

What's a Normal Human Being?

"New discoveries by evolutionarily minded psychologists, economists, and neuroscientists are propelling the cooperative side of human nature to center stage. New findings about how irrational, how emotional, how caring, and even how selfless human decisions can be are transforming disciplines long grounded in the premise that the world is a competitive place where to be a rational actor means being a selfish one. Researchers from diverse fields are converging on the realization that while humans can indeed be very

selfish, in terms of empathic responses to others and our eagerness to help and share with them, humans are quite unusual, notably different from other apes."

(Hrdy, 2009)

"Society as we know it now in the industrialised world is pathological... " (Kintz in Introduction to Zerzan, 2002). We currently live in a world in which a whole suite of dysfunctional behaviours and unhealthy states are considered to be normal or inevitable – caused by human nature, or contemporary pressures. These include burgeoning physical and mental health problems; an ever-increasing range of addictions; unhealthy sexuality; institutionalised injustice, inequality and corruption; all sorts of cruelty and violence; crime; and war. Most of us are taught, and believe, that life for human beings has always been more or less like this, that we are irredeemably aggressive and competitive; and that no other condition is possible for our species, which is doomed to this fate by Darwinian theory. This way of life and looking at the world is the *dominator* mode outlined earlier in this chapter (hierarchical, patriarchal, inequal, exploitative, materialistic).

It is the aim of this book to muster opposing evidence, and to try to prove that another – quite different – way of life is possible for human beings. Indeed, as the rest of *Do We Need To be So Screwed Up?!* seeks to show, abundant evidence from a wide range of authoritative sources indicates that *Homo sapiens* evolved as an almost entirely egalitarian and cooperative species, abundantly capable for at least 100,000 years (and probably much longer) of behaving in a largely prosocial, helpful, peaceful and – almost certainly – cheerful way! This different type of behaviour is the *partnership* way of living, again outlined earlier in this chapter. Moreover, modern scholars such as Boehm (1999), Knight (1991), and Hrdy (2009); and Kropotkin (1902) and Darwin himself before them, have mustered extensive evidence to show that our success as a species apparently entirely *depended* upon a radical leap from African Great Ape dominator-type, despotic, self-serving behaviour to cooperative childcare, food-sharing and other prosocial behaviours which enabled early humans to successfully rear children and exploit a wide range of new habitats some 100,000 years ago or more.

"Hardwired to connect". New discoveries in psychology, neuroscience, behavioural ecology, primatology and genetics are also providing increasing support for the basic premise of this book, showing that humans are "hardwired to connect" (Goleman, 2006); are biologically adapted to share, collaborate and cooperate; have an instinct for compassion; and that helpful, empathic behaviour is innate and the human default setting. Moreover, in animal studies:

> "There's now an enormous body of research on prosocial behaviour and new research is being published all the time on cooperation, altruism, empathy, reciprocity, succorance, fairness, forgiveness, trust, and kindness in animals ranging from rats to apes."
>
> (Bekoff and Pierce, 2009)

This animal research shows that humans have arisen from a mammalian past chock full of prosocial qualities; and that our own neurological underpinnings are simply an extension of those of many social animals.

Innately 'sane'. A basic premise of this book is therefore that human beings are *innately* capable of being far more sane, un-neurotic or civilised in their behaviour than contemporary Western-style dominator societies believe to be possible. In order to prove this, *Do We Need to Be So Screwed Up?!* draws upon evidence from contemporary, historic, and prehistoric hunter-gatherer[1]/partnership-style societies, and from animal studies, in order to demonstrate that most of the dysfunctional behaviour and unhealthy states which modern Westernised societies consider to be normal or inevitable are neither, but are cultural and a result of conditioning – of damaging childhoods in particular (see Chapter 7). In other words, they are a product of nurture, not nature.

Partnership and dominator people are intrinsically different. So the view taken in this book is that *undamaged*, unscrewed up human beings have always been and still are capable of living peaceful, happy, kind, cooperative lives. However, a time came around 10,000 years ago when changes occurred in human society which began to harm people's psyches and to incline them towards more despotic, aggressive, hierarchical ways of life (see Chapters 5 and 6). So began the growth of fighting, wars, hierarchical social structures, institutionalised injustice, brutality, tyranny and other manifestations of the dominator psyche which have continued, and even worsened in some ways, up to the present day.

From the point of view taken in this book, people who have been reared in unscrewed up cultures are *qualitatively* different in many ways from those who have grown up in, and been psychologically damaged by, dominator societies. Obviously there are degrees; and people are more, or less, screwed up in dominator societies. But they pretty well all have common negative traits which stem from dominator-style socialisation (see Chapter 7); whereas undamaged people are all pretty much unscrewed up, and display suites of positive characteristics and abilities which I believe stem from this unscrewed-upness (see Chapters 3 and 6).

Clearly, I am one of Boehm's 'nice' protagonists, so perhaps "I would think that, wouldn't I?"! Nevertheless, there does appear to be plenty of evidence which indicates that damaged and undamaged people are *intrinsically, qualitatively, largely irreversibly* different from each other in many key ways – different in the way that, say, a broken (even if glued-back-together) and an unbroken glass are. And I believe that the evidence also shows that this is largely a result of the deep, usually permanent, physiological, neurological and hence both physical and psychological harm which dominator-style childhoods inflict on infants (see Chapter 7). For this reason, I part company from some of my main sources because – excellent and scholarly though they are – it seems to me a real problem that they treat human history as a continuum; write as if people in dominator societies (either today or in the past) are essentially the same as undamaged partnership-type peoples; and don't see a problem in extrapolating back in time from dominator life and peoples in order to make assumptions about our prehistoric hunter-gatherer forebears.

This factor also applies more generally. For example, from this book's point of view, all standard analyses of human nature such as those which underlie personality tests or assessments of psychological health are flawed because they're based upon 'damaged goods' – on dominator-influenced people rather than upon healthy humans. They therefore treat as within the normal spectrum traits which would be considered definitely abnormal within partnership societies.

Questions This Book Seeks to Answer

To sum up this introductory chapter so far, then: the purpose of this book is to try to shed light on that most simple and straightforward of questions: *do human beings need to be so screwed up?* In order to do this, it examines the linked questions below.

- Do hunter-gatherer, partnership-style societies (in other words, those that are closest in type to the earliest – prehistoric – forms of society) create psychologically healthier, happier people than dominator-style cultures do?
- What are the values, attitudes, and behaviours which characterise such partnership societies?
- Can partnership-type values also be found in more

developed or 'civilised' cultures, or in villages, towns or cities – that is, in non-hunter-gatherer societies?

- Why and how did dominator societies first come into being? How are dominator cultures and their accompanying ills perpetuated?
- What are the chief effects of dominator culture on people's bodies, minds, and spirits?
- Why are we so unaware of our partnership history?
- What *are* health and happiness? What are their roots?
- Can we learn from partnership societies how to create saner, happier people? What's stopping us from doing so? How can we help the world move towards a happier future?

The Concepts of Partnership and Dominator are Powerful Analytical Tools

As the start of this chapter indicates, I have found the concepts of *partnership* and *dominator* to be very powerful ones; and they have been extremely useful in analysing the scientific and other material used in compiling the book. One can apply them as a kind of litmus test in order to evaluate all sorts of things or ideas – trivial, popular or low culture matters as well as serious or scientific ones – and locate them on a cooperative-competitive spectrum. In this section we give some examples in order to illustrate the usefulness of these terms. Let's also remind ourselves again that people and their works in dominator societies are always a *blend* of partnership and dominator characteristics, reflecting whatever mix of innate partnership nature, plus dominator conditioning, prevails in them.

Science. Starting with the serious side, clearly the idea of partnership or dominator approaches to life applies to the *scientific* sources that are relevant to, say, the subject matter of this book. Needless to say, because we live in a dominator culture which has been powerful for many thousands of years, the prevailing points of view or paradigms in our culture are dominator ones too. Science is no exception to this; and – as we've already seen in *Sources* above – the main sciences relevant to *Do We Need to Be So Screwed Up?!* have definitely tended to have a pro-dominator agenda, even if this is largely unconscious. So, for example, early writers such as Morgan, Engels, Kropotkin and Briffault, who experienced or described primitive communism, mutual aid, matriliny, classificatory kinship (see Chapter 2 for definitions), and the absence of the nuclear family in simple hunter-gatherer societies, have subsequently largely been sidelined by mainstream anthropology, despite the validity of their findings. Much archaeological and anthropological evidence was also viewed, analysed and interpreted from a highly patriarchal point of view. Dominator culture chooses the science that upholds its views, and has therefore tried to suppress work that supports – as in the above example – the idea of primitive communism as opposed to capitalism, matriliny as opposed to patriarchy, or mutual aid as opposed to 'nature red in tooth and claw'. This process continues today, with – for example – funding for scientific work tending to flow towards projects that sustain the prevailing pro-capitalist, pro-patriarchal agenda of modern developed states. This issue is discussed further in Chapter 8.

Politics, business. Moving on to everyday life, we can see the effects of the dominator ethos everywhere. For example, politics and big business tend by their very nature (close to the heart of the state) to have a strongly dominator flavour, and to be very hard to steer towards more partnership ways: think of the jeering, bullying, non-woman-friendly style of the English House Of Commons, or the sociopathically competitive culture of the City of London. Right-wing newspapers and news media tend to have a strongly dominator cast too, as they are key upholders of dominator norms. And business management can be seen as an interesting 'struggleground' between dominator and partnership approaches to life, with increasing – though still tentative – attempts to introduce more sympathetic, cooperative, women-friendly, non-hierarchical – that is, partnership-style – systems into the dominator-inclined world of work.

Architecture is a fine indicator of where its builders are at. For example, there are definite styles of dominator architecture – think castles, the Nuremburg stadium, Roman coliseums, Catholic churches, Egyptian temples, skyscrapers: "Monumental constructions doubtlessly proclaim an elite," (Conrad, 2011). These are structures specifically designed to vaunt the status and prestige of the possessor and to inspire awe or even fear in the beholder. Dominator governments also tend to impose particular styles of building on their subjects – faceless high-rise flats in grey concrete are popular (think Communist twentieth century and even socialist British social housing). The cubicles of US office life are another example. Dominator planning – and dominator utopias – like straight lines and grids: think how US state boundaries and street layouts cut across natural landmarks and terrain. In contrast, typical vernacular architecture is broadly partnership in flavour – low-key in style and usually low in stature, practical, homely, welcoming, unpretentious. And vernacular, unplanned settlements are higgledy-piggledy, interesting, organic and aligned with natural geographical features.

Popular culture. The concepts of partnership and dominator can also be used to locate popular or low culture items on our cooperative-competitive spectrum. So, for example, TV reality shows are typically either dominator (*Big Brother* or *The Jerry Springer Show* – confrontational, adversarial, manipulative) or partnership (*Strictly Come Dancing, Master Chef* – cooperative, friendly, gentlemanly, courteous, kind) in style. The UK's *Eastenders* is a classic dominator TV soap that showcases typical dominator values and behaviours: anger, bullying, intimidation, resentfulness, vengefulness, with bad temper as the default reaction to life's vicissitudes. Older US soaps such as Dallas, and

1970s to 1990s style blockbuster novels also typically had dominator plot lines, with ego, sex and money as the main drivers, and action involving power-plays, cut throat competition, cold-blooded manipulativeness, betrayal and so on.

Films. The genre of modern mainstream films and novels that are oriented chiefly towards a male demographic is striking in the way that it appears to (Unconsciously? Intentionally?) reflect deep dominator feelings and beliefs about the world. This is the post-apocalyptic vision of things seen in everything from *Mad Max* to *Alien, Men in Black,* the orc and fight scenes in *Lord of the Rings,* and so on. Typically, such films are shot in muted colours heavy on brown and black, and feature scenes of ruin, wreckage, explosions and burning, aliens and monsters. The emphasis is on force, terror, pain, damage and misery, anger and revenge. And the implicit message always seems to be: "This is inevitable. This is what you're going to see more and more of... so get used to it."! It's as if these filmmakers are unconsciously projecting the worst contents of a dominator psyche – a belief in a blighted, bleak, hopeless world ruled by alien forces, terror, brutality and intimidation – into their work and thence onto the viewer. Here there is little or no redemptory vision of the future; no belief in the power of ordinary human virtues of kindness and tolerance to change things for the better; no sunlight, colourful nature, light-heartedness or good humour.

"Myriad instances". So, overall, it's this gloomy dominator world view that – via the media and much popular culture – creates the psychological environment in which we swim, unless we deliberately strive to avoid it. And if you're like me, how tired one gets of it all... Nearly all the news and the majority of our culture is dominator-generated, is about dominator issues and reflects dominator values. As Henry Thoreau wrote in *Walden Pond* in 1854:

"If we read of one man robbed, or murdered, or killed by

> accident, or one house burned, or one vessel wrecked, or one steamboat blown up, or one cow run over on the Western Railroad, or one mad dog killed, or one lot of grasshoppers in the winter – we never need to read of another. One is enough. If you are acquainted with the principle, what do you care for a myriad instances and applications."

How true!

In the next two chapters we will look at a very different and much happier world – not a fairy-tale realm, fanciful golden age or imaginary utopia, but the real world of hunter-gatherer societies down the ages. Chapter 2 looks at how these societies might have arisen originally; and Chapter 3 examines their characteristics in detail.

Chapter 2

Human Origins: The 'Puzzle' of Altruism and Egalitarianism

"In the animal world we have seen that the vast majority of species live in societies, and that they find in association the best arms for the struggle for life: understood, of course, in its wide Darwinian sense – not as a struggle for the sheer means of existence, but as a struggle against all natural conditions unfavourable to the species. The animal species, in which individual struggle has been reduced to its narrowest limits, and the practice of mutual aid has attained the greatest development, are invariably the most numerous, the most prosperous, and the most open to further progress. The mutual protection which is obtained in this case, the possibility of attaining old age and of accumulating experience, the higher intellectual development, and the further growth of sociable habits, secure the maintenance of the species, its extension, and its further progressive evolution. The unsociable species, on the contrary, are doomed to decay."

Kropotkin, 1902

Why Origins Are Relevant

As was said in Chapter 1, we need to discuss the issue of human origins because this book's line of argument is based on hypotheses about what human beings and their lives were like in the beginning – at the dawn of human history.

The basic puzzle about the appearance of *Homo sapiens* is *how* early humankind – with all its new and surprising attributes – arose from our immediate primate ancestors/ relatives some 100,000 years or more ago. Typical characteristics of hunter-gatherer societies (which, we're assuming, were similar to earliest humans – see next section for the rationale for this) are described in more detail in Chapter 3; but some of the main ones which differ from our nearest primate relatives include marked egalitarianism, and cooperative food gathering, food-sharing and childrearing behaviour. In addition there is the even greater puzzle of symbolic behaviour and culture: domesticity, extended and formalised kinship, division of labour, hunting, fire, meat cooking, adornment, art, rituals, language and myth-making appeared around the same time. And to this list we can presume to add music-making, singing and dancing, social love-making, story-telling, laughing and joking, and playing – for which there is no archaeological evidence but which are such striking features of known hunter-gatherer life that it seems most unlikely they weren't part of earliest human life too. How did all these new features arise?

I discuss the animal connections first, with a look at work on animal emotions and behaviours: Marc Bekoff is a principal source here. I then draw upon my main archaeological sources for three different but complementary views on human origins: Christopher Boehm's 1999 *Hierarchy in the Forest* with its reverse dominance hierarchy theory; Sarah Blaffer Hrdy's 2008 *Mothers and Others* with its cooperative breeding/ alloparental care and provisioning evidence; and Chris Knight's *Blood Relations* with its sex strike hypothesis. These three sources all tackle the issue of primate studies, which show that – while most species do live in social groups – they are also hierarchical and despotic to a greater or lesser extent; typically display competition between males for females which is potentially or actually disruptive to group well-being and harmony; and show only limited cooperative or sharing behaviour. In contrast, the evidence that we have for the earliest human societies reveals them to be, apparently, similar to more recent hunter-gather peoples in their lifestyles and behaviour (and, we can surmise, in their beliefs and attitudes also) – that is, highly egalitarian and cooperative.

Between them, these four authors provide a spectrum of convincing ideas about the way in which Emotionally and Behaviourally Modern Humans (to use Hrdy's terms), as well as Anatomically Modern Humans, may have arisen from earlier forms.

Extrapolating back to prehistoric times. Boehm, Hrdy and Knight all assume that – in lieu of a better method – it is legitimate to extrapolate from accounts of contemporary and historic hunter-gatherer/forager peoples, and from interpretations of archaeological and palaeontological remains, back to our prehistoric forebears. This is important, since much of the argument in this book depends upon this assumption being reasonably valid. For example, Boehm develops his arguments "on the assumption that extant foragers may be used as *reasonably* accurate proxies for their predecessors... Late Palaeolithic humans in whose bands many of our genes were evolved." Hrdy makes the same assumption; and Knight believes that:

> "whilst no surviving human culture can constitute a model of earliest *sapient* life, it is not unreasonable to suppose that certain recurrent patterns – for example the striking near universality of 'classificatory' modes of reckoning kinship, or the presence of [certain] mythological patterns – convey information on traditions stretching back to the last ice age."

Table I

Human Origins: Dates and Definitions

Million Years Ago

220 Triassic: start of lactating mothers – mammals, etc

5–10 (6) Common Ancestor of humans and other apes

2.6 First unequivocal stone tools appear

2–1.8 Early Pleistocene: African ancestors of *Homo erectus/Homo sapiens* (prehumans and early human apes, now collectively termed hominins; 'Emotionally Modern Humans'

1.4 Widespread tool use; complex hand axes

Thousand Years Ago

600 *Homo heidelbergensis* emerges, with bigger brains

400–300 Unequivocal evidence for fire, hearths, cooking

140–130 Modern *Homo sapiens* emerges

130–100 Symbolic life – ochre use, deliberate burial; 'Behaviourally Modern Humans'

100 Middle Palaeolithic: Anatomically Modern Humans (with 1350cc brains – the hallmark of a breeding population of AMHs

95 Migration out of Africa

? Upper Palaeolithic: men 'hijacked' women's menstruation

50–40 The 'Human Revolution': carvings, paintings, musical instruments, sophisticated tools, beads

15 Lascaux cave paintings

10 After the Neolithic: start of farming

(partly from Douglas, 2001)

Animal Prosociality

"As we begin to look at the 'good' side of animal behaviorwe begin to take in just how rich the social lives of many animals are. Indeed, the lives of animals are shaped at a most basic level by 'good' – or

> *what biologists call prosocial – interactions and relationships. Even more, it seems that at least some prosocial behavior is not a mere byproduct of conflict, but may be an evolutionary force in its own right. Within biology, early theories of kin selection and reciprocal altruism have now blossomed into a much wider enquiry into the many faces and meanings of prosocial behavior. And, it seems, the more we look, the more we see. There's now an enormous body of research on prosocial behavior, and new research is being published all the time on cooperation, altruism, empathy, reciprocity, succorance, fairness, forgiveness, trust and kindness in animals ranging from rats to apes."*
>
> (Bekoff and Pierce, 2009)

I have chosen to begin a discussion of human origins, in relation to our *do we need to be so screwed up?* topic, with *animals,* because there is now so much evidence for prosociality as the main type of behaviour in many parts of the animal kingdom. This starts us off on a good footing about what is natural and innate in humans – because if a majority of animals exhibit predominantly prosocial behaviour, this makes the existence of similar behaviour in early humans less surprising. An important source on this subject for me has been Marc Bekoff and Jessica Pierce's *Wild Justice,* which draws on such disciplines as cognitive ethology, social neuroscience, moral psychology, and philosophy; and brings together much recent research on animal behaviour – particularly prosocial, and what the authors feel can be considered to be moral, behaviour.

Challenging the competition paradigm. Bekoff and Pierce are definitely pro-nice in their attitude, and strongly back up my book's (and Kropotkin's) basic stance that niceness, cooperation or mutual aid are very much a mainstream part of nature:

> "We challenge the domination – the hegemony, you might say – of the competition paradigm that has monopolized discus-

> sions of the evolution of social behaviour. The predominance of this paradigm in ethology and evolutionary biology is both misleading and wrong, and momentum is building towards a paradigm shift in which 'nature red in tooth and claw' sits in balance with wild justice. The innumerable situations in which we see animals working together aren't merely veneers of cooperation, fairness and trust, but the real thing. Cooperation, fairness, and justice have to be factored in to the evolutionary equation in order to understand the evolution of social behavior in diverse species."

This is interesting, as, for example, Boehm writing in 1999 (just a decade earlier) and summarising his view of the state of play at that point, claimed that, until very recently, "The capacity for genuine altruism in mammals has been denied on a widespread, often vehement basis." A paradigm shift does indeed seem to be occurring.

Bekoff and Pierce go on to take the pro-nice case further:

> "Here's a common distillation of Charles Darwin's theory of evolution. Natural selection, to borrow a popular metaphor from biology, is an evolutionary arms race. Life is a war of all against all, a ruthless and bloody battle, usually over sex and food… When we look at nature through this narrow lens we see animals eking out a living against the glacial forces of evolutionary conflict. This scenario makes for great television programming, but it reflects only a small part of nature's ineluctable push. For alongside conflict and competition there is a tremendous show of cooperative, helpful, and caring behavior as well. To offer a particularly striking example, after carefully analyzing the social interactions of various primate species, primatologists Robert Sussman and Paul Gerber and geneticist James Cheverud came to the conclusion that the vast majority of social interactions are affiliative rather than

> agonistic or divisive. Grooming and bouts of play predominate the social scene, with only the occasional fight or threat of aggression."

Moreover, there is now plentiful evidence for animals acting with altruism, compassion or kindness not just to members of their own immediate group, but also to others who aren't in their family, their clan, or even their own species. How right Kropotkin was; and how accurate and prescient his thoughts expressed in the quotation at the start of this chapter. Bekoff and Pierce go on to ask *why* cooperation has developed in so many species:

> "Cooperative behavior has always been a puzzle because it doesn't fit the predictions of Darwinian theory, which has sent us looking instead for competition and unfettered aggression. It must be that evolution, though a 'competitive' process, doesn't yield only competitive, ruthless aggressive strategies."

Evolution clearly can and does give rise to strategies of cooperation and niceness too.

Animals have feelings. The history of animal research also exhibits a resistance to accepting the extent of animals' abilities and emotions; but again this resistance is increasingly being challenged by new evidence. For example, in the earlier part of the twentieth century, many scientists still denied that animals could actually feel pain, or had emotions at all; but new research has gradually forced most of them to accept the extent not only of animal feelings and emotions, but also of their abilities and gifts. "There still remain a few researchers, even some ethologists, who have trouble with the idea that animals have emotions." Bekoff and Pierce tell us, but:

> "The tendency to focus on 'negative' emotions such as pain, fear, and aggression has given way to an increased interest in 'positive' emotions such as love, joy, and pleasure, and to complex emotional experiences such as empathy, grief, forgiveness and envy… Animals form friendships, are caught lying and stealing and lose face in the community, they flirt, their sexual advances are sometimes embraced and sometimes rejected, they fight and make up, they love, and they experience loss. There are saints and sinners, bad apples and good citizens."

In *The Emotional Lives of Animals* (2007), Bekoff gives further examples of the wide range of feelings that both wild and domesticated animals express – pleading with their eyes to be saved from dangerous situations; showing gratitude; exhibiting awe or wonder at natural phenomena such as waterfalls or thunderstorms; showing joy, jubilation and pleasure in many ways and in various situations; having a laugh, teasing, tickling, and demonstrating a sense of humour; mourning others and even dying of a broken heart; exhibiting all sorts of love and friendship – for children, mates, and friends of both the same and different species; acting embarrassed, sulking, holding grudges and getting their own back; and so on.

Temple Grandin, Doctor of Animal Science and Professor at Colorado State University, best-selling author, consultant to the livestock industry on animal behaviour, and animal welfare advocate, makes similar points to those of Boehm, and Bekoff and Pierce. As a person with high-functioning autism, Grandin claims this condition helps her to understand animals better than most neurotypical people can. And in her book *Animals in Translation* (2005), Grandin describes how the list of animal emotions which scientists have been forced to recognise has gradually grown from the most primitive (and largely negative) of rage, prey chase drive, fear, and curiosity/interest/anticipation, to include the social emotions of sexual attraction/lust, separation distress (mother and baby), social attachment, play and roughhousing, and affiliative and cooperative behaviour.

Sarah Hrdy also shows how new research is constantly extending what has been considered purely human behaviour into the animal kingdom. For example, recent work has shown that neonatal smiles, previously thought to be uniquely human, can also be found "flitting across the faces" of newborn and infant chimpanzees. "Born smiling, chimpanzees keep right on doing so," Hrdy tells us – describing the way baby chimps respond to photographs of their mother's face or that of close caregivers with "wildly enthusiastic" social smiles. This is just one example out of hundreds that one could give demonstrating how the gap between animal and human prosocial and affiliative behaviours is closing all the time.

So we applaud Bekoff and Pierce's (2009) conclusion that:

> "animals have rich inner worlds – they have a nuanced repertoire of emotions, a high degree of intelligence (they're really smart and adaptable), and demonstrate behavioural flexibility as they negotiate complex and changing social relationships... what we're saying is that arguments for evolutionary continuity – the idea that the difference between species are differences in degree rather than differences in kind – are being supported for a wide variety of cognitive and emotional capacities in diverse species... Humans should be proud of their citizenship in the animal kingdom."

On a similar theme, leading biologists are now suggesting that we might learn a lot about the evolution of social behaviour by studying not just primates, but also social *carnivores* – species whose social behaviour and organisation resemble that of early hominins (that is, prehumans and early human apes) in a number of ways such as divisions of labour, food sharing, care of young, and intersexual and intrasexual dominance hierarchies (Bekoff and Pierce, 2009). In other words, it would be sensible to look beyond solely primates in the animal kingdom in order to understand some of the roots of human behaviour. It's also interesting to note, on this theme, that Charles Darwin himself stressed the evolutionary continuity between humans and a *range* of other animals, observing that that the differences between 'us' and 'them' in all realms – including the "moral sentiments", to use his term – were of degree, not of kind (Bekoff and Pierce, 2009). This is another example of a prescient pro-nice idea suggested by a leading thinker that has been neglected, lain largely dormant, and is only now being looked at again.

Egalitarianism

> *"I write about political egalitarianism of the type Tocqueville described... But it was not Americans, two centuries ago, who invented this interesting political way of life; nor was it the Athenians of ancient Greece. The 'democratic' origins I describe are not recent and historical, but evolutionary and ancient. They date from well back in the Palaeolithic era, and were intimately involved with the development of human nature itself."*
>
> (Boehm, 1999)

> *"By any dictionary definition of communism, our ancestors were communists."*
>
> (Lee, 1988)

Christopher Boehm's *Hierarchy in the Forest: The Evolution of Egalitarian Behaviour* (1999) centres on the aforementioned puzzle of altruism and egalitarianism in humans – particularly nomadic hunter-gatherers/foragers. The puzzle in this case is that the three African great apes – chimpanzees, gorillas and bonobos – with whom we share a relatively recent Common Ancestor, are notably hierarchical. How, then did egalitarianism develop and survive among early humans from at least 100,000 until about five thousand years ago, when people increasingly began to live in more hierarchical societies such as tribes and chiefdoms?

Preadaptations. Boehm uses studies from primates and hunter-gatherers plus evolutionary theory to investigate how and why egalitarianism might have arisen. He examines possible precursors to Anatomically Modern Humans, and finds many preadaptations that seem likely to have existed in a Common Ancestor; in hominin forebears; or that are present in our ape and monkey relatives. He believes that these preadaptations were solidly in place 100,000 years ago and perhaps considerably earlier. They include: subordinate resentment of domination; the ability to form large coalitions; the capacity of such coalitions to dominate or eliminate a bully/alpha-type individual with their combined weaponry; the development of political and actuarial intelligence (strategising, risk-assessment, judgements about reciprocity and so on); communication abilities; and the advent of 'moral communities' wishing and able to proscribe unwanted behaviours and encourage desirable ones. "In effect, egalitarianism could have arisen simply because humans became culturally able to form moral communities and were prone to rebel against dominant authority," Boehm concludes.

Reverse dominance hierarchies. He then speculates that egalitarianism came about as the result of the development of *reverse dominance hierarchies,* arising when three fundamental human dispositions in our structurally tripartite human nature comprising egoism (pro-self), nepotism (pro-kin), and altruism (pro-others), are kept in balance. "Egalitarianism does not result from the mere absence of hierarchy, as is commonly assumed. Rather egalitarianism involves a very special type of hierarchy, a curious type that is based on antihierarchical feelings." This depends on the rank and file deliberately banding together to assertively deny political power to the would-be alphas in their group; or cooperating to neutralise the power of aggressive deviants.

Boehm goes on to discuss conditions which could have triggered this change to egalitarianism, including the development of big-game hunting or scavenging; and of population displacements due to strong climatic fluctuations – these being conditions which could have encouraged the development of cooperation within groups, both in the hunting of large animals, and in the subsequent fair distribution of meat. He concludes that:

> "Once one band, somewhere, invented an egalitarian order, this radical change in social ways of doing things would have become visible to its neighbours. The advantages would have been evident wherever subordinates were ambivalent about being dominated... One would expect a gradual cultural diffusion to take place, with attractive egalitarian traditions replacing despotic ones locally."

(Perhaps also expressible as the spread of a *meme*.)

Boehm's conclusions. Boehm comments that:

> "hunter-gatherer egalitarianism has involved many biases in its interpretation. These preferential approaches reflect implicit or unstated assumptions about human nature, and they range from assumptions of anarchism or of spontaneously benevolent cooperation, to theories based on endemic competitive power plays or even tolerated theft. Some interpretations appear to see equality everywhere, whereas others emphasise the existence of competition and hierarchy."

Boehm's discussions of and conclusions about human nature in fact rather favour the 'nasty' point of view, as can be seen from these concluding remarks:

> "We humans will never be able to live in relaxed egalitarian societies, in the way that squirrel monkeys do much of the time. These monkeys' innate dispositions appear to be substantially different from our own apelike dispositions, which are ethologically despotic. It is our capacity for morality, a most important cultural universal, that enables us to create egalitarianism out of what would otherwise be despotism... [The] evolutionary saga ends with a species altruistic enough to cooperate quite efficiently in large or small groups, but at the same time prone to competition and conflict. This cooperation is possible because human groups invariably act as moral communities that implement prosocial blueprints even as they suppress the aggressive egoism and dedicated nepotism that are so powerful in our nature."

My impression is that Boehm finds much of his evidence for 'nastiness' in patriarchy-influenced and therefore dominator-inclined peoples; and that this has coloured his views of what is truly original human nature. I also can't help feeling that he was influenced by the pro-nasty paradigm of those slightly earlier times during which he wrote; and that if he brought out *Hierarchy in the Forest* today he would have few scruples about casting it in a much 'nicer' light!

James Woodburn and immediate return systems. Woodburn has spent a lifetime living with and observing in particular the nomadic hunter-gatherer Hadza people of Tanzania (see, for example, Woodburn, 2005). Based on this work with foragers, he has developed the concepts of *immediate return* social systems – defined as a system of material production for immediate use without significant storage or investment, as opposed to *delayed return* systems. He claims that the social systems of hunter-gatherers – and of other societies – are best understood when seen in relation to the way in which the rights of individuals and of groups over what we term property are held and transacted.

These include rights over land and resources; tools and weapons and other moveable property; game meat and harvested vegetable food; knowledge and intellectual property; and over certain capacities of people such as their hunting labour or their reproductive capacity:

> "Most important of all, I would claim that it is through rights to property, and the ideologies linked with such rights, that structures of equality and inequality among the kin and other close associates with whom hunter-gatherers live and work are established and maintained."

Woodburn sees immediate return as one of a number of interdependent and tightly interlocked features characteristic of the contemporary hunter-gatherer peoples he has studied. He summarises it as:

> "a system of material production for immediate use without significant storage or investment; an egalitarian ideology and an egalitarian practice in which even intergenerational relationships are near-equal; a system of social relations and social groupings minimising dependence and stressing direct, individual access to material resources, to knowledge and to skills with these resources, this knowledge and these skills not controlled or allocated by people of senior generation; and emphasis on individual freedom to select on a day-to-day basis one's residential and other associates; a system of transactions focused on entitlement to share other people's recognised property, the recognised yield of other people's labour."

Egalitarian cultures. In his 2005 paper *Egalitarian Societies Revisited,* Woodburn describes egalitarian cultures as:

> "societies of equals – equals in wealth, equals in power and

> equals in status. My argument is that they are societies of equals because in these societies equality is actively promoted and inequality is actively resisted through a set of coherent interlocked and mutually reinforcing institutional procedures. These institutional procedures together constitute one particular resolution – an extreme one – of the co-existing pressure for equality and for inequality which are present in the desires of every one of us as an individual and in the operation of the political systems, and indeed of the kinship systems and the religious systems, of every human society."

Woodburn argues that certain key mechanisms are at work in egalitarian societies that together have the effect of creating a degree of human equality greater than that achieved in any other human societies. He sees the three main ones as being firstly, provision of direct access to material resources, knowledge and skills; secondly, autonomy – freedom to move around and to live and work with freely chosen associates; and thirdly, the obligation to share; and he believes that these processes disengage people from property and from the potentiality in property rights for creating dependency.

Egalitarianism among animals. It is fascinating to see how many of the social processes discussed above are mirrored in the animal world, as Bekoff and Pierce (2009), for instance, explain. So, most social animals have prohibitions – for example, against certain kinds of harm, both physical (biting, killing, violent aggression) and psychological (bullying, taunting, intimidation), under certain circumstances. There may also be expectations about helping, reciprocating, and sharing, as well as norms – that is, expected standards of behaviour within a group that are enforced by the group. So animals have rules about behaviour, and also about 'manners', such as conventions regarding grooming behaviour or eating queues – social conventions that help maintain group cohesion and cooperation. Bekoff and

Pierce also believe that at least some animals have *conscience* too, in the sense that moral rules are internalised and some self-monitoring of behaviour occurs. They see what they term moral intelligence, or morality, in animals as an evolutionary adaptation to social living; and one can see how these qualities are exactly equivalent to those which underpin or give rise to norms or an ethos about behaviour in human societies. Harm and benefit are the basic units of moral currency; and those behaviours (deceiving, cheating) that tear the social fabric are 'wrong' and those that create the kind of community in which individuals thrive are 'right'.

Animal play is also particularly interesting in the context of egalitarianism. As Bekoff and Pierce (2009) point out, play is a great *leveller*. This can be seen particularly clearly in the animal kingdom where, for example:

> "Dogs, wolves, coyotes and other animals engage in role reversing and self-handicapping to maintain social play. Each of these strategies helps to reduce inequalities in size and dominance rank between players and to promote the reciprocity and cooperation that's needed for play to occur." (Bekoff and Pierce, 2009)

Think of the Saint Bernard playing with a puppy, a Chihuahua, or your cat.

If we extend this idea into the human realm, one can see the parallels with – for example – the myriad human traditions of cross-dressing or role reversal in Lord of Misrule festivals and similar. Here, for one day or week a year, hierarchical order is overturned, the master serves the servant, men take on the dress, demeanour and roles of women, and so on. It seems that the same sort of process is operating here as in play, where the Saint Bernard pretends he's no stronger than a puppy, small-breed dog, or cat in order to facilitate play and its levelling and bonding effects. So one can speculate that human festivals which include role reversal or masquerading may also have a levelling function in hierarchical cultures – temporarily reversing the dominator order of things, and allowing a taste of egalitarianism back into the system.

Cooperation and Altruism

> *"New thinking holds that our sociability has been the primary survival strategy of primate species, including our own."*
> (Goleman, 2006)

Cooperative breeding. In *Mothers and Others* (2009), Sarah Hrdy examines human origins from the point of view of the logistical challenges facing mothers among the early hominins who were the ancestors of *Homo sapiens*. This is an issue that wasn't considered to be of much importance by evolutionary anthropologists until the end of the twentieth century; and Hrdy believes that "a fixation with mother-only care initially led evolutionists to overlook alternative modes of infant care." (Spot the patriarchal bias!) Her reasoning goes like this: babies some 1.5–2 million years ago or more had already evolved to a point where they were being born more dependant, and dependant for longer, than the young of any other ape, so that at some point human mothers began to bear offspring too costly to rear by themselves. This meant that hominin mothers definitively needed help in order to rear their slow-maturing children successfully. The solution to this was, Hrdy believes, through cooperative breeding – recruiting 'alloparents' such as grandmothers, fathers, siblings, older children, aunts and uncles, and 'as-if' kin (friends, blood-brothers, allies) to help with guarding, defending, keeping warm, cleaning, provisioning, babysitting and other childcare tasks. Hrdy then concludes that in foraging societies like those in which our ancestors evolved, support from alloparents not only improved health, social maturation, and mental development, but was actually *essential* for child survival. She also stresses that this adaptation probably preceded the development of sapient brains by well over a million years; and that, therefore, "cooperative breeding came before braininess... Brains require care more than care requires brains"!

Cooperation and empathy. Hrdy goes on to argue that our species' capacity to cooperate in groups, to empathise with others and to wonder what others are thinking and feeling probably arose in response to the selective pressures of being in a cooperatively breeding social group, and the need to be able to 'read' other people in order to assess who to trust and rely on, from babyhood on. This was the beginning of *emotionally* modern humans, defined by Hrdy as "bipedal apes born with giving impulses and empathic, intersubjective aptitudes profoundly different from those we see in chimpanzees today – people preadapted to get along with one another." She therefore sees the start of many typically human behaviours as evolving well before the development of *anatomically* modern humans (200,000 or more years ago), or of *behaviourally* modern humans. And she believes that many of the characteristics that make us different from apes evolved during those thousands of millennia during which babies who were better at gauging the intentions of others and engaging them were also better at eliciting care, and hence more likely to survive into adulthood and reproduce.

It is worth adding here that, although Hrdy doesn't discuss classificatory kinship (see next section for definitions) in those terms, many examples that she provides implicitly support the idea and importance of it. For example, she describes how: "Mothers can overshoot their capabilities to provide, and fathers can vary, because both sexes evolved in a highly fluid system where alloparents often provided the compensatory assistance."

Darwin and Kropotkin said it first. Contrary to most people's 'nature red in tooth and claw' ideas about Darwinism, Hrdy's ideas are also an extension of themes of mutual aid which had already been considered by Charles Darwin in the nineteenth century. These were subsequently fully developed by Kropotkin in his *Mutual Aid* (1902); and he stresses this same point – that Darwin didn't see evolution solely in terms of competition – in concluding his chapter *Mutual Aid Among Savages*:

> "It would be a tedious repetition if more illustrations from savage life were given. Wherever we go we find the same sociable manners, the same spirit of solidarity. And when we endeavour to penetrate into the darkness of past ages, we find the same tribal life, the same associations of men, however primitive, for mutual support. Therefore, Darwin was quite right when he saw in man's social qualities the chief actor for his social evolution, and Darwin's vulgarizers are entirely wrong when they maintain the contrary."

Kropotkin goes on to quote Darwin, who observed in *The Descent of Man* that:

> "The small strength and speed of man, his want of natural weapons, etc, are more than counterbalanced, firstly, by his intellectual faculties" [which, Kropotkin notes, Darwin remarked elsewhere have been chiefly or even exclusively gained for the benefit of the community]; "and secondly *by his social qualities*, which led him to give and receive aid from his fellow men."

The 'Sex Strike' and the Origins of Culture

Chris Knight is best-known for his theory, first set out in *Blood Relations* (1991) that human language, religion and culture emerged in our species not simply by gradual Darwinian evolution but in a process culminating in revolutionary social change. The details of his hypothesis remain controversial, but the underlying idea that symbolic culture emerged during a major transition or revolution (often termed the human revolution) has been current for many years and is now widely agreed upon. In *Blood Relations*, Knight presents a human-origins hypothesis that is complementary and supplementary to those already outlined above. His ingenious argument, as it relates to my book, goes something like this: some time between 40,000 and 100,000 years ago (Knight would adjust those dates back in light of subsequent research since he wrote his book) a tremendous social, sexual, and cultural revolution occurred. Before that, early humans were similar to their primate ancestors in having no central hearth or home and in foraging largely individualistically – males for themselves, and females for themselves and their infants. In Knight's view, a time occurred when all this changed. Palaeo-women were already coping with increasingly immaturely-born, helpless babies; and if *Homo sapiens* was to become more sapient, it was crucial for the women to have a secure base in which to rest and nurture their young and – somehow – to encourage their menfolk to go off, hunt, and return with food for the women and children.

The sex strike. In Knight's scenario, women encourage men to provision them by synchronising menstruation and inaugurating monthly 'sex strikes' – the deal being that until the men return with meat, the women of the group won't allow them sexual intercourse; but that concomitantly, neither will the women allow any other males access to them either. Safe in this knowledge, and with their honour, plus sexual gifts (and cooked food) dependent upon it, the men go off to hunt, return with food to camp, and are rewarded with feasting, rejoicing, and physical love. Men hunt around the time of the full (hunter's) moon, and the period of feasting and uniting with women follows. Then women reassert their mutual solidarity via the sex strike during the last quarter of the waning moon, building up to the next cycle of hunting as the moon waxes again. The moon is thus society's calendar, and life revolves around a roughly fortnight-on, fortnight-off lunar time frame.

Knight summarises the effects of this revolution on women's lives like this:

> "Child-burdened females were no longer caught between the need to gain help from one another and the need to avoid excessive travel... They had broken through the entire framework of such constraints, establishing a completely new mode of living. Groups of related women were now in a position to stay in one place for weeks or perhaps months on end, assisting one another in the tasks of household management, gathering, storing food, preparing meals, cooking, distributing provisions and caring for children – whilst drawing on the continuous economic and social support of men who could comb an immense area for game... Each gender group was freed by the other to perform its distinctive role, the two benefiting jointly from the human revolution's gains."

Knight goes further, and sees women as also being primarily responsible for originating human culture in its widest sense – culture which was later 'hijacked' by men (see Chapter 5):

> "Men invented none of the basic principles of kinship, ritual action or cosmological belief... At best, masculinist ritual activity and its associated mythology represents only a politically distorted imprint made from a pre-existent template... Far from producing culture... male power enters tardily on to the scene, transforming and politically colonising a cultural landscape long since formed by others."

This short summary doesn't do justice to Knight's remarkable book, but is intended to give the bones of his main ideas and some of their ramifications. Subsequent research has confirmed most of its hypotheses. From the point of view of *Do We Need To be So Screwed Up?!*, it provides a lot of support for my basic thesis (that we *don't* need to be!).

Matriarchy, Matrilocality, Matriliny and Classificatory Kinship

Before concluding this chapter, the subject of matrilocality, matriliny and classificatory kinship need to be firmly flagged up as part of our discussion of human origins because abundant evidence shows that this form of social structure was the original type for all humankind (for example, see Briffault, 1927; Knight, 2008; Alton 2011).

Definitions. *Matrilocality* is a social system in which women live near their mothers rather than moving away to live with their husband's family; and children stay with their mother and her family rather than with their father and his family (the latter being the norm in patriarchal systems). A *matrilineal* clan is a group of related people in which descent is reckoned through the mother and the female line. The more old-fashioned term *matriarchy* covers both matrilocality and matriliny. A classificatory kinship system is likely to be present within a matrilineal or matrilocal community. A *classificatory kinship* system is one in which a woman's chief allegiance throughout her life is to her blood kin, in particular to her mother, her siblings, and their children. The same applies to men, their alliance being to their own blood kin; while children are raised by their mothers and her family, rather than by their fathers and *his* family. It can be seen, therefore, that marriage or sexual pairing cuts across these alliances; and that such pairings in traditional hunter-gatherer and other matrilineal societies is inevitably a weaker bond than those with one's blood relatives. Roughly speaking, it means that a child calls all its mother's brothers 'father' and sees them (classes them) in that role; calls all its mother's sisters 'mother' and sees them in *that* role; an uncle calls all his nephews 'son' and treats them as his biological children, and so on – hence the use of the term 'classificatory'. Indeed 'father' is a concept that isn't even recognised in many such societies (see also Chapters 6, 7, 13).

And because a father doesn't raise his own children but has more influence with his sisters' children, marriage doesn't break up the biological family, as it tends to do in patriarchal systems. Nor does a breakdown in marriage involving separation or divorce between wife and husband break up a family: children continue to live with and be brought up by their mother, grandmother, uncle, aunts, cousins and so on – that is, with their classificatory mothers, fathers and siblings.

Briffault and *The Mothers*. The authoritative source on matriarchy is Robert Briffault's 1927 three-volume *The Mothers*. Alton (2011) explains how Briffault:

> "gathered together every last reference from Genesis to Herodotus and from China to the Torres Straits, to argue that nearly all the world's indigenous peoples show evidence of being matriarchal in key respects... Briffault's aim in listing all the matrilineal and matrilocal tribes he could find was to explode the fallacy that the nuclear family and lifelong monogamy had always been the normal pattern of marriage. In the process of doing this... he began to build up his argument that the forms of patriarchy found so commonly in the world were always preceded by matriarchy and that women almost everywhere had much more solidarity and power than was generally acknowledged."

Those who want to assert the centrality and original nature of the nuclear family attempt to deny, ignore or challenge the primal nature of matriliny and classificatory kinship, but objective scholarship demonstrates that this point of view is incorrect.

Characteristics and benefits of classificatory kinship. Some thirty or so matrilineal cultures still exist today, and in them we can study living examples of classificatory kinship and its benefits. A most striking example is the tribal Na society of China, described by Cai Hua in *A Society Without Fathers and Husbands* (2001). With the Na, a sister sets up a household with her brother. There is no marriage; men visit women's homes for sex, but don't reside; and any resulting children are part of their mother's home. Hua stresses how different such a system is from the traditional nuclear family:

> "The Na kinship bond is eternal. This feature puts their system into direct opposition to the marriage relationship in other societies: marriage, as a rule, while uniting outsiders and making them relatives, occasions a split between blood relatives in every generation... the bond between brothers and sisters, created by their mother and their shared consanguineal identity, is immutable, whereas the matrimonial bond is mutable, as the possibility of divorce shows."

This description applies to all classificatory kinship societies; and because of this immutable bond, such systems have many advantages – particularly for women and children. (These are described very well in by Knight, 1991; 2008; and by Alton, 1984.) In particular, mothers and children always have a support structure of their own kin, regardless of how supportive or otherwise *spouses* may be. For example, the matrilineal Na make fun of the adjacent nuclear-familied Han: "Because the Han family (based on the nuclear family) is always limited, the Na joke that the couple is left to take care of everything and that their house is always a mess."! This is in contrast to their own households, where – typically – grandmothers look after the children while mothers and sisters look after the household and brothers work the land. Alton (1984) makes the point that – compared to classificatory kinship systems, which can *rightly* be called 'extended' families – traditional Western-style kinship systems would be more appropriately called 'restricted' families – "a form which resulted when kinship links were systematically severed, shorn off and reduced to the minimum levels consistent with certain reproductive and other necessities... thoroughly marginalised, privatised, emasculated and shorn of all public weight or political power... "

Another key advantage of classificatory kinship systems is that having brothers on one's side and in one's camp means that husbands can't physically dominate wives or children: the men of one's own kin can stand up to them.

> "A sexual equilibrium therefore prevails in place of male dominance... Matriliny works against the likelihood of the nuclear family developing and makes its existence unstable. This is always to the advantage of women... The matriliny rule is just one aspect (which has tended to survive longer than other aspects) of a complex of rules whose effect is to counteract male dominance."
>
> (Alton, 1984)

No wonder patriarchal societies want to pretend matriliny never existed!

And though marriage is usually found in some form within matrilineal systems, there is also scope for sex outside marriage within the social structure, so that the vexed issues of monogamy, faithfulness, infidelity, divorce, broken homes, hurt children and so on, which are such a problem in Western societies, don't arise with any force. (This is discussed further in Chapters 6, 7 and 13.) Nor do couples in matrilineal societies have the unrealistically extensive expectations of each other that couples tend to have in the developed world, for their wider needs for friendship, companionship, support and so on are largely met by the clan as a whole. This is touched on again in

Chapter 12; and other significant implications of classificatory kinship are considered throughout this book.

Effects of Partnership Life on Our Genes

This concludes our review of some leading theories about human origins that have a bearing on this book. Before leaving the subject, however, this seems an appropriate time to survey the effects which our presumed partnership origins, and our more recent dominator history, might have had on *natural selection* and our *genes*.

We were partnership-type people for at least 90,000 years. A point that needs to be stressed again at this stage is *the very long period of time* (at least 95% of our time on earth) during which our hominin forebears lived as partnership-style egalitarian, and evidently largely peaceful, hunter-gatherers. Indeed, for thousands of years – from at least 100,000 years ago and maybe over two million years ago, until about 10,000 years ago and the beginnings of horticultural, pastoral and agricultural lifestyles – it seems likely that this is how *all* early humans lived. In other words, it is worth stressing again that a hunting-and-gathering, egalitarian, partnership-style way of life appears to be the one we *evolved* to exist in – it is our Environment of Evolutionary Adaptedness (see Chapter 6). It is therefore reasonable to ask, what effect some 100,000 plus years (equivalent to more than a thousand generations) of egalitarian, altruistic life is likely to have had on our species' genetic makeup?

Selection for altruistic traits. This issue is discussed in detail by Boehm (1999), who examines the evidence for selection for altruism in human beings – that is, selection for behaviour which apparently doesn't directly benefit the breeding group concerned (also called between-group selection). His general view is that there is a strong case to be made for the proposal that Darwinian selection acting on intentionally egalitarian groups of people over perhaps 500,000 years, or 20,000 generations, has selected for altruistic traits. His hypothesis is therefore that:

> "the spread of palaeolithic egalitarianism had a profound effect on basic mechanisms of natural selection. Specifically, selection at the between-group level was empowered at the expense of selection at the within-group level, a shift that profoundly affected human nature. This was the case because between-group selection supports the altruistic traits that have been so vigorously denied for three decades."

Boehm therefore believes that the evidence contradicts the stance held for well over twenty years previously by evolutionary biologists, sociobiologically-inclined anthropologists, and evolutionary psychologists who had agreed, nearly unanimously, that natural selection can support nepotistic helpfulness but *not* altruistic helpfulness.

Boehm concludes that between-group selection and altruism probably operated as a significant factor in the 100,000 or so years during which cooperative, egalitarian life flourished on earth. In other words, in those cultures, which valued cooperation highly, there must have been positive breeding selection for people with those traits: women would actively seek hospitable, generous, peaceable, kindly men as mates, for example. Those traits would also be valued and supported in the population as a whole; and since Boehm wrote in 1999, increasing amounts of evidence have confirmed his conclusion – highlighting the importance of between-group altruism among hunter-gatherers, including prosocial contacts with networks of non-kin friends, 'allo-kin' and so on (Hrdy, 2009). In her review of human prosociality in *Mothers and Others* (2009), Hrdy also stresses the general and ongoing influence of the human desire to connect – found among all peoples, whether significantly dominator-influenced or not; and up to the present day. The likely effects of these factors, and of the subsequent 10,000 years of dominator-influenced life, on selection and our genes, is discussed further at the end of Chapter 5.

'Real People' rather than 'High Priestesses'? Finally, it is interesting to speculate about the differences between the picture of prehistoric peoples, based mainly upon historic hunter-gatherers, which we've developed in this book so far compared to the perhaps rather overblown impressions given by some authors championing the idea of women's powers in those mysterious times. The latter tend to paint a picture of society then as something rather solemn, in which women were 'revered' as 'earth mothers', 'venerated priestesses' or 'respected elders'. However, such terms imply a degree of seriousness and non-egalitarianism that – on the evidence given in this book – was very unlikely to have existed. On the contrary, it seems much more probable that pristinely matriarchal ancient societies were like current hunter-gatherers crossed with Marlo Morgan's 'Real People' mentioned in Chapter 1 – living simple but cheerful hunter-gathering lives full of fun and laughter, music-making and dancing, chatting, story-telling and visiting, hunting and cooking, love-making and games-playing. These would undoubtedly have been societies based on absolute trust in the universe and its willingness to provide for humankind; but everyday life, I believe, would have been more like what's found in a Hadza camp than in the Catalhoyuk or Cretan settlements described by authors such as Eisler (1987) or Gimbutas (1991).

Chapter 3

Hunter-Gatherer Societies: Do They Create 'Saner' People Than Dominator-Style Civilisations?

Key Characteristics of Hunter-Gatherer Societies

> *"I asked the Pirahãs once during my early missionary days if they knew why I was there. 'You are here because this is a beautiful place. The water is pretty. There are good things to eat here. The Pirahãs are nice people.' That was and is the Pirahãs' perspective. Life is good. Their upbringing, everyone learning early on to pull their own weight, produces a society of satisfied members. That is hard to argue against."*
>
> (Everett, 2008)

Partnership societies tend to be different in many ways from what contemporary dominator-style cultures consider to be normal or inevitable. This fact is the jumping-off point for this book, and invites us to question dominator assumptions about what societies and individuals 'have' to be like. This chapter concentrates mainly on hunter-gatherer societies – cultures characterised in particular by what nineteenth century researchers Morgan and Engels termed primitive communism and Kropotkin called mutual aid; and by egalitarianism. Those authors, and the many others who have written about foraging peoples sympathetically, show how different normal behaviour is or was in such societies compared to the dominator-type cultures which have been the norm for the past few thousand years.

Two surprising features. Two things stand out in particular in making this sort of review. One is how surprising and even counterintuitive many features of hunter-gatherer life are compared to the usual stereotypes or received wisdoms. This applies particularly to the forager approach to childrearing, which is radically different from what's taken in dominator cultures and yet produces very satisfying results (see below; and Chapter 6). Other aspects, such as life without clear leaders, or the 'live for the day, keep nothing for the morrow' attitude to food, also go against Western ideas of what's sensible or necessary in life.

The other surprising feature is how *widespread* – in fact evidently universal – many hunter-gatherer characteristics are, including some of the more unusual or puzzling ones. This certainly seems to apply to basic childrearing styles – perhaps not surprisingly, as these are presumably what underlie and are the foundation for subsequent adult hunter-gatherer character and behaviour.

***Not* primitive.** Before going further, it is also important to stress one point which may or may not seem obvious: hunter-gatherers and other formerly-termed 'primitive' peoples are absolutely *not* primitive in their faculties, but display the same range of intelligence and abilities as would be found in modern developed-world peoples. However, their upbringings and socialisation are very different from Western peoples' (see Chapter 6 for details), their views of the world are therefore also quite different, and their hunter-gathering way of life is obviously very different too. Hence different qualities and skills are valued; and it is these that get developed the most – possibly at the expense of others that Westernised cultures consider to be more important such as left-brain-type learning. (This fact is in direct opposition to the views of even some modern scholars such as Colin Renfrew, who have continued to contend that simpler peoples are indeed 'primitive' in the worst sense of the word – sub-human, unintelligent and so on.)

Abundant admirable qualities. We can set the scene for our review of forager characteristics with Kropotkin (1902), who cites a quotation from the early eighteenth century explorer Kolben in which the latter says of the South African Hottentots that "they are certainly the most **friendly**, the most **liberal** and the most **benevolent** people to one another that ever appeared on the earth." Kropotkin then goes on to say that in describing the Hottentots in this way, Kolben "wrote a sentence which has continually appeared since in the description of savages." In other words, observers and researchers from the early days of ethnographic and anthropological work onwards have repeatedly been struck by the many positive features of 'savage' life. And this point is still valid today, with many contemporary authors – professional anthropologists and others – who have lived with unspoilt tribes, describing them in the same enthusiastic way. For example, in *Don't Sleep, There Are Snakes* (2008), Daniel Everett says of the Amazonian Pirahã tribe with whom he lived in the 1970s: "Since my first night among them I have been impressed with their **patience**, their **happiness** and their **kindness**." While extreme sports writer Christopher McDougall, who was unexpectedly exposed to the reclusive contemporary Tarahumara people of Mexico while researching his best-selling *Born to Run* (2009), described them as the "kindest, happiest people on the planet"; and wondered at the fact that:

> "In Tarahumara Land, there was no crime, war or theft. There was no corruption, obesity, drug addiction, greed, wife-beating, child abuse, heart disease, high blood pressure, or carbon emissions. They didn't get diabetes or depressed, or even old: fifty-year-olds could outrun teenagers, and eighty-year-old grandfathers could hike marathon distances up mountainsides. Their cancer rate was barely detectable."

Attitude to childrearing. This is discussed in greater depth in Chapter 6. Suffice it to say here that the forager approach to childrearing is very different from what's normal in Western society. It appears to be based on a fundamental trust that babies will grow up into agreeable adults in their own time if nurtured fully as children, given good examples of proper grown-up behaviour by others, gently encouraged towards acceptable behaviour (particularly food-sharing) and discouraged from unwanted traits. The understanding is that babies and children themselves know best what they need – when to eat, when to sleep, when to play – and that their requests should therefore be fulfilled as well as possible by older people around them. There is no concept of 'spoiling' children or of chastising or punishing them. Nor is there any idea that children should obey others, be forced to do so, or be punished for not obeying, as there is (overtly or covertly) in dominator societies. The same personal freedoms are granted to children as to everyone else in these cultures, and children respond to requests if they want to, not if they don't (though they mainly seem to want to). Babies are held close to caregivers for most of their early years; are the object of abundant affection and attention; and typically aren't weaned till around age two. The implication of the forager approach to early childrearing is that the infant has a right to absolute indulgence; that its wants are the same as its needs and should be satisfied; and that in due course satisfaction of its wants will lead it to become an adult with the ability to take on adult responsibilities, including those of satisfying the wants of children (Hamilton, 1981).

The physical development of hunter-gatherer children is also far ahead of what's typical in Western cultures. This is partly because some behaviours are encouraged from very early on – such as the ability to sit unsupported on a mother's shoulders, or to walk – because it enables women to go foraging with youngsters as soon as possible. Children in these societies are also trusted far more to be around 'dangerous' things; and – if necessary – to learn by experience that fires burn, knives cut and so on. And, remarkably, despite this minimal adult intervention, children largely avoid serious harm. Peer group play from the age of four or five also encourages physical development, with activities like running, climbing, swimming and throwing being helped and spurred on by fellow children.

The result is – unexpectedly, to exponents of a 'spare the rod' philosophy – generally highly prosocial behaviour among hunter-gatherer children compared to those in Westernised societies, coupled with remarkable physical abilities. Liedloff (1975), and Everett (2008), both provide good descriptions of these traits in Amazonian tribal children. Liedloff, for example, observed of the Yequana that:

> "The children were uniformly well-behaved; never fought, were never punished, always obeyed happily and instantly... I saw little Yequana girls from the age of three or four (sometimes they looked even younger) taking full charge of infants. It was clearly their favourite occupation, but did not prevent them doing other things at the same time, tending fires, fetching water and so on."
>
> (Liedloff, 1975)

And Hamilton (1981) sums up the development of Arnhem Land children like this:

> "By the time children are 5 they have become independent, self-possessed creatures... closely involved in adults' everyday affairs. They have received no formal training from adults in skills, beliefs or moral values and occupy their days with little supervision. They are generally considerate of each other, willing to help younger children, and find much of their emotional support in the peer group, where they spend much of their time. They have learnt the rudiments of many adult activities by watching closely and practising themselves

> but have no experience of intensive, goal-directed communication. They are masters of their own social world, tolerated and indulged in their demands, with an assured place beside a number of different adults and children to whom they are tied by bonds of kinship, aid and daily interaction."

And all this has been achieved with a minimum of 'don'ts or 'mustn'ts and with absolutely no smacks, naughty steps, bribes or threats – surely something to give pause to modern parents!

Hamilton goes on to stress the point that:

> "Such was the environment within which the human race evolved and to which the relations between adult and child were for thousands, perhaps even hundreds of thousands, of years adapted. No one to my knowledge has yet produced evidence of a hunting and gathering society which fails... to treat its children in a similar fashion, as if following the same theory. On the contrary, all accounts suggest a basically very similar picture... "

One therefore pretty much has to conclude that it is this sort of upbringing that results in adults with the largely admirable characteristics described in this chapter. Clearly each factor leads to the other: hunter-gatherer style childrearing produces hunter-gatherer grown-ups and communities that, in turn, rear children in a way which continues to carry on hunter-gatherer values and behaviours. And as we've already said above, it's also hard not to be struck by how similar the basic approach to childrearing is or has been in forager cultures all over the globe and from different eras, indicating how fundamental and intrinsic it is to this way of life.

Egalitarianism. James Woodburn is a leading thinker on egalitarianism and its central role in hunter-gatherer society, and some of his ideas have already been outlined in the previous chapter's section on that subject. We have also described Christopher Boehm's (1999) views there. For Boehm, egalitarianism is the most striking quality – and chief puzzle – about hunter-gatherer society. He defines it as "status equivalency among the decision-makers of a group"; views egalitarian hunter-gatherer society as being what he calls an intentional moral community; and sees egalitarianism as something that is kept in place by a community's traditional, largely unspoken, pro-egalitarian ethos.

In order to maintain egalitarianism, foragers seek **freedom for individuals**, **equality** and a **horizontal social structure** by encouraging prosocial blueprints, and discouraging or proscribing upstarts, freeloaders, cheats or excessively competitive or aggressive behaviour. The former is done by requiring or encouraging acceptable or admirable behaviour, including **generosity**, **honesty**, **helpfulness and even-temperedness**. The latter is done largely by discouraging unwanted behaviours such as stinginess, aloofness, arrogance, boastfulness, lying, theft, violence – mainly through mild shaming methods such as teasing, banter and ridicule (see *Group Harmony and Settling Disputes* below for more about sanctioning methods). The personal qualities that suggest someone is ambitious for power or wealth in and of themselves exclude such a person from the possibility of leadership (Woodburn, 1981). Overall, the effect is to encourage behaviour that is **honourable** and **just**. All adults usually have a right to contribute to decision-making, and this is intended to be as consensual as possible. Male and female, old and young, are usually able to contribute meaningfully to the process.

Perhaps it is worth making the point here that hunter-gatherers' ability to dispense with leadership – indeed, to actively fight upstartism – may be the result of their satisfactory childrearing practices (Chapter 6). Their nurturing upbringings don't leave them with unsatisfied longings for parenting, whereas many dominator-reared people want to be looked after and led, even in adulthood – desires which make them seek parental figures or be willing to submit to leaders, bosses, hierarchical systems and so on.

Individual autonomy. Another feature of forager life that is particularly noted by modern authors such as Brody (2001), Liedloff (1975) and Woodburn (2005) is the value that hunter-gatherers place on individuals' freedom to make decisions. "Individual autonomy is valued above all else... No one has the right or means to direct, order, or coerce another individual to do anything against his or her wishes," (McCreedy, cited in Taylor, 2005). Woodburn associates this with a disengagement from binding commitments or dependencies in close social relationships; and it applies to everyone, regardless of age or sex. Everyone's freedom to *not* comply, to do their own thing, and to move away from an upstart or despotically-inclined individual if necessary is also a key factor in discouraging upstarts or those attempting to take power.

'Leadership' by those best qualified. In hunter-gatherer cultures, 'leaders' are temporary – adopted for specific circumstances because of their particular abilities. Rather than being leaders, they are people who others defer to about the topic at issue, and are also expected to display all of the required or admired prosocial qualities in spades – to be "modest in demeanour, generous to a fault, and egalitarian" (Woodburn, 1981). Of either sex, depending on the task at hand, they may plan or lead hunting expeditions; broker disputes within the group or discussions between groups about issues such as use of waterholes; arrange suitable matches, and so on:

> "the combined hunting, healing, and political skills of 'elder statesmen' diffuse tensions, promote solidarity, attract useful group members, and otherwise promote the group's solidarity and continued access to resources."
>
> (Hrdy, 2009)

"There are experts rather than leaders, men or women whose skills are revered; but decisions about whether to follow their lead or take their advice are matters of individual choice," confirms Brody (2001).

Women's role. Briffault, writing in the 1920s, emphasised the influential role that *women* played, for example, in North American tribes – quoting a source who reported of the Eskimo that "the women appear to stand on a footing of perfect equality with the men, both in the family and in the community," and quoting the missionary Lafitau who avers that:

> "Nothing is more real than the superiority of the women. It is in the women that properly consists the nation, the nobility of blood, the genealogical tree, the order of generations, the preservation of families. It is in them that all real authority resides; the country, the fields, and all the flocks belong to them. They are the soul of the councils, the arbiters of war and peace."

Briffault then comments: "That description has been thought to be highly coloured, but we have evidence to show that it is strictly accurate," and cites numerous examples to show that "woman's influence was absolutely paramount." And no doubt this was true of many other hunter-gatherer and tribal peoples in the past – the more so as we move back in time.

Hospitality and **generosity** with a strong **cooperative** and **sharing ethos**. Knight (1991) relates these qualities directly to his sex strike scenario, whose main aim is to encourage exactly these behaviours (ones which are weak in our ape relatives and therefore surprising in *Homo sapiens*). Alloparenting is also a prime example of sharing resources – in this case regarding the provisioning and care of children.

Hrdy stresses the importance of *giving* generally in hunter-gatherer society, and the major role that exchanges of gifts and services plays in maintaining the extended kin and as-if kin networks common among hunter-gatherers living a precarious existence in marginal lands. Favours are remembered; and networks of mutual goodwill are maintained across time and space in these ways, even to the extent of being inherited, with people understanding that their most important resources are their reputation and the stored goodwill of others. Children in many forager societies are also specifically taught to give and share from a very early age (Hamilton, 1981; Hrdy, 2009); and this obviously contributes to their subsequent abilities to be hospitable and to share, and to their expectations that others will share also.

The ways in which equitable sharing is achieved are described by many authors:

> "In a small and tightly knit hunting band survival can only be achieved by the closest co-operation and by an elaborate system of reciprocal obligations which ensures that everyone has some share in the days' catch. Some days one gets more than others, but nobody goes without. There is, as often as not, a great deal of squabbling over the division of the game, but that is expected, and nobody attempts to take what is not his due... Disputes are generally settled with little reference to the rights and wrongs of the case, but more with the sole intention of restoring peace to the community... This is perhaps one of the most remarkable features of pygmy life, the way everything settles itself with apparent lack of organization. Co-operation is the key to pygmy society; you can expect it and you can demand it and you have to give it." (Turnbull, 1961).

Norberg-Hodge (1991) confirms this in regard to the tribal Ladakh of the Himalayas, describing how "a concern not to offend or upset one another is deeply rooted in Ladakhi society;

people avoid situations that might lead to friction and conflict." Again, ensuring harmony and peace is more important than the rights and wrongs of a case.

However, we also need to bear in mind a point that Woodburn and Hamilton stress: that sharing is seen as an absolute *obligation* in hunter-gatherer societies and one which doesn't require or seek reciprocation or gratitude. Woodburn and Lewis (2008/9) also emphasise the hunter-gatherer viewpoint that accumulating resources beyond what is required on the day is actually immoral, and that everyone has an obligation to give away whatever is not being used at that moment.

This obligation to share extends beyond the physical to the sharing of knowledge, skills and abilities; and encompasses the concept that group involvement can enhance or increase what's being shared. Speaking of trance dance healing, Woodburn (2005) observes:

> "A man pays no fees to the healers who teach him to become a healer, and when he is qualified he shares the yield of his ability to heal with everyone in the community without fee or expectation of reciprocation. His ability to heal is believed to derive from *n/um*, a personally owned substance or force within him which is said to be warmed up and made available for curing with the help of other dancers and singers. He shares *n/um*, or the yield of *n/um*, in a way that is directly analogous to the sharing of a personally owned carcass of a game animal he has killed. But I should go further than this. Sharing in this context is not merely analogous to the secular sharing of meat. It is consecrated sharing produced in the context of the joint participation of the entire community, a potent dramatisation of the production of the egalitarian community... "

Supportiveness. Within egalitarian groups, everyone –

including the sick, weak, old and young – are entitled to a share of the community's resources, up to the point where actuarial intelligence recognises that continued support is endangering the group. "Everyone has responsibility for the community and everyone is cared for by the community," (Everett, 2008). One particularly significant aspect of the forager pattern of supportiveness and sharing is the alloparenting discussed in Chapter 2; but mutual support and sharing of resources continues from cradle to grave, and is a central feature of hunter-gatherer life. So, in regard to the old and infirm, Lee has this to say of the !Kung Bushmen:

> "The aged hold a respected position in Bushman society and are the effective leaders of the camps... Long after their productive years have passed, the old people are fed and cared for by their children and grandchildren. The blind, the senile, and the crippled are respected for the special ritual skills they possess... "
>
> (Lee and DeVore, eds., 1968)

Unsentimental Woodburn sees these practices as illustrations of the fact that – in the case of the Hadza – society is open and there is simply no *basis* for exclusion, rather than as demonstrating sympathy or humaneness *per se* (Woodburn, 1981). He illustrates this further by describing how the Hadza don't exclude lepers from their community (behaviour which is very different from the excluding behaviour of adjacent, settled, communities) – again because their culture's ethos has no basis for excluding anyone. Woodburn does discuss instances of neglect or abandonment – among the Hadza, for example; but believes that these are relatively rare. He also makes the point that such examples are more visible in forager societies because they can't be hidden behind closed doors as they be can in more 'civilised' communities.

Community spirit. Close cooperation and a tightly knit community is characteristic of many traditional tribal societies. It is a feature of the Ladakh, for example, who exemplify the type of traditional self-governing village society described so well by Kropotkin (1902):

> "The Ladakhis have been fortunate enough to inherit a society in which the good of the individual is not in conflict with that of the whole community; one person's gain is not another person's loss. From family and neighbours to members of other villages and even strangers, Ladakhis are aware that helping others is in their own interest… A healthy society is one that encourages close social ties and mutual interdependence, granting each individual a net of unconditional emotional support. Within this nurturing framework, individuals feel secure enough to become quite free and independent."
>
> (Norberg-Hodge, 1991)

The lack of crime – from anti-social behaviour to petty theft to murder – in traditional societies is also commented on by many visitors. For example, in 1840 the Russian missionary Veniaminoff wrote of the Inuit-related Aleoute that:

> "… one murder had been committed since the last century in a population of 60,000 people, and that among 1,800 Aleoutes not one single common law offence had been known for forty years… scolding, scorning are absolutely unknown in Aleoute life. Even their children never fight and never abuse each other in words."
>
> (Kropotkin, 1902)

Not materialistic. Nomadic hunter-gatherers by definition have to travel light for practical reasons: "Mobility and property are in contradiction," (Sahlins, 1966). But it is notable how little they are attached to material objects for their own sake, and how willing and able they are to pass valued objects along to others. Woodburn relates this more to sanctions against accumulation than to questions of practicality; and describes, for example, the Hadzas' practice of gambling on a game of chance which inevitably results in valuable objects getting redistributed around the society (Woodburn, 1981). Many observers have also commented on how little care foragers typically take of their possessions or of presents they've received. This is very different from what pertains in dominator-style cultures, including our current Westernised one, which is almost defined by materialism and attachment to 'stuff'. Certainly, one can view materialism as a by-product of screwed-upness – a point which is touched on again in Chapter 4. And one can view the hunter-gatherers' casual or unattached attitude as stemming from a fundamental spiritual belief that their world is a loving, kind place which will always give them what they need when they need it if they treat their environment right (Lewis, 2007/8). This is surely trust at its finest; and equates to the Lord's Prayer's enjoinment to "give us this day our daily bread" – no less, but also no more!

Not driven by a work ethic; plentiful leisure time; 'living well'. This feature of hunter-gatherer life has been much commented on (negatively) by Protestant-work-ethic-driven visitors and colonisers down the ages; and is discussed (sympathetically) by many recent authors such as Lee and Zerzan. Foraging societies usually don't view 'work' as an activity distinct from life in general, or even have the concept of or a word for 'work'. They certainly don't see life's necessary activities as being something specific – 'work' – whose execution is laudable in its own right or intrinsically confers virtue on the doer. Theirs is a joined-up world, in which gathering, hunting, childcare, music and dance, artistic or ritual activities and so on are carried out as needed, or as enjoyed, or in their due season.

Marshall Sahlins, in his now famous paper *The Original Affluent Society*, and Richard Lee in his *What Hunters Do for a Living* paper (both presented at the 1966 *Man the Hunter* conference (Lee and DeVore, 1968)) were among the first to show how foragers – even in apparently harsh environments – can provide themselves with a rich and varied diet for relatively little input, the result being abundant leisure time to spend on 'non-essentials'. A passage from Lee about the !Kung Bushmen from the same conference is quoted by Sahlins in order to illustrate this point:

> "A woman gathers on one day enough to feed her family for three days, and spends the rest of her time resting in camp, doing embroidery, visiting other camps, or entertaining visitors from other camps. For each day at home, kitchen routines such as cooking, nut cracking, collecting firewood, and fetching water occupy one to three hours of her time. This rhythm of steady work and steady leisure is maintained throughout the year."

Such a pattern is typical of foraging peoples: their wants are few and usually easily obtained; they enjoy 'work' and play both; and have abundant leisure time to spend on what these days we'd call socialising and hobbies(!). Hardly a nasty, brutish life... Here's another example, from an Amazonian tribe:

> "For the people of Santa Clara, 'living well' is the ideal of everyday life. It means living without malicious gossip, living without fighting, living in a peaceful village surrounded by helpful and generous kinspeople, living in good health, and especially eating abundant quantities of what Piro people call 'real food', plantains from the gardens and game animals from the river and forest, and drinking lots of manioc beer."
>
> (Gow, 2001)

To be fair to Westerners, this ideal is very similar to what many developed-world people would wish for in their lives too. Indeed, I've lived in an English village which came pretty close to this ideal in many respects, with the community allotments and two village pubs playing a vital role in 'living well' therein!

Peaceableness. Hunter-gatherers and many tribal peoples are largely peaceful and peace-loving, calm and uncompetitive. For example:

> "In traditional Ladakh, aggression of any sort is exceptionally rare; rare enough to say that it is virtually nonexistentthere has been no fighting in the village within living memory. Even arguments are rare. I have hardly ever seen anything more than mild disagreement in the traditional villages – certainly nothing compared to what you find in the West." (Norberg-Hodge, 1991).

Hrdy, one of many now arguing against the longstanding Darwinian view that human hypersociality developed as a within-group response to threats or competition from competing groups, corroborates this book's view that peaceableness is a feature of unscrewed up humans:

> "Far from being competitors for resources, nearby members of their own species would have been more valuable as potential sharing partners. When conflicts did loom, moving on would have been more practical as well as less risky than fighting… Nevertheless, from the early days of evolutionary anthropology to today's textbooks in evolutionary psychology, the tendency has been to devote more space to aggression and our 'killer instincts' or to emphasize 'demonic' chimpanzee-like tendencies for males to join with other males in their group to hunt neighbouring groups and intimidate, beat, torture, and kill them… [Yet] in spite of abundant evidence documenting

intergroup conflict over the past 10,000 to 15,000 years, there is no evidence of warfare in the Pleistocene. Such absence of evidence is not evidence of absence, but it helps to explain why many of those who actually study hunter-gatherers are skeptical about projecting the bellicose behavior of post-Neolithic peoples back onto roaming kin-based bands of hunter-gatherers."

(Hrdy, 2009)

Hrdy goes on to suggest that it takes high population levels, competition for the same resources, long-standing conflicts of interest, and major provocations to persuade hominins that neighbouring people are sufficiently alien, evil or potentially dangerous to warrant face-to-face killing.

Cheerfulness, love of fun, playfulness, good temper, sense of humour. This is an aspect of hunter-gatherer life which tends to be under-reported in scientific anthropological accounts. However, it features very strongly in more popular writings such as Turnbull's *The Forest People* (1961), Liedloff's *The Continuum Concept* (1971), and Everett's *Don't Sleep, There Are Snakes* (2008). Turnbull's description of everyday life with the Mbuti pygmies is typical:

"usually everyone is talking and laughing and shouting rude remarks from one end of the camp to the other... The pygmy is not in the least self-conscious about showing his emotions, and he likes to laugh until tears come to his eyes and he is too weak to stand. He then sits or lies down on the ground and laughs still louder."

Daniel Everett's descriptions of the Amazon basin Pirahã people tells the same story:

"Pirahãs laugh about everything. They laugh at their own

misfortune: when someone's hut blows over in a rainstorm, the occupants laugh more loudly than anyone. They laugh when they catch a lot of fish. They laugh when they catch no fish. They laugh when they're full and they laugh when they're hungry."

Or take the Amazonian Canela tribe:

> "Canela culture is radically divergent from European-based cultural expectations, values and perspective, even though their common humanity is apparent. They live a joyous life of festival, ceremony, and ritual that is inconceivable from the perspective of a work- and time-oriented Westerner. The Canela spend hours and days engaged in symbolic re-enactments of their cultural meanings, and parts of every day engaged in what seems like plain everyday fun – such as racing around the village perimeter carrying heavy logs on their shoulders (a great way to keep in shape, it seems)."
>
> (Crocker and Crocker, 2004)

This aspect of forager life is discussed further in Chapters 9 and 11.

Carefree, free of worry or depression. Everett notes how carefree and generally mentally healthy the Pirahã are: "The Pirahãs show no evidence of depression, chronic fatigue, extreme anxiety, panic attacks, or other psychological ailments common in many industrialized societies." And he goes on to make the good point that this isn't due to a literal lack of cares:

> "But this psychological well-being is not due, as some might think, to a lack of pressure. It is ethnocentric to suppose that only industrialized societies can produce psychological pressure, or that psychological difficulties are only found in such societies. True, the Pirahãs don't have to worry about

> paying their bills on time or which college to select for their children. But they do have life-threatening physical ailments... And they have love lives. And they need to provide food every day for their families. They have high infant mortality. They regularly face dangerous reptiles, mammals, bugs and other creatures. They live with threats of violence from outsiders who frequently invade their land. When I am there, with a much easier life than the Pirahãs themselves have, I still find that there is plenty for me to get worked up about. The thing is, I do get worked up, but they do not. I have never heard a Pirahã say that he or she is worried."

The same point is made by McDougal (2009) and many other authors.

Unhung-up about sex, the body, or bodily functions. While many things in forager life are subject to taboos – some of which can seem peculiar or unfathomable to Westerners – hunter-gatherers overall tend to have an accepting, pragmatic or jocular view of the body and bodily functions, including sex. This is very different to what is found in patriarchal societies, including developed and ostensibly liberated cultures such those of the West. This subject is discussed further in Chapters 11 to 13.

Kind, warm. Visitors almost invariably speak of the kindness and warmth which they've experienced while living with hunter-gatherers, even when times and conditions were difficult. For example, see Everett (2008); McDougall (2009); and the quotation from Kropotkin given at the start of this chapter. "People interact closely and warmly all the time both in subsistence and non-subsistence activities," affirms Woodburn (2005).

Affectionate to children. The vital importance of giving affection to children, and its role in unscrewed-upness is discussed in more detail in Chapters 6 and 7. It is a marked feature of hunter-gatherer societies and has been studied and measured by many:

> "A brief survey of caretaking practices across traditional hunting and gathering peoples – the closest proxies for Pleistocene hominins we have – reveals that even though nomadic foragers differ in where and how they make a living, babies are universally treated with warm indulgence... Babies are never left alone and are constantly held by someone."
> (Hrdy, 2009)

These are classificatory kinship societies, so the whole community plays a part in caring for everyone's children. For example, Turnbull (1961) describes how a pygmy child can turn to anyone in times of need, for he will always be found and carried back "to the safety of a hut. It does not matter which hut, because as far as the child is concerned all adults are his parents or grandparents." And Everett observes how: "Pirahã children roam about the village and are considered to be related to and partially the responsibility of everyone in the village." This attitude is exemplified by the story quoted by Briffault (1927, citing Lafitau, 1724) of an old North American tribesman upbraided by a Jesuit missionary who was dismayed by his tribe's apparent sexual promiscuity and hence the uncertain paternity of its children. The tribesman responded:

> "You white people love your own children only. We love the children of the clan. They belong to all the people, and we care for them. They are bone of our bone and flesh of our flesh. We are all father and mother to them. White people are savages; they do not love their children. If children are orphaned, people have to be paid to look after them. We know nothing of such barbarous ideas."

Older children too may be treated indulgently in some cultures:

for example, Lee says of the !Kung Bushmen:

> "Another significant feature of the composition of the work force is the late assumption of adult responsibility by adolescents. Young people are not expected to provide food regularly until they are married... It is not unusual to find healthy, active teenagers visiting from camp to camp while their older relatives provide food for them."
>
> (Lee and DeVore, eds., 1968)

Benign world view; trust. "What is striking about the world-views of foragers... is that they tend to share a view of their physical environment as a 'giving' place occupied by others who are also liable to be well-disposed and generous. They view their physical world as being in line with benevolent social relationships. Thus, the Mbuti [of Central Africa] refer to the forest as a place that gives 'food, shelter and clothing just like their parents'," (Hrdy, 2009). Turnbull (1961) also describes this benign world view well when recounting a nocturnal trip he made with the Mbuti pygmies into the Congo forest:

> "It struck me with a sudden shock that not one of them carried a spear or bow and arrow... As they peered into the dusk and cocked their heads... satisfying themselves that we were really alone, it seemed that they felt themselves so much a part of the forest and all the living things in it that they had no need to fear anything except that which is not of the forest. One of them said to me, later, 'When we are the children of the forest, what need have we to be afraid of it? We are only afraid of that which is outside the forest.'"

This aspect of forager mindset also relates to their views on sharing, for it seems quite clear from authors such as Woodburn (2005) and Lewis (2008/9) that primitive peoples' attitude of living for the day and seeing accumulation as immoral is based on a deep belief that their world will provide for them, as long as they in turn treat their world and each other right:

> "The Yaka... [like] many other forest hunter-gatherers... have a faith that the forest will always provide them with what they need. Abundance is taken as natural. Should people not experience abundance, it is not because resources are diminishing but due to improper sharing."
>
> (Lewis, 2008/9)

This attitude is explained well in *Mutant Message Down Under* (Morgan, 1991):

> "I learned that the appearance of food was not taken for granted. It was first requested, always expected to appear, and did appear, but was gratefully received and genuine gratitude was always given... The tribe carried no provisions. They planted no crops; they participated in no harvest. They walked the blazing Australian Outback, knowing each day they would receive bountiful blessings of the universe. The universe never disappointed them."
>
> (Morgan, 1991)

Many tribal peoples, too, share this benign world view – their feelings of happiness and security springing partly from a sense of deep connection to their land, and their community:

> "I have never met people who seem so healthy emotionally, so secure, as the Ladakhis. The reasons are, of course, complex and spring from a whole way of life and worldview. But I am sure that the most important factor is the sense that you are part of something much larger than yourself, that you are inextricably connected to others and to your surroundings."

(Norberg-Hodge, 1991)

Positive spiritual life. A belief in different realities and magical, sacred or supernatural entities and forces – spirits, the Dreamtime, *n/um* and so on – is an intrinsic part of hunter-gatherers' lives (and indeed of most peoples' lives down the ages.) It interweaves through every aspect of their existence, is inherently involved with their view of the world; and it goes without saying that experiencing the world as a place imbued with real magic helps makes it meaningful and vibrant. The less patriarchal the culture, the more positive and 'healthy' (free from unnecessary fearfulness, guilt, shame and so on) the spiritual world view seems to be; and one can certainly see this type of animistic world view as another of the positive traits to be found in hunter-gatherer cultures.

As I said in Chapter 1, I don't have a problem with accepting that hunter-gatherers and many other simpler peoples have perceptions or abilities which Westernised cultures don't recognise, such as enhanced intuition or a 'sixth sense'; shamanic and healing powers (see for example, the book and film *The Horse Boy* by Rupert Isaacson); or the ability to directly experience the magic in nature as described so beautifully by Turnbull in *The Forest People*. I am glad that anarcho-primitivist Zerzan shares this view to at least some extent, and is brave enough to nail his colours to the mast about, for example, telepathy – citing several authors who claim to have witnessed it among indigenous peoples (Zerzan, 2002).

Liedloff (1975) certainly believes that the unscrewed up, continuum-style childhoods experienced by the Amazonian tribes she lived with give them enormous advantages if they deliberately seek to develop spiritual abilities by practicing spiritual techniques – providing them with:

"a huge head start over us on the road to serenity… The

> proportion of Sanema who have attained truly impressive states of joy and harmony with their surroundings is remarkable, and would be impossible to match anywhere in the West or East."

Steve Taylor, too, suggests that all unfallen peoples have a strong sense of the "sacredness and alive-ness of nature" coupled with a natural state of connectedness/higher consciousness; and that most children have this as well, before it is socialised out of them (Taylor 2005; 2009). Taylor's and Liedloff's observations square well with the basic thesis of this book, which is that unscrewed up humans exist in an innate state of happiness which includes being spiritually tuned-in, perceptive, aware of higher vibrations or energies, and connected to a wider reality beyond the immediate physical world accessible to our five senses. This 'naturally spiritual' aspect of partnership life is discussed further in Chapters 11 and 13.

Bravery and fortitude. Calm stoicism in the face of hardship or suffering is the norm among hunter-gatherers. For example, here Hugh Brody (2001) describes his Inuit companions in the last stages of an exhausting, fruitless, and potentially fatal hunting expedition he took with them:

> "Despite exhaustion, hunger and disappointments, they had expressed neither disingenuous optimism nor disgruntled pessimism. The mood never changed. The same balance of quiet conversation, jokes and friendly silence had continued each day."

The harsh physical realities of forager and tribal life, plus the sound values they espouse, tend to naturally develop strength of character, integrity and authenticity in their peoples. Or – to use the terminology employed by the esoteric teacher Gurdjieff (Ouspensky, 1950) – it tends to foster the development of *essence* as opposed to *personality* in their characters. This is particularly apparent in situations where quiet fortitude and courage are required. For example, in describing Ladakh shepherds facing attacks on their flocks by wolves, Norberg-Hodge (1991) says,

> "I knew that attacks like this had to be accepted in the mountains, but even so the Ladakhis' attitude was remarkable. I saw no sign of bitterness or self-pity. Nothing, it seemed, could affect their equanimity."

The tremendous hardiness and fortitude of hunter-gatherer and tribal peoples is commented upon by many authors. For example, Kropotkin (1902) cites the Russian missionary Veniaminoff on the Aleoute:

> "Endurability is their chief feature. It is simply colossal. Not only do they bathe every morning in the frozen sea, and stand naked on the beach, inhaling the icy wind, but their endurability, even when at hard work on insufficient food, surpasses all that can be imagined."

Good lifestyle and quality of life generally. Further characteristics of foraging cultures which aren't central to the thesis of this book but are well worth mentioning include **good health** and **fitness**. These are a natural result of hunter-gathering life, with its varied exercise and diverse diet; and this would have been the case even more in the less stressful (non-marginal, or unharassed) conditions which must have been available to foraging peoples more widely in the past. The abundant **leisure time** which is likely to have pertained for foragers in such conditions has already been mentioned above. Lee (1968) summarises foraging as "a persistent and well-adapted way of life"; and Woodburn (2005) concludes:

> "Much of my own and other people's work in recent years in societies with immediate return systems has demonstrated that their systems are internally coherent and viable, that they make sense politically and economically for their members and allow them to live reasonably rewarding and satisfying lives... [providing] reasonable security, good health and nutrition and a greater amount of leisure than is available in most societies."

Group Harmony and Settling Disputes

Equanimity. This aspect of hunter-gatherer life has already been touched on earlier in this chapter, but it deserves further discussion. A partnership-type ethos encourages restraint in expressing negative emotions, and this contributes greatly to the harmony of tribal life compared to ours. In addition, group living also helps to encourage high standards of behaviour; and there seems to be a healthy and rewarding balance between habits of positive self-restraint, and the ability to be joyful - between 'The Good Life' and 'The Pleasant Life' (Seligman, 2003). For example, as Brody (2001) explains:

> "Inuit elders are remarkable for their equanimity. Smiles and laughter are used to deal with many forms of disquiet, and a judicious withdrawal is the proper way of responding to conflict. Anger was understandable in children but quite unacceptable in adults."

Everett (2008) also describes this well, showing the Pirahãs as a group which is both hard-nosed, realistic and stoical about the hardships of life, but also playful, joyful and good-humoured. "Life for these people is not easy. Yet they live as if it were, greeting people with grace, good humour, and helpfulness." He, and other observers of forager or tribal life, describe various ways in which disputes are settled and justice is done with little or no violence, aggression or coercion, and few explicit rules:

> "In a small primitive society, much of social life is smoothly regulated by these codes, rules, expectations, habits and customs that are related to etiquette, ethic and role. And because these are not explicit, nor revealed by frequent breaches, the society might give the impression of freedom and lack of conflict, as Rousseau would have it."
>
> (Service, 1975, quoted in Boehm, 1999)

Sanctioning methods. Boehm has paid particular attention to this aspect of egalitarian life, especially to sanctioning methods. He notes a continuum from "moderate" method which range from gossiping to criticism, ridicule, or disobedience (if someone tries to order others about), to "strong" methods starting with various forms of ostracism, then expulsion from the group, deposition, or desertion (from an upstart's group, for example), which are used only in cases of repeated offences against group *mores*. The "ultimate" sanction of execution is also applied *in extremis* against social deviants and those who transgress against universal prohibitions. These include incorrigible bullies, people with despotic tendencies, adulterers, rapists, and those who commit incest, or murder within the group; but this sanction is rarely needed or used.

Other authors stress teasing and mild ridicule as being the sanctions most used and most effective, plus group withdrawal from an offender, and withdrawal of food-sharing (Everett, 2008; Turnbull, 1961). Turnbull (1968) and Woodburn (2005) also emphasise the freedom that hunter-gatherers have to simply move away from unpleasant people or situations to other households or camps, and the fact that this autonomy and social mobility plays an important role in defusing problems, particularly by subverting authority. Letting litigants argue things out between themselves, or engage in a mild fight are other methods described by Colin Turnbull. Or else supernatural powers such as spirits may be invoked to make a judgement about a dispute. And it is a testament to egalitarian life that these mainly relatively mild methods – which are potent just because of the importance of group harmony in tribal life – are usually effective. Hunter-gatherers don't use a large proportion of their resources on police forces, law courts, or locking a significant percentage of their population up in prisons as more 'civilised' societies do… It is also interesting how similar these methods are to those described for social animals by Bekoff and Pierce (2009): physical punishment, social ostracism, future payback (like refusing to play when next invited) or being treated with less generosity if one has been stingy or unfair are examples from chimpanzees and coyotes – demonstrating evolutionary continuity again between humans and our social animal relations.

Harmony in communal life. Kropotkin's description of communal life among the Inuit of his day (drawn from studies which are chiefly from the late nineteenth century) depicts the even-tempered tenor of everyday life under even the harshest and most trying of circumstances:

> "The families… remain united in clans, and how could it be otherwise? How could they sustain the hard struggle for life unless by closely combining their forces? So they do, and the tribal bonds are closest where the struggle for life is hardest, namely, in North-East Greenland. The 'long house' is their usual dwelling, and several families lodge in it, separated by small partitions of ragged furs, with a common passage in the front… The German Expedition which spent a winter close by one of these 'long houses' could ascertain that 'no quarrel disturbed the peace, no dispute arose about the use of this narrow space' throughout the long winter. Scolding, or even unkind words, are considered a misdemeanour, if not produced under the legal form of process… Close cohabi-

tation and close interdependence are sufficient for maintaining century after century that deep respect for the interests of the community which is characteristic of Eskimo life."

(Kropotkin, 1902)

Kropotkin describes the Inuit and their close congeners in the North as "one of the nearest illustrations of what man may have been during the glacial age" – implying that the behaviour he recorded was probably similar to what our Ice Age ancestors displayed, and confirming the longevity of this type of harmonious community life. (As an aside, we may perhaps see relics of life in the long house or the communal camp in society's continuing love of the 'third place' – cafes, bars, pubs, diners, plazas, malls, bookstores, libraries – welcoming semi-public places where we can hang out with others in a communal setting, engaging with our fellows as much or as little as we like, meeting old friends and making new ones, gossiping, chatting, eating and drinking…)

Conclusions

Not perfect – but still pretty damn good! This is not to say, of course, that hunter-gather peoples are perfect. For example, some treat their children at times in a way we might consider harsh (because they see this as essential to the child's learning), and many are indifferent to the suffering of animals. Infanticide and the abandoning of the elderly to die also exist, as do executions, as mentioned above – but these behaviours are always adaptive responses to harsh climes or times, usually performed reluctantly. Overall, the consensus of observers is that good humour, laughter and kindness prevail in most hunter-gatherer societies. A further point that is worth emphasising here is that recent and modern hunter-gatherers tend to live in the harshest environments on earth, such as deserts and the frozen North, because they have largely been forced out of more hospitable lands into marginal habitats by agrarian communities (Brody, 2001). This makes the fact that they are generally so hospitable, kind, equable and good humoured – even in exceptionally difficult conditions – even more remarkable.

What a difference, one can't help but think, between the values and behaviours of foraging peoples and those that TV programmes like *Big Brother* and *East Enders* showcase (and therefore seem to espouse). Here 'emotional unintelligence' seems to be vaunted; and a lack of restraint and uninhibited expressions of negative or puerile emotions – resentment, anger, vengefulness, boastfulness and so on – are the main behaviours shown. "In the parallel universe of TV land you do not negotiate or joke your way out of conflict – you shout and swear and kick ass," (Martin, 2005). Moreover, these are the behaviours which are increasingly being adopted by alienated and antisocial people throughout the 'civilised' world today, particularly by young people wanting to seem tough.

Suppressing or misunderstanding the facts about hunter-gatherer life. In concluding this chapter, we also need to remind ourselves that (as was mentioned in Chapter 1) acknowledgement of the admirable characteristics of hunter-gatherer peoples has often been suppressed, hidden or denied down the ages and into the current day. Instead, 'savages' have often been described as 'ignorant', 'miserable' or 'brutish' – as scarcely human, closer to animals than people, and so on. Even where good points were acknowledged, there has still often been a great gulf in understanding between the dominator viewpoint of Western-oriented observers and that of the indigenous peoples. As Brody (2001) explains:

> "Many writers, from explorers to missionaries to ethnographers, have referred to the difficulties or inspiration or awe they experienced as radical differences were revealed between

> the hunter-gatherer way of life and their own. Missionaries could not understand why people welcomed gifts with shouts of excitement and delight, then left them behind or threw them away. Explorers were amazed that parents never chided or disciplined their children. Administrators puzzled over a profound reluctance to exchange a condition of 'unemployment' as an 'impoverished' hunter for a job that would bring a regular and secure income. Political organisers exclaimed in despair when men and women whom they had designated or trained as 'leaders' remained committed to anti-political individualism. And everyone commented on the generosity and hospitality that prevailed even when supplies were minimal."

So hunter-gatherers continue to surprise us with their different world view. But their abundant admirable qualities must surely make at least some of us want to be a bit more like them?

Chapter 4

What Else Makes for a Partnership Society?

Can Partnership Societies be Found in More Developed or 'Civilised' Cultures?

The previous chapter described mainly *hunter-gatherer* societies, and aimed to show that these seem to produce very sane, happy peoples with abundant admirable qualities. The next question to ask is whether equally sane societies have existed or are possible in more developed societies too – ones conventionally associated with increasing levels of 'civilisation' (a term that is queried later in this chapter). Could the same values and behaviours exist generally in tribes; in settled, non-nomadic or agrarian societies; in villages, towns or even cities? This is a complex question, with many variables and many unanswered questions. All sorts of permutations have been found of societies that are more, or less, egalitarian or hierarchical/despotic; matrilineal or patrilineal; nomadic or settled; rural or urban. And reasonably egalitarian cultures have been found among peoples who exhibit some degree and mix of all these variables. One thing that stands out is that *nomadic hunter-gatherer societies* definitely seem to exhibit the most purely partnership lifestyles.

Women-power continues in tribes. Egalitarianism is one thing, but matriliny and women-power is another. Knight (1991) and other authors (for example Eisler, 1987; Stone, 1976) suggest that the evidence indicates that very early human culture was highly equal between the sexes. However, at some stage in prehistoric times, it seems that women's powers were hijacked by men, and that some degree of patriliny then began to emerge (this is discussed further in Chapter 5). From then on, nearly all known cultures – including hunter-gatherer societies – have exhibited some level of patriarchy. Nevertheless, many tribal cultures in particular continued to be relatively egalitarian between the sexes. So while a more settled lifestyle and accumulation of property – including rights to land – seem linked to an increase in patriliny, they don't necessarily entail a complete move away from at least some degree of freedom and power for women.

Agrarian, town-dwelling *and* peaceful. Nor does a settled or even town-dwelling way of life need to entail a loss of partnership ways, for if Gimbutas is right in her interpretations of Old Europe, then settled, sophisticated, urban cultures were evidently both highly women-centred *and* egalitarian *and* peaceful. Her extensive research into the civilisations of Neolithic Old Europe paints a picture of long-lasting, settled, agrarian, peaceful, town-dwelling societies which definitely seem to have been of the egalitarian, partnership type (Gimbutas, 1991). And these in turn appear to have stemmed from earlier societies in nearby Anatolia – most notably that of the remarkable town of Catalhoyuk – and the later Minoan civilisation of Crete. So, certainly in Europe and parts of the Middle East, sophisticated partnership civilisations existed from the Upper Palaeolithic up until the Bronze Age. Max Dashu's *Suppressed Histories Archive* also supports the type of view put forward by Knight and Gimbutas. Dashu has worked hard at refuting naysayers in this field; and her critique of Cynthia Eller's *The Myth of Matriarchal Prehistory* (2000), for example, effectively reaffirms the likely existence of peaceful and egalitarian prehistoric matrilineage societies, including town-dwelling ones (Dashu, 2000).

Prosocial behaviour persists, even in dominator-influenced societies. Coming forward into historic times, Lee tells us how:

> "Before the rise of the state and the entrenchment of social inequality, people lived for millennia in small-scale kin-based

social groups, in which the core institutions of economic life included collective or common ownership of land and resources, generalized reciprocity in the distribution of food, and relatively egalitarian political relations. This basic pattern, with variations, has been observed in literally hundreds of non-state societies... including bands, tribes and some chiefdoms."

(Lee, 1988)

Kropotkin's *Mutual Aid* amplifies Lee's contentions, and describes in detail how habits of cooperation and egalitarianism have survived and persisted even in completely patriarchal regimes ostensibly driven by selfish greed; and in all forms of social organisation – including towns and cities – down the ages. The point being made here is that – as we've already stressed earlier – partnership behaviour still persists to some extent at least, even in Western societies whose overall nature is a dominator one. Think of the long list of clubs and societies, and communal meetings and events, to be found in most local newspapers, to give one simple example of our species unquenchable desire to connect and cooperate. Or how nearly every community celebrates its own special fete or festival – creating a new one if there isn't an existing event.

Our behaviour: nature or nurture? The effects of over 100,000 years of prosocial behaviour on our genes were discussed at the end of Chapter 2. The possible effects of the subsequent 10,000 years of dominator-influenced life on our genes are considered at the end of Chapter 5. Suffice it to say here that even though dominator culture has been in supremacy for the last ten millennia, and presumably *has* encouraged selection for dominator-type traits, this is still a relatively small percentage of human beings' time on earth. We can therefore presume that our genetic makeup is still largely that of partnership people; that the influence of dominator-influenced natural selection on our genes has a lesser influence; and that any dominator-type behaviour we display derives significantly from nurture (see Chapter 7) rather than nature.

Modern Communism and Socialism; Communes and Intentional Communities

> *"The rapid spread of communism, on the basis of an ideology that glorified the empowerment of the rank and file, provides us with possible model for how the egalitarian syndrome diffused from band to band in the late Paleolithic (or whenever it occurred). We humans are attracted to political 'deals' that free us from domination and exploitation precisely because we are innately prone to resent authority. However, in practice, the Paleolithic 'deal' was a far better one than Marxism."*
>
> (Boehm, 1999)

Modern Communism and Socialism. At this point it seems appropriate to examine how, or whether, modern Marxian communism and socialism have contributed to the development of partnership society in modern times; and to also look at modern non-state communes and other attempts at communal living today. Marx, Engels and fellow nineteenth century left-wing thinkers strove to understand the dynamics underlying capitalist (dominator) societies in order to attempt to change them into more partnership-like forms (although those terms weren't used). Communism can be defined as a socio-political movement that aims for a classless society structured upon communal ownership of the means of production, and the end of wage labour and private property. Socialism is seen as a transitional stage on the way to communism. Communist theory generally states that the only way to solve the problems existing within capitalism is for the working class (proletariat), which is the main wealth-producer, to replace the capitalist ruling class which exploits it. Pure communism, or the stage in history after socialism, refers to a classless, stateless society in which decisions on what to produce and what policies to pursue are made in the best interests of the collective society, with the interests of every member of society given equal weight. (Does this sound familiar?!)

Engels and Morgan. Engels in particular was, as we have seen, strongly influenced by the pioneering nineteenth century American anthropologist and social theorist Lewis Henry Morgan. Morgan is best known for his work on kinship and social structure, his theories of social evolution, and his ethnography of the Native American Iroquois. The "liberty, equality and fraternity", and "communism in living", which Morgan perceived and described in Native American peoples, directly influenced Engels as he developed the idea of modern communism. In other words, the theory of modern communism sprung from, and is intellectually directly linked to, contemporaneous partnership-type peoples and their egalitarian ways of living which the founders had read about. It stemmed from primitive communism; and North American hunter-gatherers are therefore the template on which modern communism is based. This is a fact that has largely been forgotten by, or has never registered with, most people today – the majority of whom believe that communism arose entirely as a response to the perceived injustices of industrial nineteenth century Europe.

Modern communism isn't! Turning the discussion the other way round, this book takes the view that any society which is of the partnership type is displaying some form of communism; but that the reverse is certainly not necessarily true. Indeed, it seems that most, if not all, attempts at Marxian-style communism or socialism in the last century and a half have *not* managed to create egalitarian or partnership-style societies. This is probably because it is more or less impossible for people who have been brought up in dominator societies – with all the psychological problems and dominator attitudes that inevitably go with them –

to create partnership-style lives. Most of us are so damaged by dominator life, and so deeply imbued with all the wrong values and behaviours, that we find it nearly impossible to live anything approaching a really partnership type of life. And our issues are so deep-seated that we can't change them just because we want to (see Chapters 7 and 10).

So, most hard-core communist states are or were deeply dominator in style – far more so than most Western-style democracies. This is partly because their attempts to create communism (whether in good faith, or in cynical *Nineteen Eighty-Four* fashion) have mostly ended up as top-down, typically dominator-style hierarchical, coercive states. As Boehm continues in the passage quoted above:

> "Marx and Engels were sincere altruists and political reformers, but as visionary democrats they were unrealistic... [and they] were not alone. In their anthropological naïveté, visionary communists everywhere failed to see that human hierarchical tendencies are simply too strong to allow dominant competition to evaporate and the state to wither away on its own. The image was compelling, and it captured the hearts of resentful underdogs everywhere. But the social engineering was inept: the blueprint was not laid out with an accurate view of human political nature."

Boehm believes that those "too strong" hierarchical tendencies are innate, while I believe they are caused more by nurture and dominator conditioning than by nature. But as things stand at the moment, Boehm's conclusions are correct, and a different sort of social engineering – or different influences on humankind – would indeed be needed to make communism work (see Chapter 14).

Communes and Intentional Communities. Another obvious way of trying to reintroduce more partnership ways into modern life is through some form of communal or community living. Indeed, many older readers of this book will, like the author, have had some experience of this through living in communes or similar establishments in the 1960s or 1970s, and will know how hard it actually is to make this work. The fact that only a few communes have survived from that era testifies to the difficulty modern first-world people have in living communally. (The Fellowship for Intentional Community listed less than 200 communes worldwide for 2009.)

Many of us who have attempted communal living wished to create living arrangements which were more egalitarian and less nuclear-familied than those prevailing in conventional society – arrangements that involved more sharing and fewer rules about how people should combine in households. But as with travel, we 'couldn't leave ourselves behind'! We were putting old wine in new bottles – trying to create new forms of cohabitation and community, but peopling them with us and our same old hang-ups and character faults: dominator-reared people playing at partnership life. We hadn't grown up with the attitudes, traditions, and unspoken rules of behaviour which make communal life natural and relatively smooth-running in hunter-gatherer societies; and any screwed-upness within us made this type of life even harder. We usually had to resort to explicit rule-making methods – arduous meetings to discuss issues, the setting up of housework rotas, and so on – in order to try to make these alternative households function at all. And often, in the end, our individualistic desire to manage our own home lives unhindered, to *not* share our belongings, to make our own rules, and to not have to take others' desires into account, made us quit these experimental arrangements. Where communes *have* worked for longer periods, it appears to be because members subscribe to some strong overarching belief system such as exist within Christian or Steiner communities or Israeli kibbutzim. These can evidently substitute for the belief systems and *mores* of traditional partnership societies.

This discussion shows, I hope, that we need to understand the *real dynamics* underlying dominator societies in order to stand a chance of changing them into more partnership-like forms.

Questioning Conventional Views of Civilisation; Reappraisals of 'Primitive' Societies

"Civilized society is insane."
(Lawrence, 1928)

This chapter seems to be the appropriate one in which to spend some time looking at the concept of *civilisation*. Anarcho-primitivist and anti-civilisationist John Zerzan is a leading modern critic of civilisation and its effects on the world; and his views – as expressed in numerous books, essays and interviews – coincide with much of what is posited here. Indeed, he is seen by some as doing a job which archaeologists and anthropologists could, and perhaps should have done already, in critiquing modern life and civilisation in the light of their research findings. As archaeologist Kintz says in her introduction to *Running On Emptiness* (Zerzan, 2002):

> "Archaeologists themselves could become very effective social critics of rampant technological change, hierarchical class systems and unsustainable technological development if they chose to interpret the evidence they study in such a light."

Another archaeologist, Marija Gimbutas, certainly did make use of the insights gained from her work to critique society. Her views, based largely on her investigations of Old Europe and the Near East, are highly critical of the pro-dominator biases in her profession:

> "I reject the assumption that civilisation refers only to androcratic warrior societies. The generative basis of any civilisation lies in its degree of artistic creation, aesthetic achievements, non-material values and freedom which makes life meaningful and enjoyable for all its citizens, as well as a balance of power between the sexes... Archaeologists and historians have assumed that civilisation implies a hierarchical political and religious organisation, warfare, a class stratification, and a complex division of labour [whereas] if one defines civilisation as the ability of a given people to adjust to its environment and to develop adequate arts, technology, script, and social relationships it is evident that Old Europe [for example] achieved a marked degree of success."
>
> (Gimbutas, 1991)

Defining civilisation. It is interesting to note that aspects of Gimbutas' definition of civilisation apply to 'primitive' cultures as well as to the more developed, town-dwelling, Old Europe societies which she was discussing. So, if we use the term *civilised* as it is commonly employed in everyday speech, most people would surely equate civilisation with behaving in a civilised way generally – that is, with being kind, sharing, hospitable, tolerant, just, and so on. And as we have seen from Chapter 3, such behaviours are ones that are particularly notable in hunter-gatherer and many tribal cultures. However, it is actually surprisingly difficult to find formal or official definitions of civilisation – or what it means to behave in a civilised way – that reflect this sort of common usage.

For example, the Concise Oxford English Dictionary (COED) is not much help, defining civilisation as "an advanced stage or system of human social development". Other definitions from historical or archaeological literature also seem strangely detached from the values on which concepts of civilisation should surely be based. They relate, for example, to archaeological criteria such as the presence of metal tools; to the presence of mental/intellectual accomplishments such as writing; or to the level of social organisation/complexity reached (as with the COED definition), or with the State, as political scientists use the term. Unfortunately, the civilisations to which these definitions relate are usually also *dominator* cultures, and are characterised by typical dominator traits such as hierarchy, inequality and exploitation – which most people would *not* consider inherent characteristics of the concept of civilisation or of being civilised. So, it is pleasing to see that the 2010 Penguin edition of Engels' *The Origin of the Family* concords with our non-dominator view, as in its *Glossary* it has this to say of the old-fashioned term 'primitive':

> "The term for peoples living in a hunting and gathering, or horticultural, economy is awkward due to its negative connotations in popular use. Suffice it to say, as Engels' book documents so thoroughly, primitive peoples are more 'civilized' than more 'advanced' societies if the term is used to denote human interpersonal relations."

Hear, hear!

Indeed, one can make a case for seeing civilisation in its conventional sense, and its products – including those which are most vaunted, such as the 'high' culture of sophisticated art, architecture, music and so on – as just compensatory activities for what has been forfeited in the fall from our original partnership state. In that fall we have lost physical and psychological unscrewed-upness; connection with nature, the sacred and the magical; and happiness generally (topics which are discussed further in later chapters and which *Mutant Message Down Under* (Morgan, 1991) illustrates particularly well). Or one can see the products of civilisation as simply manifestations of our state of dominator-induced unease and unhealthiness: "all the so-called achievements of man are only monuments to overwhelming pride and hubris," (Kintz in Introduction to Zerzan, 2002).

Reappraising the past. So it is encouraging to find a significant new trend in recent years which is questioning conventional views of the primitive or uncivilised nature of ancient and tribal cultures. For example, in the last twenty years, many authors have produced TV series or books that present a more sympathetic and accurate view of these societies. Richard Rudgley's *Lost Civilisations of the Stone Age* (Rudgley, 1998) set out to debunk the 'nasty, brutish and short' myth of the ignorant, shivering savage – showing instead how technologically advanced prehistoric societies were, and asserting that "more and more evidence is tipping the scales further back and is showing that prehistoric cultural achievements are more profound, complex and multifarious than has been hitherto suspected." (And for those who are interested in the wilder side of this topic, Michael Cremo and Richard Thompson's *Forbidden Archaeology* (1993) or its abridged version *The Hidden History of the Human Race* (1996) is a must-read!) Terry Jones in his 2006 *Barbarians* TV series and book made a similar point about more recent societies, and showed that peoples conventionally portrayed as barbaric in the worst sense of the word were anything but. Alice Roberts has performed a similar service for the Anglo-Saxons and the so-called Dark Ages recently in the British TV series *Digging for Britain*. For example, in one of these programmes, archaeologists were 'surprised' to find evidence of caring for the disabled, elderly and young in the community they were excavating, and were encouraged by this to consider the Anglo-Saxons as being more humane than had previously been thought! (Roberts, 2010). And though adventurer and TV personality Bruce Parry doesn't set out to sell partnership values, he can't help but convey many of them naturally through the medium of his UK *Tribe* TV series and book (Parry, 2007), and subsequent programmes.

Some conventional interpretations of mainstream archaeology are also being re-evaluated. So Native American, European Neolithic, Egyptian and many other cultures are being reconsidered in the light of a more partnership perspective (for example Wright, 1996; O'Callaghan, 2004). This trend is important, as it contributes to the growing mutual-aid perspective which is countering current dominator world views.

Chapter 5

How Dominator Cultures Came Into Being

Replacement of Partnership by Dominator Cultures

When, why, how and where did dominator societies first arise? And how have they managed to replace nearly all partnership cultures during the last 10,000 years or so? These are questions that need to be examined before going any further, so that we have some idea why partnership societies – with all their apparent advantages – have died away or become diluted or degraded throughout most of the world during this period.

At the end of Chapter 2 we described matriliny and classificatory kinship; and noted that this type of social organisation has many advantages for women and for the maintenance of partnership values and egalitarian life generally. The balance of power in such systems is as much in women's favour as it is in men's, or more so. Women have high status (Briffault, 1927), and are esteemed for a wider range of abilities, qualities and powers than they are in traditional patrist societies – for being knowledgeable or wise, or a shaman or healer, as well as for being a skilful craftswoman, good cook or singer. In such societies, women may also have the additional advantage of possessing (or being perceived to possess) specific sacred or magical powers. Any weakening of a blood kinship system therefore tends to weaken women's position in society and their associated strength and freedom, and to tip the balance of power in favour of men (Alton, 1984; 2011).

So how and why has this tipping occurred? For we find few, if any, purely matrilineal systems today; and of all those that we know about from historic accounts, none seem to have retained women's powers as they apparently existed in early prehistory.

Originally, women, as we can surmise they were from myths and legends, would have been seen as magical and powerful; and it is also possible to make a good case (as Knight (1991) does) for women's powers to have derived from or be linked to their menstrual blood.

'Male menstruation'. But somehow, this situation changed, and we see only vestiges of those powers now. For many origins myths seem to show that a time came, far back in prehistory, when women's menstrual-blood-derived powers began to be represented by men as unfair or oppressive, as Knight (1991) describes:

> "Through their bodies and, in particular, through their reproductive organs, women [were] felt to have a peculiar and privileged mode of access to 'medicine', 'magic' or witchcraft of a kind which is all the more dangerous for being linked with the moon, rooted in nature *and therefore ultimately beyond male cultural artifice or control.*"

This changed perception then gave men the justification for stealing or replacing women's particular powers with male-created equivalents – typically initiation rites involving blood-letting of some kind to mimic women's menstruation. (See Chapters 13 and 14 of Knight's *Blood Relations,* in which a range of origins myths across several cultures are analysed.) Knight believes that:

> "'male menstruation' is the secret of our set of matriarchy myths, and that such pseudo-menstruation is a means of robbing women of their actual menstrual power… these myths… are expressions of the fact that in all the societies we have been examining, menstrual synchrony is not – or is no longer – the basic ritual organising principle of social, sexual and economic life. For reasons which have yet to be under-

stood, men have learned to supplant and displace women in synchrony maintenance… As the men's counter-revolution is accomplished, male 'menstrual blood' becomes sacred and life-giving, while women's becomes polluting and feared, the first symbolising solidarity and power, the second, isolation and exclusion from power."

(Knight, 1991)

Since writing this, Knight and his colleagues connected with the Radical Anthropology Group have developed clearer explanations for this displacement, and these are outlined below.

Men supplant women. From the time of that supplanting onwards, Knight suggests, men have maintained their position "through an endless process of vigilant suppression, exploitation and *ideological deception* of the female sex." He proposes that men would have claimed that women didn't know how to handle menstrual potency when they had it, and that the men therefore had to appropriate it for themselves. As a consequence, women not only lost their rightful menstrual power but it was, in fact, actively taken from them by men. And from then on, women become increasingly marginalised, castrated of their powers and rendered second-class citizens – with men in a position to justify their oppressive or dominating behaviour by claiming that women were less capable or deserving than them. Or as Shuttle and Redgrove put it, informally but succinctly, in *The Wise Wound* (1978):

"There is much evidence that the original shamans were women, from whom the men learnt ecstatic techniques, perhaps at first more controlled, because not natural, like the women's, then later stolen enviously, and the female origins ignored."

The development of dominator ways. Knight and colleagues such as Camilla Powers and Ian Watts feel that the evidence implies that women's original loss of power derived from a loss of menstrual synchrony; and postulate that this probably occurred when **harsh conditions** and **scarce game** forced hunter-gatherer bands to split up in order to survive, and that this helped to weaken or destroy classificatory kinship structures, the ability of women to unite in mutually agreed sex strikes, and a life organised around lunar cycles (Conrad, 2011). Other scholars support this or similar views. For example, Hrdy (2009) suggests that patrilocal residence patterns (which indicate a move away from matrilineality and gynocentricity) may have arisen after the Ice Age as hunter-gatherers began to colonise more northerly areas in which women could no longer gather wild plants year-round, or as groups settled into circumscribed areas. And new, harsher, ways of rearing children may then have arisen from changes in society – particularly warfare – which moved them away from matrilineal life: "Only in the past 10,000 or so years has interclan warfare become an integral part of human lives, necessitating patrilocal residence patterns and in the process changing the way that children are reared."

Population growth. Another key factor leading to the weakening of partnership ways is likely to have been population growth in certain areas gradually leading to pressure for space, and then the relinquishment of a fully hunter-gatherer way of life in favour of practices which produced more food per unit area – initially, probably, small-scale horticulture; and then agriculture and/or pastoralism. This is a process that began in the Neolithic about 11,000 to 12,000 years ago, has been observed throughout the ages, and still goes on today in those parts of the world where hunter-gatherers persist but are under pressure to settle down and grow crops or husband animals.

> "The post-glacial cultures associated with the origins of farming were later to prove relatively intensive in their uses

of space. From then on, history was essentially made by cultures which discovered ways of fitting ever more people into ever more restricted areas."

(Knight, 1991).

We could ask why early hunter-gatherers ever allowed populations to reach the point of overcrowding, as it is a feature of these cultures that they seem able to maintain stable population levels. In addition, earlier Upper Palaeolithic cultures would have had no need to experience overcrowding, for "they were space hungry and resistant to any intensification of land use. Their first answer to problems of resource scarcity would have been simply to move on," (Knight, 1991). Subsequently, as Brody (2001) points out, the first diaspora of *Homo sapiens* the hunter-gatherer from Africa required at least 100,000 years, and perhaps as much as 250,000 to spread out around the globe. In other words, this first colonisation of the earth by forager humans was very slow, and population levels were presumably kept largely in balance with available resources as it occurred. Whether rapid population growth became a feature as soon as settled life and farming began, we can only surmise. But, certainly, populations soon began to grow much faster than they tend to among hunter-gatherers. The comparable diaspora of *Homo sapiens* the farmer over the same distances, and with a commitment to transform the landscape of each new region, required less than one-tenth of this time.

A settled way of life. Boehm (1999) ponders the transition from egalitarianism to more hierarchical systems, describing it as one of the great mysteries of social evolution. He suggests that a move away from nomadism to a more settled way of life is often linked to this change, remarking that extant foragers seem to be invariably egalitarian as long as they remain basically nomadic. This may perhaps be connected to the point stressed by James Woodburn (2005) that hunter-gatherers with a mobile lifestyle tend to evade attempts to dominate them by simply moving away from anyone who is acting despotically. But this becomes harder in more settled communities, and is probably one of the factors that encourages the growth of more despotic behaviour and the development of hierarchies in such societies. Boehm summarises the permutations and combinations described above by pointing out a general tendency for sedentary life, coupled with population expansion, to spur an increase in competitive behaviour and social hierarchy that may or may not coexist with egalitarianism. Zerzan believes that humanity basically took a wrong turn with the advent of animal domestication and sedentary agriculture, and that these "laid the foundation for the exploitation of the earth, facilitated the growth of hierarchical social structures, and subsequently the ideological control of the many by the few," (Kintz in Zerzan, 2002).

Some formerly nomadic foragers have become sedentary and have collected into larger groups; and some of these have gone on to develop hierarchical lifestyles and to accept competition, social stratification, and authority at the group level even if they still forage for a living. Thus hunter-gathering doesn't – of its own accord – guarantee egalitarianism. But neither does nomadism. For example, research has shown that, in the past, after the domestication of animals, some pastoral nomads remained egalitarian but others became hierarchical. So the picture isn't simple.

The point can also be made that humans were only able to tolerate increasing population densities *because* we are good at cooperating and getting on with each other: in that sense, our cooperative natures have actually made us vulnerable or amenable to dominator life.

Division of labour. Zerzan argues that division of labour was associated with the changeover from egalitarian to more hierarchical societies – "a slow slippage" that happened so gradually as to be almost imperceptible and which entailed increasing alienation from fellow humans, nature, our bodies, until it "reached some sort of critical mass, giving rise to its apotheosis in what we've come to know as civilization," (Zerzan, 2002).

Yet forms of egalitarianism persist even in more hierarchical societies... Most hunter-gatherers in the past evidently eventually became tribesmen, but it seems that most of them transferred their egalitarian ways directly to this new type of society. Indeed, even half a century ago, thousands of these egalitarian tribal societies still existed (Boehm, 1999). Much of Kropotkin's *Mutual Aid* (1902) is also devoted to discussing the intriguing ways that egalitarianism has persisted in societies even as they gradually succumbed to hierarchical or dominator influences. His Chapter 4 is particularly relevant to this process, describing as it does tribal societies ('barbarians') worldwide and through the ages; and discussing at length the democratic processes used by them to maintain their egalitarianism and mutual-aid cultures in the face of encroaching despotic pressures. Kropotkin's commentator and supporter John Hewetson brings the concept further up to date in his essay on *Mutual Aid* (1946) by observing that:

> "the principle of mutual aid still survives as the motive force in all vital institutions of society, despite all the State's attack on local initiative. However ruthlessly governments attempt to eradicate mutual combination and support... they can never succeed in uprooting it altogether, for it provides the cement which binds society together and gives it whatever degree of social cohesion it may possess."

This observation is still very valid today – indeed the current British Conservative government's promotion of the idea of a "Big Society" entirely depends upon it.

Sun-based life replaces moon-based. Another aspect of the move from matriliny to patriliny – from partnership to dominator culture – was also, evidently, the change from a moon-based calendar and way of life in favour of a sun-based one. "Solar rhythms assume an ever-growing importance with agriculture. After all, people would now labour while there was daylight and sow and harvest according to the solar-governed seasons," (Conrad, 2011). Lionel Sims's (2006) work on Stonehenge in the UK, for example, indicates that this major Neolithic monument is one of a number whose design seems to show an attempt to introduce a sun-based orientation into a primarily moon-oriented religious site at a time of transition from hunter-gathering to pastoralism and simple agriculture. Sims claims that: "The aim of the monument builders was to juxtapose, replicate and reverse certain key horizon properties of the sun and moon, apparently with the intention of investing the sun with the moon's former religious significance." The implication in this particular situation seems to be of a relatively benign 'steering' of the population by spiritual leaders away from their traditional moon-based lives towards acceptance of farming, with its sun-based ways. And maybe this process *was* gradual, peaceful and more or less voluntary. Indeed a sun-based world view might have been a *zeitgeist* whose time had come and which was adopted gratefully by communities (or men, at least) exposed to it – a meme that gradually caught on.

Relics of this power-balance change from moon-based to sun-based life may also, perhaps, be found in the aforementioned cross-dressing or role-reversal traditions such as Lord of Misrule-type festivals. In other words, these traditions allowed people to revert back to lunar ways temporarily – upsetting the new sun-based order of things for a short while during which masters switch roles with servants, men dress as women, humans pretend to be animals and so on.

Farming drives out foraging. On the other hand, it also seems highly likely that the lunar-based nomadic/foraging ways of our prehistoric ancestors were *forcibly* suppressed or overcome in many places. Certainly, this is the process that we largely see at work in historic times, and which is the central theme of Hugh Brody's *The Other Side of Eden* (2001). Brody's view is that:

> "The model of a growing population with a recurrent demand for new farmland and pasture may reveal the process by which hunter-gatherers, despite the strengths and achievements of their forms of economy and social life, disappeared. The implication is that they did not adopt agriculture so much as lose to it."

Brody believes that the change from hunter-gathering to settled farming is pretty much inevitable once horticulture, agriculture or pastoralism had been established in an area; and that this largely entails a process of *enforced* change – indigenous foraging peoples being marginalised, driven out, assimilated or killed by the encroaching farmers. And once begun, farming has its own inexorable momentum: increased productivity of land feeds more people; more people then seek more land, using force if necessary; and this goes on until all easily-farmed land has been taken from its first peoples.

Nor does Brody think that this process is likely to have been a gentler one in the unrecorded past than it has been in historic times. Writing of those prehistoric eras, he speculates that:

> "The fate of many hunter-gatherers may well have been 'terrible' if only because farming makes little, if any, allowance for rival ways of using the land. There are no records that yield any insights into what took place. But there are many reasons for supposing that it was ruthless, and few for thinking it might have been benign."

And Zerzan (2002) parallels this view: "Scholars who used to ask, 'Why did it take so long for our ancestors to adopt agriculture?'

now wonder, 'Why did they ever do it?'"!

To be fair, however, in relation to this issue, we do also need to bear in mind the fact that many nineteenth and even twentieth century citizens of Western industrialised countries genuinely believed that 'primitive' peoples were stuck on a 'side branch' of the main evolutionary tree; and that more developed nations therefore had an absolute moral obligation to help them advance and 'join the main trunk' – even by such extreme methods as the forced State 'assimilation' practised on the Aborigines in Australia:

> "the imperial-colonial powers, while most certainly out for power and profit were also – the best among them – on a massive mission to bring the benefits of civilization to their less fortunate brethren."
>
> (Fox in Morgan, 2000 [1877])

Defending resources and property. Hrdy (2009) also supports Brody's point of view outlined above – painting a picture of growing populations which inevitably seem to lead to increasing conflict and violence in societies because of their perceived need to defend resources and property:

> "... with more reliable food sources from unusually rich coastal or freshwater habitats or with food surpluses from horticulture or herding... higher population densities and increasingly stratified societies become possible, along with the need to protect such resources. As groups grow larger, less personalized, and more formally organized, they would also be prone to shift from occasional violent disagreements between individuals to the groupwide aggression that we mistakenly take for granted as representative of humankind's naturally warlike state... Over the past 10,000 years or so, matrilocal and matrilineal societies have increasingly given

way to pressures from expansionist, patrilineal neighbours and invaders so that patterns of conquest are widely documented across Europe, Africa, Asia, and South America."

'Delayed return' leads to patrilocality and patriliny. One can see how, increasingly, novel features of settled, delayed return life such as owning land, storing food, or starting to accumulate valued objects for their own sake, in and of themselves tend to promote conflict because of the perceived need to protect such resources. Hrdy (2009) describes this process well:

> "In the Middle East, people began to herd livestock and became increasingly dependent on growing crops, storing the surplus, and accumulating property. As group sizes along with population densities increased, people adjusted their behaviour to these new demographic, dietary, epidemiological, and social realities. For settled people, shorter birth intervals and faster population growth, along with the accumulation of resources and the emergence of social stratification, brought with them the need to protect livestock and cultivable land as well as wives and children. Protecting such valuable resources became a higher priority than maintaining cordial and reciprocal exchange with neighbors. As outside invasions became more routine, men needed allies they could count on. Who better to rely on than close male kin? Increasingly, men sought to remain near father and brothers, obtaining wives from other groups. Only in the past 10,000 or so years has interclan warfare become an integral part of human lives, necessitating patrilocal residence patterns and in the process changing the way that children are reared... As in all primates, mothers without support from matrilineal kin lost some of their autonomy. The reproductive interests of patrilines increasingly took priority."

Erosion of individual freedom via 'onslaughts' on autonomy. Woodburn (2005) also suggests that, in order to move from immediate to delayed return economies, one would expect an undermining of the considerable autonomy which women and young men enjoy in immediate-return systems. This process would involve increasing incorporation of women and young men into committed kinship and affinal (marriage-related) relationships, and into structured kinship groups in which ideological control was vested predominantly in older men; and would culminate in societies in which women and young men were fully incorporated into household units with heads who exercised control over a significant part of the yield of their labour. This process can be seen in part in some Australian Aboriginal cultures.

Erosion of individual autonomy via spiritual beliefs and practices. Woodburn again suggests that a move away from egalitarianism has been connected to or effected by the development of religion and "forms of ideological elaboration which deny the autonomy of participants." Examples of these include beliefs in practices such as blessing, cursing, bewitching or contaminating, whereby one's own power and autonomy are strongly affected by someone else's actions. Woodburn believes that "the religious route, prolonged and tortuous though it is, is likely to have been a major route, perhaps even the major route, in the repeated historical transitions from immediate to delayed return."

Whether or not religion is a prime cause of transitions from immediate to delayed return, there is certainly no doubt that religious ideas and practices are a most effective means for encouraging or coercing people to relinquish some of their autonomy and move towards social forms which are more hierarchical.

Patriarchy Now Affects All Societies to Some Extent

> *"The periodic sex strike would put wives with their blood kin in one great camp or coalition, husbands with their matrilineal kin in an opposing coalition... We need only assume a subsequent weakening or patrilineal overlaying of this logic – detailing the causes and consequences of this for each culture or locality – for the ethnographic record as actually found to be explained."*
>
> (Knight, 1991)

As Knight observes in the passage above, the actual picture of human societies as they have been found down the ages – with all their combinations and permutations of egalitarianism versus hierarchy, matriliny versus patriliny, and so on – can be explained by this "weakening or patrilineal overlaying" of originally purely matrilineal and egalitarian cultures. And as we have also seen in the previous section, a variety of factors probably contributed to the process. Moreover – whatever the causes were in particular times and places – the erosion of egalitarianism and the growth of patriarchy was probably a very gradual and subtle process in many parts of the world. Nevertheless, all societies that have been studied in historic times do contain some element of patriarchy, including true hunter-gatherer societies. In other words, it seems that patriarchy, or a degree of dominator-style change, has affected *all* societies on earth – however geographically remote or pristine – compared to our original prehistoric condition.

Invasion of settled partnership societies by dominators. However, just to complicate matters even further, if Marija Gimbutas is right in her interpretations of Old Europe, then those sophisticated urban cultures were apparently both settled, *and* highly gynocentric and egalitarian. So while a more settled lifestyle and accumulation of property, including rights to land, usually seem inexorably linked to an increase in patriliny, this evidently isn't inevitable; and nor do they necessarily entail a move away from egalitarian ways. In fact, the evidence from

Eurasia, where there is much good archaeological evidence from which to draw conclusions, seems to show that the eventual changeover from partnership to dominator life there was a revolutionary – or, rather, a *counter-revolutionary* – one, achieved by forceful takeover rather than through a gradual process of change. Replacement of partnership by dominator cultures in this part of the world is essentially the subject of Eisler's classic work *The Chalice and the Blade* (1987). It is also a topic that is central to much of archaeologist Marija Gimbutas' work, on which Eisler drew heavily.

Both scholars paint a picture of peaceful gynocentric prehistoric partnership civilisations in Old Europe and the Near East – which, it needs to be stressed, included highly developed cultures, notably Crete at the peak of its development – being attacked and subjugated by nomadic dominator hordes. Where these conquering dominator peoples came from originally we still don't know for sure – apparently they were tribal, probably pastoral people who came from the east and were already fully versed in the skills of warfare and of subjugating other cultures through the use of force. It seems that in many cases their attacks were periodic, with intervening terms of conqueror-conquered assimilation during which the preceding partnership-style culture still maintained some of its partnership characteristics before it was subjugated further by a fresh assault. The point to be made about these cultures is that they evidently didn't gradually transform away from partnership ways but, rather, were *compelled* to change – perhaps much as many foraging cultures have been forcibly made to settle and 'assimilate', or else be driven off their lands, or killed.

Eliminating partnership ways in cultures like Old Europe. In order to subjugate or assimilate such cultures, invading dominators would have needed to change the very foundations of the conquered community's culture. The evidence we have seems to show that the original Old Europe-Near Eastern partnership societies were gynocentric, and that within them women had status at least equal to men's. So society was no doubt matrilocal; women were proprietors of their own homes, belongings and land; played an equal part with men in everyday secular life; were artists and craftswomen, healers or doctors, shamans or priestesses. Once having conquered a partnership society, therefore, invading dominators would have needed to change these things in order to enforce and consolidate their position and to change the society from partnership to dominator mode. This gynocentric-to-androcratic aspect of the changeover is what Eisler (1987) and Gimbutas (1991) concentrate on in their works; but the changeover would also have entailed the destruction of classificatory kinship systems – those systems which are so supportive of women's rights and of women and children's well-being. And, in light of Kropotkin's (1902) discussions, a major part of this changeover must also have involved subduing egalitarianism generally, and introducing more hierarchical social structures.

Aspects of this process are discussed in detail by Merlin Stone in *The Paradise Papers* (1976), by Eisler in *The Chalice and the Blade* (1987) and by Hrdy in *Mothers and Others* (2009). It seems that – quickly or slowly, subtly or violently – priestesses were removed from positions of authority; women's spiritual gifts derided or denied; their ability to take an equal (or any) part in governance or business queried and removed; their rights to property and land taken over by men; and their power as life-creators belittled and made secondary to men's.

Furthermore, in order to begin to enforce patrilineage, men also had to ensure their own rights to and ownership of *children*. So began the suppression of women's free sexuality which is a feature of patriarchy everywhere – with men imposing faithfulness and monogamy on women in order to ensure that a woman's children were his and his alone. In patrilineal systems, women tend to be used primarily for men's reproductive interests even at the expense of their own well-being or that of their children. At the extreme, they may be treated largely as childbirth 'vessels' – machines for producing 'heirs and spares' – rather than as free human beings with equal rights. As Hrdy (2009) says of this process in human history:

> "As in all primates, mothers without support from matrilineal kin lost some of their autonomy. The reproductive interests of patrilines increasingly took priority... As cultures emphasising female chastity flourished, women's freedom of movement was severely curtailed. No longer could women use sexuality to line up extra 'fathers' [see Chapter 13]; no longer could daughters move to be near kin at birth, or mothers move to be near daughters who needed their help... Whereas people with matrilineal/matrilocal histories award high priority to maternal interests, those in patrilineal, and especially full-fledged patriarchal, societies where property is passed from fathers to sons are more concerned with ensuring the husband's paternity and preserving patrilineal access to resources, even when this entails practices detrimental to the well-being of mothers (and children too)."

This is in clear contrast to women in matrilineal societies, who have considerable control over their own reproduction and usually have babies at well-spaced out intervals of years. As Engels famously put it in 1884, "The overthrow of mother right was the *world historical defeat of the female sex*."

Entrenching Patriarchy

Once in charge, the job that dominator conquerors had on their hands was to change partnership cultures' hearts and minds to dominator ones; and the struggle was a long and brutal one which – in one way and another – still goes on today. As we've already said earlier, this is a battle which *can never be completely won*, because human beings' hearts, minds and bodies are genetically largely partnership in nature. Dominator culture therefore has to keep imposing its ideas on, and moulding its citizens to, dominator ways anew, and against the grain of human nature.

Eisler sees the changeover to dominator culture as an enforced change in our *cultural evolution*, and discusses this shift in terms of the replication of ideas (again, what many today would call memes). She expresses her views on the subject in strong terms:

> "It is impossible in a few pages to even begin to describe a process that went on for millennia and is still going on in our own time: the process whereby the human mind was, sometimes brutally and sometimes subtly, sometimes deliberately and sometimes unwittingly, remolded into the new kind of mind required by this drastic shift in our cultural evolution. It was a process that... entailed enormous physical destruction that continued well into historic times. As we can still read in the Bible, the Hebrews, and later also the Christians and Muslims, razed temples, cut down sacred groves of trees, and smashed pagan idols. It also entailed massive spiritual destruction, again a process that continued well into historic times. Not only through book burning but through the burning and persecution of heretics, those who did not perceive reality in the prescribed way were killed or converted. Directly, through personal coercion, and indirectly, through intermittent social shows of force such as public inquisitions and executions, behaviors, attitudes, and perceptions that did not conform to dominator norms were systematically discouraged. This fear conditioning became part of all aspects of daily life, permeating child rearing, laws, schools."

Again, Kropotkin supplements this story by describing in detail the sustained attack on egalitarianism and mutual aid cultures that has continued through recorded history with – if anything –

ever-increasing (though often hidden) ferocity.

Sidelining women's powers; suppressing women's power. Much of this conquering process was aimed specifically at suppressing, removing, ridiculing or sidelining women's powers. The mechanisms which keep a power balance between the sexes in classificatory kinship societies were broken. Now women were to be put down and kept in their place through seclusion, purdah, the burkha, or a strict mother-in-law to obey. Where once a man was honour-bound to provide meat for his wife and her family, and gained prestige and respect by how well he fulfilled his provisioning duties, now his duty lay with his own blood kin – his wives and even his children (certainly girl children) having a lesser claim on his resources. Where once women's sexuality was respected and her role in the community's sex life seen as equal to men's, free sexuality now became a prime target for patriarchal religions, was declared wicked and dirty and was stamped out as much as possible. Indeed, as James Prescott (1975) points out, "Violence against sexuality and the use of sexuality for violence, particularly against women, has very deep roots in Biblical tradition, and is spelled out very early" – a discussion justifying rape actually occurring in Genesis.

The aim was to make women as powerless as possible – and in particular – to deprive them of any specifically female (menstrual-blood-derived?) powers. So wherever or whenever patriarchy harshened, even the most benign manifestations of female abilities, as expressed in such skills as herbalism and midwifery, were treated as witchcraft or similar, and suppressed. Christianity was probably the worst persecutor in this sphere, as Shuttle and Redgrove (1978) contend:

> "witchcraft is the natural craft of the woman [and] has been denigrated ceaselessly by men, who fear women and who wish them to under-achieve... In the Middle Ages it has been

estimated that nine million women were burned as witches for exercising their natural crafts of midwifery, hypnotism, healing, dowsing, dream-study and sexual fulfilment. They were persecuted and burnt by the Christian Church of that time, who wished only men to have power and ability."

Suppressing knowledge of partnership history. Another vital way in which dominator cultures transmit and propagate their norms is through suppressing knowledge of partnership history, and this is discussed further in Chapter 8.

The Effects of Dominator Life on our Genes

A further factor which needs to be considered here in our review of the changeover from matriliny and partnership to patriarchy is the extent to which the paramountcy of dominator life during the last several thousand years has affected natural selection and our genes. As we saw at the end of Chapter 2, Boehm (1999) analysed the evidence for between-group selection and altruism; and argues cogently that this probably operated as a significant factor in the 100,000 plus years during which cooperative, egalitarian life flourished on earth. And Hrdy, in her review of human prosociality in *Mothers and Others* (2009), stresses the ongoing influence which the human desire to cooperate must have had on selection, up to the present day. The interesting idea of *human self-domestication* may also be relevant here. Wild animals may self-domesticate if tame behaviour enhances their survival near humans; and it seems likely that we have done the same thing in order to increase our ability to cooperate – including, probably, selecting for a particularly prosocial emotional/behavioural profile during our evolution.

On the same basis, presumably *pro-competitive, pro-selfish, pro-warlike* genes have also been selected for within dominator-style cultures since these appeared? Dominator ways favour the ascendancy of and selection for dominator character traits and behaviours, so – one can hypothesise – these must have been strongly favoured in the past 10,000 years or so. As Hrdy (2009) puts it: "Altruists eager to cooperate fare poorly in encounters with egocentric marauders." Genghis Khan springs to mind; but if we consider modern life, just think of the personality profile of a typical successful businessman today. Psychologists readily acknowledge that many are sociopathic, yet such people are role model figures for many people in our culture, and usually also a success story with women (the sex-appeal of power). The same applies to dictators, many of whom are clearly clinically unbalanced if not outright insane, yet hold positions of disproportionate influence and power in the world, including in reproductive matters. Such people are among today's successful breeders, so how will this have affected our genes? Are these noticeably less partnership in style than they were before the beginnings of dominator life? Could significant genetic changes have occurred during these last ten millennia? To what extent might the two processes – selection for prosocial traits, and selection for dominator-style traits – be co-existing and interweaving in modern populations?

Hrdy (2009) takes quite a pessimistic view of this question in light of the pathologies of modern life, and believes that:

> "If empathy and understanding develop only under particular rearing conditions, and if an ever-increasing proportion of the species fails to encounter these conditions but nevertheless survives to reproduce, it won't matter how valuable the underpinnings for collaboration were in the past. Compassion and the quest for emotional connection will fade away as surely as sight in cave-dwelling fish."

This is a worrying thought, and makes the challenging of current dominator cultural hegemony all the more vital. In any event, and whatever the underlying causes may be, one key effect of humanity's shift from partnership to dominator-style *mores* has been to create people whose psyche and soma are harmed. This book contends that much of this damage is the result of a new approach to *childrearing*; and in the following two chapters the old, nurturing, hunter-gatherer way of bringing up children is contrasted with the new, damaging dominator way.

Chapter 6

Creating Undamaged People: Natural Upbringings

It is a key contention of this book that benign childrearing is a vital factor in the well-being and happiness of partnership-type peoples; and that, conversely, harmful upbringings underpin and help maintain dominator society. In taking this stance, the book is proffering a version of the 'noble savage' view of life by suggesting that the closer we are to the physical and psychological condition of pristine hunter-gatherers or early *Homo sapiens* the happier we are likely to be. In this chapter we will look in more detail at the way that children grow up in hunter-gatherer societies and how this affects them; while in the following chapter we examine dominator-style upbringings and their effects on people.

Stone Age Childrearing Practices

Family life is within a classificatory kinship structure. We have described classificatory kinship and some of its advantages for children in Chapter 2; and noted that this type of structure seems to be the one which originally existed in human society. The most important aspect of classificatory kinship as far as childrearing goes is that it provides a secure, stable, cradle-to-grave physical and emotional support structure for mothers and children.

The Environment of Evolutionary Adaptedness or Continuum Concept. US author Jean Liedloff's influential ideas – in particular her notion of the *continuum concept* – are central here; and closely parallel those of developmental psychologist John Bowlby (best known for his work on attachment) who introduced the idea of the '*Environment of Evolutionary Adaptedness*'

(EEA) in the mid twentieth century. Both terms are intended to convey the idea of generations of human beings living naturally millennia after millennia in the environment and culture with which their innate instincts and behaviours had co-evolved. This co-evolution meant that there was a good fit between our species' internal biological needs and 'behavioural equipment' on the one hand, and the external environment – particularly the social environment created by our fellow humans – on the other. Since even modern humans are very similar genetically to our prehistoric hominin forebears, this means that we're still genetically designed to develop from birth onwards in a social and environmental context that is essentially Stone Age. As Annette Hamilton (1984) puts it:

> "For the baby fresh from the womb is normally a wholly natural creature and its biological being brooks relatively little cultural interference in any but superficial fashions. No doubt this is why the newborn appear to be such terrifying creatures to many 'civilised' persons."

Bowlby understood that the EEA would vary according to exactly which human trait or 'system' was being considered. It is the child-development system which we're considering here; and child development expert Hrdy (2009) stresses that, in the case of early childhood and the human infant's emotional attachment to its mother, the EEA has changed relatively little over the course of hominin evolution. The point to be made is therefore that human babies still need, and thrive best on, Stone Age-style mothering. In particular, what Liedloff calls in-arms nurturance is vital – mother or alloparental love in all its natural, physical, instinctual forms – cuddling, holding, rocking, stroking, breast-feeding, talking, looking at the baby and young child. This key concept has been steadily reinforced by a stream of research since Liedloff first stressed it in 1975 (for example, see Prescott, 1975;

Hamilton, 1981; Hrdy, 2009 and 1999; Gerhardt, 2004; Goleman, 2006; Chilton Pearce, 2007; Young, 2009).

Basic Attitudes to Children and Childrearing

This topic was introduced in Chapter 3 and is examined further here. First of all, perhaps it is worth saying how strangely uninterested we seem to be in cultures (such as hunter-gatherers') which produce contented, prosocial children and adults. We complain about our own societies' difficulties in this sphere ('problem children', anti-social behaviour and so on) but don't seem keen to examine cultures which *don't* have these problems, and evidently have the secret of happiness instead! Annette Hamilton is an exception; and her intelligent, thoughtful and fascinating book *Nature and Nurture* (1981), based on her studies of Arnhem Land Aboriginal childrearing, is one of the few studies carried out specifically to look at the underlying beliefs and subsequent practices involved in indigenous childrearing. Also well in advance of its time is social worker Hilary Alton's excellent 1984 unpublished paper on alternative approaches to adoption which draws its main inspiration from Hamilton's and other anthropological works on hunter-gatherer childrearing.

Fulfilling needs, not spoiling. Hamilton's research led her to believe that the forager approach to child development is quite different from all those discussed in standard Western textbooks and based upon 'civilised' ideas of childrearing (and upon dominator peoples). Instead, she found that the childrearing belief system or 'theory' of the hunter-gatherer people she studied:

> "fails to suppose that the child is innately greedy and wicked, out to get whatever he/she can, nor yet infinitely malleable. Instead it supposes that the child is born with a set of needs, which can only be supplied through social interaction; that

the child indicates those needs to others, and the duty of others is to respond; that there is no difference for a small child between want and need, and that these things remain hard to differentiate throughout life; that the older and stronger must be responsible for the younger and weaker; that dependency behaviour is perfectly right and proper; that the child is naturally sociable and wishes, from its innermost being, to do the same thing that others do provided that others treat it with fairness and equality; that reward is not necessary to produce acceptable behaviour providing everyone behaves well... It denies that the baby is born a tyrant or that the adult's role is to control its tyrannical wishes. It denies that indulgence will produce selfishness and lack of sociability and asserts instead that indulgence is the right of everyone when a child, and indulgence is the duty of everyone when an adult."

Births. Hunter-gatherer approaches to giving birth vary widely, but most accounts show how much easier births are for women in these cultures and, often, very little fuss is made of the whole event. This in itself means that babies are less stressed by birth than is considered normal in Western cultures.

Breastfeeding. From birth on, babies are in close contact with mothers or others, breastfed on demand (or "on request" as Hamilton suggests we should more kindly and accurately put it!), and sleep with their family. Breastfeeding has many advantages, and promotes infant health and helps to prevent disease in numerous ways in both the short and longer term. Breast milk is free, is sterile, and is a complete, perfect food with many subtle ingredients not found in formula milks. These include colostrum (initially), and hormones such as oxytocin and prolactin, which relax the mother and help strengthen the bond with her child. Breastfeeding boosts the infant's immune system and so helps it to fight infections. Breastfed infants are less likely to become overweight or to develop diabetes; may be more intelligent; and so on.

Affectionate physical and emotional contact with babies. Affectionate treatment of infants is a strong feature of foraging peoples' behaviour, and has been highlighted by many authors. For example Hrdy (2009), in her comprehensive review of hunter-gatherer caregiving, describes how much loving contact there is between infants and others in these cultures – observing that forager babies spend "far more time in contact with their mothers than is typical of infants in farming or post-industrial societies"; and that "Babies are never left alone and are constantly held by someone." In one example, she describes life for typical Bushman babies – sometimes sitting in a sling on their mother's hip, perhaps "exchanging looks, smiles and 'vocalizations' with admiring prepubescent girls"; at other times being passed from hand to hand around a camp fire for similar interactions with one adult or child after another:

> "They are kissed on the faces, bellies, genitals, sung to, bounced, entertained, encouraged, even addressed at length in conversational tones long before they can understand words. Throughout the first year there is rarely any dearth of such attention and love."
>
> (Konner, 1972, quoted in Hrdy, 2009)

Similarly, among the Hadza, Hrdy describes how a baby is "in continuous contact with someone, frequently the mother, but is also held by grandmothers, great-aunts, older siblings, fathers, and even visitors from neighbouring groups." And babies also sleep with a member or members of their family, never alone.

Infants are usually breastfed till about age two, "on request". Cultures vary in their approaches to weaning, which often depend upon the arrival of a baby sibling; and this tends to be unwelcome to toddlers, as it is to most mammal infants. Nevertheless, hunter-gatherer children have usually had a good innings before this occurs, with unlimited access to their mother's breast for food or comfort or both for far longer than is normal in developed societies. And as Root (2005) points out: "Although babies who are carried more are also fed more frequently, they feed no longer in total, and so there is no evidence that greater parental responsiveness makes babies greedy." In other words, even infants are self-regulating if allowed to be, rather than bottomless pits of needs and greed!

Results in relaxed babies. Liedloff (1975) comments on the difference between continuum and non-continuum babies:

> "There is a remarkable contrast between the behaviour of Yequana infants in-arms and our own infants, most of whose time is spent in physical isolation. The Yequana babies are soft and easy to handle, unresistant to being carried in any convenient position. Our infants, on the other hand, kick their legs out straight, wave their arms violently and stiffen their backs into strained arches."

She sees this as being due in part to the natural energy exchange which occurs between continuum caregivers and their in-arms infant – the caregivers being able to discharge any excess energy through their normal everyday activities. In addition, of course, continuum children don't have screwed up physiology (Chapter 7), and therefore don't have the excess stress-produced unassimilable energy found in non-continuum children.

Many 'parents' are better than just two (or one). Another factor which is important in hunter-gatherer childrearing is that – because some form of classificatory kinship operates in all these societies – children have many caregivers. Allomothers, allosisters, allofathers and so on treat all children largely as their own (and this is regardless of the presence or absence of biological fathers), so that love, nurturing and play are available from many – not just one or two – caregivers. An older generation of grandmothers is also on hand to help and guide in these cultures. Babies and children in forager societies therefore have an abundance of the physical and emotional contact with adults which tends to be in short supply in Western homes. Then as they grow older, from the age of four or five, children usually spend a lot of time playing with their peer group, so are looked after naturally and relatively effortlessly by other children at this time.

Tribal cultures too may be very similar to hunter-gatherers in their approach to shared childcare. Speaking of children born to the Ladakh, Norberg-Hodge (1991) says that "they have continuous physical contact with others, a factor that plays an important role in their development." An infant spends more time with his mother than anyone else, sleeps in her arms, feeds whenever he wants:

> "but caring for the baby was not her job alone. Everyone looked after him. Someone was always there to kiss and cuddle him. Men and women alike adore little children, and even teenage boys were not embarrassed to be seen cooing over little Angchuk... The traditional way of life allows mothers and children to remain together at all times. When villagers gather together to discuss important issues, or at festivals and parties, children of all ages are always present. Even at social gatherings that run late into the night with drinking, singing and dancing, and loud music, young children can be seen running around, joining in the festivities until they simply drop off to sleep... Children receive unlimited and unconditional affection from everyone around them."

One can see how this environment of alloparents takes the load off any one caregiver and also allows the child to be itself and 'do its thing' without being the intense focus of one – perhaps worried, overconcerned or stressed – nuclear couple or single parent, as is common today in Western families:

> "One of the overall effects of such an extended kinship system is a dilution of the powerful relationship between parent and child evident in our society…it is hard for those of us whose personal knowledge of kinship has been moulded by the experience of European 'family life' to imagine a society where each one of us is considered to be interchangeable with any one of a large number of 'brothers and sisters'. Where my children are yours and yours are mine and in which each one of is said to be loved from infancy onwards by not one but a multiplicity of 'mothers', 'mother's brothers', 'fathers' and other relatives."
>
> (Alton, 1984)

Yet it is this scenario which is a part of the all-important EEA or continuum, for which we are designed and to which we are genetically adapted. "It takes a whole village to bring up a child," says the African proverb: and this sort of all-enveloping yet relaxed and diffuse care is evidently better for children than stressed, scheduled, restricted 'quality time' with a single parent (Root, 2005).

Learning child care. Another advantage of the 'whole village' approach to childrearing that is found in traditional societies is that there are far more opportunities to learn how to look after children, from early childhood onwards. Everyone in the community learns by direct observation and participation:

> "In societies that live more simply, babies and children are ever present. The opportunities to hold babies, soothe them, discipline them and learn about them are ample. In other words, there is psychological preparation for becoming a parent through social learning and observation."
>
> (Gerhardt, 2004)

Little or no controlling behaviour. Hunter-gatherers worldwide have what the West would see as an extraordinarily *laissez faire* attitude to bringing up children. For example, Hamilton describes how the Arnhem Landers she studied appeared to employ all the practices that are supposed to 'ruin' children: "they didn't toilet train, they breast-fed as long as possible, they made no effort to schedule or control children." She found that no special efforts were made to incorporate children into camp life beyond attending to their immediate needs/wants; no rearranging of life and its activities was considered necessary; and other than the injunction that babies must never be left to cry but must be fed immediately: "no stated rules govern their treatment. They are seen merely as inevitable and necessary extensions of the camp's social life. No one complains at the inconvenience they cause, and no one makes any special fuss of them." Dirt and mess are likewise ignored: "This, like most other Aboriginal childrearing practices, is governed by the principle of never interfering in a child's activities until it, or another, indicates distress." Rather than following any set rules, it is the child's current expressed desire which is met:

> "Aboriginal child-training practices are on almost all points 'permissive'... authoritarian practices are entirely absent. No demands are made for unquestioning obedience or externally regulated development; adults expect little of children, while children can demand all from adults, at least up to a certain age."

Children may get angry with adults – even physically angry – but this is tolerated as acceptable childish behaviour and shrugged off. The child may even be admired for standing up to grown-ups and exerting his right to resist them. There is certainly no retaliation or attempt to control or punish children for such behaviour: the assumption is that they will outgrow it in due course:

> "Most youthful transgressions are explained by remarks like 'children have no sense' or 'their intelligence hasn't come to them yet.' Behaviour is judged, commented on and occasionally criticised, and scoldings are not uncommon, but parents basically believe children to be utterly irresponsible. There is no doubt in the parents' minds that as children grow up they will learn to act with sense, with or without deliberate training, simply as a result of maturation, social pressure and the desire to conform to group values. Since most !Kung adults are co-operative, generous and hardworking, this theory is evidently right, at least for them."
>
> (Marjorie Shostak, 1983, *Nisa: The Life and Words of a !Kung Woman* quoted in Alton, 1984)

No violence to or abuse of children. Hunter-gatherers are horrified at Western-style strictness towards children, and even more so by actual physical abuse of young people. For example, Hamilton (1981) says of the Aborigines: "Needless to say, no one ever physically abuses an infant by hitting, smacking or otherwise violently hurting it," and goes on to explain how adult disincentives to perceived frowned-upon behaviour, such as the hitting of one child by another, are achieved by a stern stare, or at most a clenched-fist threatening gesture – certainly not by any physical force or punishment.

The Wider Childrearing Environment

Stimulating surroundings. Liedloff (1975) and Hamilton (1981) both stress how much sensory stimulation tribal infants experience as opposed to first-world babies:

> "While European babies spend much of their time in cots and cribs, and even alone in a room with the door closed, Anbarra

> children are constantly exposed to the sights and sounds of the camp. Consequently, they receive much more sensory stimulus from the environment, as well as more physical stimulus from other people."
>
> (Hamilton, 1981)

Liedloff (1975) highlights the active-observer role of infants in forager societies – describing the casual way in which Yequana babies are carried about on carers' hips. The infants aren't specifically being played with or talked to, but are alert, and able to look about and absorb the life around them. So infants are present in, can observe, and are part of the whole social and natural scene, without any specific efforts necessarily being made to engage with them or keep them occupied. TV isn't needed to keep them quiet, nor is 'quality time' an issue. (For some reason, Western societies seem to struggle with the challenge of carrying infants. Instead of the traditional eons-old baby-in-a-sling-on-the-hip technique, we use inappropriate devices that crush babies' faces into parents' chests or backs and prevent them seeing anything! Or else expose them face forward on the parent's front.)

Moreover, this passive involvement in everyday life plays an important part in the child's informal education:

> "The infant's business in arms is to have experiences which will ready him for further development towards self-reliance. The witnessing and passive participation in those startling, violent and menacing events, which are the daily lot of a babe in the arms of a busy mother, are essential building blocks for confidence in himself. It is an important part of the stuff of which the sense of self is made."
>
> (Liedloff, 1975)

As the baby grows, so new, enjoyable forms of stimulation and of safe separation are introduced: imperceptibly, the child becomes increasingly independent and resilient – stimulated, enriched and strengthened by its experiences close to parents and alloparents.

As they get a little older, and can leave camp on foraging expeditions with their carers, children are exposed to even more new, exciting, interesting and fun things as part of their everyday life. Then they become increasingly independent, spend more and more time with their peer group, and are relatively free to roam and choose the surroundings they wish to be in.

Part of a kind, caring community and world. Much has been written about the relationship of hunter-gatherers with their environment, and few authors describe this more sympathetically than Colin Turnbull. For example, he describes how a Mbuti baby in the womb is treated as a person whose relationship with forest and community has already begun; and how, shortly after birth, infants are passed around a variety of complementary 'mothers' so that the child's experience of parenting expands to incorporate a "plurality of mothers and safe territories," (Turnbull, 1978 cited by Finnegan, 2009/10). Hrdy (2009) too is struck by the world views of foragers, and the way that they tend to view their physical environment as a 'giving' place occupied by others who are also liable to be well-disposed and generous – a physical world in line with benevolent social relationships. For example, she notes how the Mbuti refer to the forest as a place that gives "food, shelter and clothing just like their parents," (Hrdy, 2009); and observes that:

> "Among our hunter-gatherer ancestors, food was often scarce, predators ever present... Yet by definition, individuals who *did* survive would have done so surrounded by others who cared for and shared with them. This endowed them with a personal confidence notably different from that of many modern people who grow up in environments with more

available resources but less caring."

Alton (1984) reinforces this fact, pointing out that in classificatory kinship systems the presence of kin means that 'home' is all those places in which we have such kin, and that this gives us the right to eat or sleep in any one of an immense number of homes at any time and as a matter of course. Because of this, "it is impossible for a child to grow up deprived of love." Moreover, within such societies:

> "love is not dependent on sexual intimacy and is not a personal, private matter at all but is the very kinship-stuff of which society (the society of all our known and unknown kinsfolk combined) is made… It is possible that it was on the basis of immense space-enfolding kinship networks, generated from sibling solidarity, that the human species once enveloped the globe."

What a lovely thought, and how different from dominator culture's grasping, competitive, adversarial view of neighbouring peoples and nations.

Physical abilities; accelerated motor development. The remarkable physical abilities which forager children develop very young have already been mentioned in Chapter 3, and are discussed in detail by Hamilton (1981) in regard to the Anbarra Aborigines. For example, Anbarra children of six or seven months can ride on their mother's shoulders, clinging on to her hair, while European children of the same age would have trouble even sitting unsupported on the ground. These abilities are probably accelerated by children being held and carried in positions which foster rapid physical development, and encouraged to perform activities beyond their physical capabilities, Hamilton describes how:

"By the time they reach 5 they are physically graceful and

skilful from constant running, throwing and swimming, and through the absence of cautions and warnings about physical danger they have learnt to feel entirely at home in the environment."

There is usually a lack of cosseting in hunter-gatherer cultures, with little special provision being made for protecting or separating young children from danger – to a point which Western parents would find alarming. However, as Hamilton suggests, this can be seen as "rigorous selection imposed unconsciously by people with few technological aids for maximising the survival of the human infant." In response, most children *do* survive, and even thrive – acquiring life skills and arts of self-preservation precociously (as we would see it) early. But it seems that these children are actually developing normally, from an evolutionary perspective; and that it is our Western unnaturally overprotected children who are *not* normal, and who have evidently lost their innate abilities in part through a regime of 'Be careful!s and 'Don't do that!s as well as through the effects of harmful childrearing practices. As the explorer, Frederick Schwatka said in 1888 about the elusive Tarahumara people of Mexico, who have evaded persecution only by retrenching deep into precipitous mountain terrain and now live among deep gorges and chasms: "How they can rear children on these cliffs without a loss of one hundred percent annually is to me one of the most mysterious things connected with these strange peoples." But rear them they do, and apparently without any particular effort or angst – as Christopher McDougall, author of *Born to Run* (2009), found out when he visited them a century later.

Freedom to move about. In all hunter-gatherer societies – as Woodburn, for example, discusses – freedom to move about seems to be one of the factors which underpins the key qualities of these cultures such as their egalitarianism, relative peaceableness and lack of discord, for people can simply move away from quarrels, uncongenial relatives or neighbours. In stark contrast to dominator societies, this applies to children too: they also can move freely among their classificatory kin, and so evade oppressive behaviour from a particular adult by going to live with, say, an uncle or a grandmother. Contrasting the relatively strong pressures on individuals to behave in socially acceptable ways in Australian Aboriginal cultures, Hamilton (1981) notes that:

> "Pressures to conform are lessened by the freedom with which individuals can move from one group of people to another. Unbound by possessions of a durable, material kind, free of the obligation to work in a particular place in a particular manner, the individual who is inserted into a situation of potential conflict between his own needs and those of others can resolve the situation by simply moving away. This must be the deepest and most significant freedom of Aboriginal society."
>
> (Hamilton, 1981)

This is clearly a huge and important freedom for children – particularly compared to most Western children, for whom the walls of the nuclear family home may be both a prison and a torture chamber from which there is no ready escape.

Learning, play, and socialisation. In hunter-gatherer communities, learning comes chiefly from observation and participation rather than from specific instruction. For example, speaking of the Australian Anbarra, Hamilton (1981) observes that:

> "Anbarra children from 5 to 9 continue to receive little or no instruction in social codes or beliefs. There are no verbal explanations of the behaviour expected of them and no systematic means of displaying approval or disapproval.

> Girls become proficient in understanding and exploiting the environment, while boys devote their energies to exploring and perfecting their physical skills."

However, one of the few 'life skills' which *is* deliberately taught in forager society is *sharing*:

> "Adults start from a 'modelling' rather than a 'training' approach, however. You do not train a child to share by withholding yourself. The first principal in encouraging unselfishness is the unselfishness of the adults, most especially the mother. By never denying the child's wants (which are considered identical to its needs) the adults demonstrate unselfish behaviour. The child is not exhorted to carry out behaviour which is seldom to be seen around it – the requirement that it share its food is no more than the requirement that it act the same way as everyone else, and such requests for sharing go in two directions... When a child refuses to share his right to do so is unquestioned, but he is described as odd, ungenerous and 'deaf'; people talk and act as if they are surprised by such behaviour and treat it in a wondering kind of way. By starting with the assumption that generosity is natural, it becomes so."
>
> (Hamilton, 1981)

Learning to share. Hamilton describes the gesture of supplication which is:

> "used by adults and young children of all ages to obtain something the other has, usually food. It is never used between adults. The arm is extended with the palm up. The gesture may be used alone or may be supplemented by the word *guno* – give. It is remarkable how often the gesture is complied with, and a child will give up a treasured piece of

food without protest."

Alton (1984) comments on how: "This willingness to share even among toddlers is remarkable to European eyes, accustomed to debates about 'this is mine', 'this is hers', 'you've got the biggest'. Such behaviour is often put down to human nature at the same time it is deplored." However, hunter-gatherer childrearing shows that gentle encouragement of children in a context of culture-wide sharing behaviour can steer even very young children into the habit of sharing. The same seems to be true of tribal communities too, being found, for example, in the Ladakh (Norberg-Hodge, 1991).

Hrdy (2009) describes similar encouragement of sharing behaviour among African hunter-gatherers; and, as a general point, observes how children seem to want to help and to please innately – describing how even modern psychologists studying first-world children are:

> "increasingly struck by how early and eagerly children seek to establish connections with others and how connected to others children feel right from an early age. They are eager to help and to share, not just with their mothers but with various others, even strangers, as long as their mother or a familiar companion is close by and they feel safe."

This seems to prove that much of the prosocial behaviour seen in forager children is normal and innate to humans. If it is reduced in non-forager children, presumably this is because of Western-style socialisation.

In forager society, compliance in general isn't praised or rewarded, because it is *expected*. Nor is non-compliance punished. It is assumed that people do what they do because they wish to, and that if they don't want to they'll refuse – that they are as they are, and if they don't want to obey a request, that is down to their nature or how they're feeling at the time. "Perhaps they are deaf," as the Anbarra say. Nor do they usually have words for 'good' and 'bad', or use judgmental terms to label people or behaviour.

Learning through watching and doing. From around age five to puberty, Hamilton describes how Aboriginal boys, in particular, spend much time playing in peer groups; and how some of this play may involve developing abilities such as tracking, or practising or imitating other adult skills. Boys can accompany older male relatives on a hunt; and younger boys, or girls, can go on gathering expeditions with the women. However, there is no formal instruction or pressure on children to learn, so this is achieved mainly by doing or watching. Hamilton (1981) points out that this form of learning may well enhance people's ability to acquire the kind of enhanced cognitive skills specifically required by hunter-gatherers – such as the ability to recognise tracks and plants, sense weather events, hear and see keenly and be aware of a whole range of sensory data far beyond the range of most non-foragers.

Overall, hunter-gatherer-style childrearing appears to largely empower children, make them feel loved, at home in life, capable, confident, supported by kin, friends and peers, and part of a benevolent natural world in which they become increasingly physically competent. As Everett (2008) says:

> "I believe that the Pirahãs are so confident and secure in their ability to handle anything that their environment throws at them that they can enjoy whatever comes their way. This is not at all because their lives are easy, but because they are good at what they do."

Carl Jung had a similar impression of natural dignity, grace, confidence and pride in one's life when he visited the pastoral Ugandan Elgonyi in 1925–26. In his autobiographical *Memories,*

Dreams, Reflections (1963), he describes the elder sister of one of his guides within her home context in a typically Jungian way:

> "I had the feeling that the confidence and self-assurance of her manner were founded to a great extent upon her identity with her own wholeness, her private world made up of children, house, small livestock, *shamba* [small-holding] and – last but not least, her not unattractive physique.... My hostess was plainly and unproblematically the embodiment of stability, a veritable *pied-a-terre* for the husband. The question did not seem to be whether or not *he* was there, but rather whether *she* was present in her wholeness, providing a geo-magnetic centre for the husband who wandered over the land with his herds."

Little or no fighting. Children may challenge each other to be the best in running, throwing, balancing, climbing, swimming and so on, but there is little fighting. Hamilton (1981) says of an Anbarra boys' 'kid mob':

> "Within the group there was no bickering or quarrelling. The ethic of generosity and mutual help that started to appear before the age of 5 was strengthened and boys shared food, weapons and other treasures freely with each other. There was no system of superior or inferior status based on relative age. As a younger child 'graduated' into the older boys' group he was helped and supported by his older brothers and cousins who acted as his 'sponsors' until he was comfortable with the others... I never saw the teasing and aggressive horseplay common among European boys of this age and I never saw a violent quarrel or fight (although adults said these did sometimes occur)... The boy who attempts to organise and control his peers is either ignored or ridiculed, or both, and learns that there are no rewards for it."

Transition into adulthood. Eventually, around puberty, children stop being indulged so much and are recruited into the world of adults. For example, among the Anbarra "the child has freedom, the adult has responsibility." Girls take on more women's work such as childcare, food and wood gathering, and cooking, and may be betrothed or married; and boys are initiated into the men's group and male activities. By this stage, children are physically adept and have become skilful at many adult occupations appropriate to their sex, Hamilton describing Anbarra girls as "resourceful, independent and tireless in carrying out useful tasks"; while boys can run, climb and swim, track and hunt. In other societies, children of both sexes may start to take on adult roles from the age of five or so – looking after other, younger children, herding flocks and so on – but demonstrating a similar ability to be responsible at a remarkably young age (Norberg-Hodge, 1991).

In conclusion, it seems that hunter-gatherer childhoods are immeasurably easier and more enjoyable for all concerned compared to the painful, protracted battleground which is accepted as normal childrearing by most people in the developed world.

Physiological and Psychological Results of Natural Upbringings

> *"Human touch and love is essential to health... For over a million years babies have enjoyed almost constant in-arms contact with their mothers or other caregivers... receiving constant touch for the first year or so of life."* (Young, 2009)

Effects of physical and emotional affection on child development. Positive physical and emotional contact between caregivers and babies has profound beneficial effects upon them on every level – from brain development to hormone production and limbic regulation. These in turn have lifelong effects on individual mood and behaviour; which, in their turn, obviously have profound implications for societies as a whole. (The reverse is also true; and this is what is discussed in the following chapter.) Specialist in this field Sue Gerhardt explains the process in scientific terms in her enlightening book *Why Love Matters* (2004). From Gerhardt's point of view, nurturing is important because human babies need others in order to help regulate the complex interacting 'orchestra' which is the physiology of the developing child. The human organism has many systems which are constantly oscillating according to their own particular rhythms and timings – the sympathetic and parasympathetic nervous systems, blood pressure, sleep patterns, breathing, excreting, all follow different patterns simultaneously, while influencing each other and signalling to each other and the brain via electrical, chemical and hormonal systems. This internal 'symphony' of fluctuating inhibitory and excitatory activity is self-organising through a process of feedback loops, so that influences are mutual and constantly adjusting to each other. Cells and organs regulate themselves and each other: they have their own functions but are part of the whole system. The system also adjusts to its external environment; and a crucial part of this for babies – the main part, indeed – is their mother or caregiver. Positive, nurturing interactions with alloparents are as important to the infant's physical, neurological and emotional development as are the homoeostatic adjustments that are going on internally.

Touching, holding, rocking and breastfeeding help a baby's system balance and harmonise while it is developing; and have a role in actual physical development itself. For example, affectionate contact between mother and infant entrains their heartbeats, and helps the infant heart develop as it should. Touching and stroking the baby activates dormant sensory nerve endings and the peripheral nervous system, which is also a primary extension of the brain. Pleasurable interactions with mothers switch on the infant's senses of smell, touch, hearing and vision, and help develop healthy dopamine and norepinephrine systems in the brain, so ensuring a positive attitude to life, the ability to concentrate and sustain effort, to delay gratification, and so on (the basis for a good balance between the 'Pleasant Life' and the 'Good Life' mentioned in Chapter 3). And the orbitofrontal cortex, which is so much about being human, develops almost entirely post-natally. The polyunsaturated fatty acids in breast milk are also involved in the production of these neurotransmitters. In turn, mothers' nurturing responses are activated by skin to skin contact, "making bonding a reciprocal dynamic of awakening and discovery," (Chilton Pearce, 2007). And, as authors such as Gerhardt (2004), Hrdy (2009) and Chilton Pearce (2007) discuss, babies are designed to interact with human faces; and positive interaction with an affectionate human face is needed to switch their body-brain system on properly.

Physiological effects of nurturance. Gerhardt describes these sorts of nurturing processes as 'cooking' the delicate ingredients which make up the baby; and particularly crucial is the developing nervous system, to which "the very early stages of cooking make all the difference." So, while physical factors like poor nutrition *in utero* or lack of oxygen at birth will obviously affect the child, styles of infant care are crucial too:

> "Early care actually shapes the developing nervous system and determines how stress is interpreted and responded to in the future... Human babies are born with the expectation of having stress managed for them. They tend to have low levels of cortisol for the first few months, as long as caring adults maintain their equilibrium through touch, stroking, feeding and rocking."

Babies who are touched and held a good deal in babyhood and receive plenty of positive attention in early life develop plentiful cortisol receptors, which means that they are well prepared to deal with stressful situations, and also to turn off the stress response system when it is no longer needed:

> "Pain and illness, the deaths of those one loves, discomforts and disappointments mar the happy norm, but they do not alter the fact that happiness *is* the norm, nor affect the tendency of the continuum to restore it, to heal it, after any disturbance."
>
> (Liedloff, 1975)

Appropriate *responsiveness* to babies is also very important: Gerhardt calls it "the mystery tonic that enables babies to flourish as soon as they get it." This is not over-anxious love but is about responding to infants' wishes and needs appropriately, and showing that you care and enjoy your interactions with them. Psychologists believe that such responsiveness not only satisfies babies' requirements for physical care and love, but also helps them to develop a proper sense of self because it demonstrates a recognition of the baby's *psychological* self – its feeling and thinking self.

Conclusions. We can see from the discussion above that both physical and emotional contact and affection are crucial to an infant's proper development at every level; and that their effects – far from being short term or superficial – are profound and often permanent. For example, actual brain structure and body chemistry are altered in babies subjected to stressful childrearing styles. Our prehistoric forebears, or modern hunter-gatherers, obviously didn't need to comprehend these scientific facts in order to know how to treat babies properly: they were and are guided by millennia-old instincts, participation and emulation. But the bottom line is that babies who are brought up in the hunter-gatherer way develop as (presumably) nature intended into unscrewed up young people and adults who fit into group living easily and well. This is the foundation upon which the good qualities found in forager societies is built. And the corollary is that the forager approach to childrearing makes life immensely much easier and more pleasurable for caregivers too.

The very different way in which dominator cultures rear their children, and the effects which this has on all society, is the subject of the next chapter.

Chapter 7

Creating Damaged People: Harmful Childhoods

Harmful Childrearing Replaces Natural Upbringing

> "[if a child] *feels safe, loveable and 'at home' before he can think, his view of later experiences will be very distinct in character from those of a child who feels unwelcome, unstimulated by the experiences he has missed and accustomed to living in a state of want, though the later experiences of both be identical.*"
>
> (Liedloff, 1979)

Just as continuum childrearing is a key contributor to the psychological and physical health of hunter-gatherers, so one can argue that harmful upbringings play a crucial role in screwing up people subjected to them. From the evidence that we have, it seems that methods of childrearing which are less natural, Stone Age or continuum go hand-in-hand with the emergence of patriarchy and more dominator-inclined cultures. And one can certainly also make a good case for claiming that the damage done to babies and young children, through lack of in-arms nurturing in particular, is a major cause of screwed-upness. This book therefore suggests that:

1. this screwing up is caused chiefly by non-continuum childhoods
2. there is a direct cause-and-effect connection between screwed up people and dominator society
3. dominator cultures actively *need* screwed up citizens in order to keep going, and therefore have a vested interest in ensuring that their childrearing practices are harmful

(even if they are unaware of this, and if the harming process is accomplished largely unconsciously).

The corollary of these three points is that – if we want to improve things – it's fruitless to address only part of the situation. If we wish to change matters for the better *we need to challenge the validity of dominator society itself.* In this chapter we therefore aim firstly to describe the harmful affects that non-continuum childrearing has on children and subsequently on the adults they become; and then to show how screwed up people contribute to dominator-style society and are also actively required by it in order to keep it going.

We saw in the previous chapter how nurturing childrearing has a huge positive effect on children's development and well-being. The converse is also true, for it seems that any significant departure from this continuum way of doing things is harmful to a child to some extent. Childrearing in Western cultures is very different – quite opposite in some respects – from what pertains among hunter-gatherers, however; and it does indeed appear to be harmful. The following discussion therefore goes through the main factors in dominator-style or non-continuum childrearing which seem to be damaging to infants, children, and the adults they become.

A "Basic Distrust Orientation"

Helena Norberg-Hodge told a Ladakhi mother "how much time some babies in the West spend away from their mothers and how at night they might sleep in another room and be fed cow's milk from plastic bottles on a schedule rather than when they cry. She was horrified: "Please, atche *Helena, when you have children, whatever you do, don't treat your baby like that. If you want a happy baby, do like we do."*

(Norberg-Hodge, 1991)

Rejection of attachment; 'toughening them up'. Annette Hamilton (1981) reviews Western-style childrearing and the main theories about it in order to compare these with hunter-gatherer upbringings. She concludes that Western childrearing has tended to believe (and still does, to an extent) that children aren't innately good; that they need rewards and punishments to condition or socialise them; even that the infant is limitlessly egotistical and the child is 'greedy' – full of insatiable cravings and desires that must be curbed. As we have seen in Chapter 6, this is very different from the attitude to children that exists among hunter-gatherers.

Foragers, for example, treat children's innate attachment behaviours such as the smiling, sucking, crying, clinging and following responses as natural, and respond to them unstintingly and uncritically. Dominator-style societies, however, tend to treat these evolutionarily-sensible behaviours as evidence of being a nuisance, naughtiness, wilfulness, badness, and so on, rather than as the perfectly natural and reasonable (from a Stone Age point of view) responses that they are. Or at best they are seen as restricting parents' freedom, and to be 'got over' as quickly as possible (Root, 2005). Children's attachment behaviours can also elicit disturbing feelings in adults who had *their* attachment behaviours curbed as children, making them avoidant of emotional intimacy or reluctant or unable to respond sensitively to babies' needs for care and attention. Or it may make the grown-up in turn wish to suppress these signs of dependence in the child and speed them on the road to independence over-quickly (Root, 2005).

However, contrary to the ideas which dominator society fosters, being properly coddled, nurtured and made to feel secure in childhood makes children *more* secure and independent as they grow up, not less. Many specialists concur on this:

"The desire of adults to promote independence in the child

> seems to underlie the rejection of attachment; this assumes that the only way to stop an infant or child from eternal demanding dependency is to ignore all but the obvious material needs right from the start. I would argue that this has the opposite effect... only by completely fulfilling the small infant's desires for dependency can the next step towards relative separation be taken."
>
> (Hamilton, 1981)

> "A baby confident of a rapid response by a mother committed to his well-being is likely to become a child who will be quicker to soothe and adapt to new situations, and likely to grow up to feel confident about human relations generally... over the long haul babies with more responsive mothers are going to cry and cling to their parents less, not more."
>
> (Hrdy, 2009)

> "Unfortunately, leaving a baby to cry or to cope by himself for more than a very short period usually has the reverse effect: it undermines the baby's confidence in the parent and in the world, leaving him more dependent, not less... The paradox is that people need to have a satisfying experience of dependency before they can become truly independent and largely self-regulating."
>
> (Gerhardt, 2004)

This is quite different from the beliefs underlying, say, old-fashioned British boarding schools. Here, separating children from parents and treating them harshly by subjecting them to emotionally cold and physically Spartan regimes was meant to toughen children up and produce the unbending, stiff-upper-lipped, well-behaved citizens of tomorrow. It might, indeed, have apparently toughened children up in their external behaviour – but at a cost, since it weakened them emotionally and psychologically. Few people go to this type of boarding school these days, but a milder form of this attitude to children persists in all dominator societies, particularly in regard to boys: "Don't cry"; "Don't be a sissy"; and so on. Indeed, even today in relatively enlightened post-Victorian times, it is surprising how many children still grow up with parents who – if not actively cruel – are cold, stern, controlling, overcritical or in other ways unloving. And many children also go to schools where peer pressure tends to create a similarly harsh environment – competitive, jeering and bullying at worst – a microworld in which the 'culture of hard' flourishes, and where tender, affectionate or kind behaviour is considered to be 'soft'.

Power imbalance. Another vital difference between Western-style and forager childrearing is that a *power imbalance* between adults or older children on one hand, and younger children on the other, is broadly assumed – even if this is not explicit. Certainly, until quite recently, *fear* underlay most of children's 'good behaviour' at home, at school and in the community. We did our chores, kept quiet, behaved in class and didn't cheek the neighbours not from good nature but from fear of the reprisals (physical or emotional or both) if we didn't. And though physical force or violence is used less against children these days, emotional reprisals certainly still are, with withdrawal of affection or approval; use of judgmental language ("Bad girl!"; "Naughty boy!"); or conditional reward and punishment being common.

Hamilton (1981) points out how, in Western childrearing:

> "the suppression of individual desires and submission to adult authority occurs at a very early age in conjunction with bodily routines such as feeding, cleanliness and other 'attachment' behaviours. The child's acceptance and sense of self-worth depends on it accepting the dictates of others, almost invariably its parents, who have absolute and unques-

> tioned control even to the point of physical attack... In this relationship the adult is seen to have power and society sanctions that power, where the child is expected to be powerless and obey."

And Alton (1984) adds:

> "Where all the dependency needs, nurturing, trust and love as well as discipline and disapproval are tied up in two parents this gives them enormous powers of coercion and control. The child feels as powerless as he experiences his parents as powerful. By contrast, in traditional cultures the diffuse emotionality of the wider kinship system means that biological parents cannot monopolise the child in the same way."

These in-family power imbalances exacerbate the many others which make children feel relatively powerless in everyday life; and contribute to the production of citizens within dominator society who go on to feel innately disempowered for the rest of their lives. Moreover, one has to point out that this must surely be to the advantage of hierarchical cultures, as it ensures that most citizens journey through life in a disadvantaged state which can be exploited to keep them in their place, intimidate them, exploit them and so on. This is in clear contrast to hunter-gatherer-style childrearing which, as discussed in the previous chapter, appears to empower children.

'Stages' in child development. It should now be clear that Western ideas about child development and what is normal for children at different stages in their lives are based on faulty evidence – on the lives of children reared in dominator-style homes and societies rather than on those raised in hunter-gatherer, continuum-style cultures. Alton (1984) points this out, and quotes from literature on developmental progress in infants and young children which lists the type of stages which we consider to be standard in Western society. These include:

> "At 2 years: Constantly demanding Mother's attention. Defends own possessions with determination. As yet no idea of sharing. Plays near other children but not with them. Resentful of attention shown to other children. At 2.5 years: Throws violent tantrums when thwarted or unable to express needs and less easily distracted. Watches other children at play interestedly and occasionally joins in for a few minutes, but little notion of sharing play-things or adults' attention. At 4 years: Needs other children to play with and is alternately cooperative and aggressive with them as with adults."

Alton comments that: "I would submit that not one of these manifestations in social behaviour is the normal condition of childhood. (Indeed, as an example of desirable upbringing, such a child would be regarded as severely disturbed by many peoples of the world.)"! The same applies to the adolescent upheavals and teenage misbehaviour that modern society accepts as normal and unavoidable: again, this isn't a phenomenon that occurs in traditional hunter-gatherer or tribal societies.

In fact, it's extraordinary what we've come to accept as acceptable in the sphere of childhood disorders and abnormal or bad behaviour. For example, fairly recent statistics tell us that:

> "A quarter of British pre-school children are considered by their parents to have problem behaviour. Three-fifths of 3-year-olds with behaviour problems have troubled behaviour five years later... Between 20 per cent and 30 per cent of school children have serious behaviour/psychological problems. [and] the psychological symptoms underlying these problems tend to persist, resulting in antisocial or other

disturbed behaviour in adolescence or adulthood."
(Root, 2005)

This is shocking, surely – yet we continue to "normalize the craziness", as Zerzan puts it.

Western-style childrearing is unpleasant for parents compared to hunter-gatherers. But perhaps the main message arising from this discussion is how immensely much more difficult and unpleasant childrearing is in Western cultures compared to hunter-gatherers! At best it's seen as rewarding but also "a long, hard job [with] lots of hard work and deprivation... repetitious, tedious, wearing and extremely demanding," (Root, 2005). Perhaps more often it's experienced as a nightmare of trying to soothe babies back to sleep, exhaustion, projectile vomiting, screaming tantrums in supermarket aisles, battles of wills over sweets and toys, complete lack of 'me time' and so on. And at worst, post-natal depression, psychosis, or other breakdowns in mental or physical health blight the experience for mother and infant, or frustration and exhaustion result in violence and abuse to the child. Yet our culture doesn't seem to think it odd that bringing up children is routinely found to be so hard; or to wonder if it couldn't and shouldn't be less stressful...

Other Negative Factors

Less natural pregnancies. During pregnancy, the developing foetus is vulnerable to harmful influences passed across the placenta from mother to child. Dominator life is stressful: and if mothers are stressed, cortisol passes readily into the womb and the baby's body with particularly harmful results (see below). In this way, mothers may pass on their own heightened stress responses to their baby and set them up in turn for a lifetime of oversensitised responses to life. (No wonder that most traditional cultures have strong customs about keeping mothers calm, untroubled and stress-free as this makes good sense in light of the underlying biochemistry.) Drugs such as alcohol, caffeine and nicotine (plus, of course, illegal drugs), which are more likely to be used by stressed mothers to 'self-medicate' can also stress the baby directly. In this way, a chain of overdeveloped stress responses can be set in motion – stress-sensitive babies growing into readily-stressed mothers who pass on excess cortisol to their child in turn.

Less natural births. Western-style births are usually far less gentle, natural and instinctual than hunter-gatherer or tribal births; and may perhaps be more difficult compared to those in simpler cultures partly because our culture encourages us to 'live in our heads' rather than in our bodies: too much consciousness probably fights the body's own instinctual wisdom and ability to do its thing in its own way in its own time. Births have also become increasingly medicalised and intrusive over the centuries: "consider how common it is for our newborn to be removed from their mothers' bodies by the obstetricians forceps then taken away to be washed and ensconced in a plastic trolley like so many products fresh from the assembly line," (Hamilton, 1981). Opponents of the over-medicalised approach continue to try to introduce more natural birthing systems, but we don't appear to be making much headway overall, despite the lasting harm caused by unnatural methods. Joseph Chilton Pearce, for example – an outspoken critic of over-medicalised childbirth – recognises the lasting harm that inappropriate methods can cause and believes that:

> "The ruinously expensive take-over of all birthing by hospital-medical procedures has brought into play an equally huge and expensive cradle-to-grave therapeutic operation, undertaken in our efforts to repair the damage we are blindly causing at the same time."
>
> (Chilton Pearce, 2007)

Less or no breastfeeding. Breastfeeding for more than a few months is not the norm in most developed-world cultures – despite its generally-acknowledged benefits, which are attested to by all major health bodies, including the World Health Organisation and the American Academy of Pediatrics, and were outlined in Chapter 6. These bodies both recommend exclusive breastfeeding for at least the first six months of life, and beyond for as long as is mutually desired by mother and child, say up to two years or more. Despite this, many babies in Western societies still aren't breastfed at all, or only very briefly. This has huge negative implications for babies' and mothers' bonding and for the infants health, well-being and general development.

Less opportunities for parents to learn childcare naturally. As we said in Chapter 6, there are ample opportunities in hunter-gatherer or tribal life to learn how to care for children. But the way that modern life is organised means that many first world people don't get a chance to learn how look after children before becoming parents themselves:

> "... in Western societies where people are cut off from each other physically by their elaborate houses and apartments, and work is rigidly separated from domestic life, these opportunities do not arise. There is little chance to observe how an experienced mother deals with a baby or toddler, and less chance of practising with other people's children." (Gerhardt, 2004)

We can see the effects of this in the increasing call for parenting classes today.

Lack of stimulation; lack of opportunities to practice life skills. Liedloff and Hamilton both contrast the natural sensory stimulation available to hunter-gatherer children with the relatively limited stimuli that many (most?) modern babies and children receive – laid out on their backs in cots and prams staring at the ceiling or sky (or thrust into parents' chests or backs!); playing on the same old dull floors; sat alone in front of the TV; interacting only occasionally with non-parents; and – increasingly – being more or less prisoners in houses because of fears about their safety in the outside world.

These sorts of restrictions on children feed in to a vicious cycle, with the child who is prevented from experiencing challenging or dangerous things, becoming increasingly unable to deal with them, feeling increasingly incompetent, powerless or scared, and so on. And clearly, the growing need that many parents feel to restrict their children imposes an added workload on caregivers, puts family members in each other's pockets excessively, and may cause outbursts of ill-judged recklessness if the child evades the curbs on its freedom. Yet modern parents who are brave enough to allow their children reasonable freedoms seem to find that an innate wisdom and judgement operates in Western-culture children much as they do in foragers: "If young children are trusted by being given freedom of movement, they are able to use their judgement to avoid hazards," (Root, 2005).

Isolation. The relative isolation of the mother/carer-child pair in most Western-style families for much of the time is emotionally unhealthy and unnatural too, compared to our EEA and the 'whole village' which is childhood's natural habitat. However loving the carer, "The unit is too small and the relationship within it consequently too intense," (Alton, 1984). Moreover, at worst, all sorts of abuses can go on in the privacy of these isolated households:

> "People are all lumped together, but in such a way as to maximise the divisions between them. This way, it is possible to ensure that we really do get the worst of all worlds: we can hear the neighbours shouting and screaming and the children crying through the thin walls and yet the walls mean that we

> are meant to be cut-off and indifferent, unable to do anything to help. Would men abuse or batter their wives if they weren't able to do it in the 'privacy' of their own homes? If it was taken for granted that children could run into their neighbours' homes, would we have *any* children battered by their parents? Isolation is a very real contributing factor to oppression of all kinds."
>
> (Alton, 1984)

It is certainly much harder to perpetrate abuses in the communal settings typical of hunter-gatherer or tribal life, and under the collective disapproval of the group, than in the privacy of the nuclear family home characteristic of dominator cultures. Even where life was lived indoors in cold climates, the Inuit and Native Americans, for example, inhabited communal long houses in which most of everyday life was shared, and within which acceptable behaviour was ensured.

Lack of In-arms Nurturing, and Harmful Separation: What They Do to Us

> *"Expressions of in-arms deprivation checker our lives and color the personalities around us so frequently that we tend to view them as part of human nature."*
>
> (Liedloff, 1975)

But perhaps the most crucial difference between hunter-gatherer and Western-style childrearing, as we've stressed in Chapter 6, is that forager caregivers keep babies and children close to them – in arms – from birth and usually for about the first two years of life. Babies born in developed-world situations, in contrast, are typically separated from their mothers immediately after birth for more or less amounts of time; and spend increasing amounts of their early months physically apart from carers. Most modern infants and toddlers spend a great deal of their time *not* being held; and often without much interaction with other people. Or – worse – carers may be stressed, distracted, neglectful, irritated or even actively hostile to the child.

Separation in animals and humans. However, before examining the subject in detail, let's first consider it in the context of the whole animal kingdom, and particularly in regard to our mammal relatives. Animal ethologist Bekoff has this to say on the subject:

> "The bonding process between mother and infant facilitates the development of neurophysiological structures that underlie normal social behaviors such as empathy. We know that in humans a disruption of this bonding process can result in reduced capacity for empathy and an increased propensity towards violence. Early trauma has permanent effects on the brain, and thus on behavior. Trauma such as separation of the infant from its mother, or abuse or neglect by the mother, can lead to a permanent impairment in empathic social interaction."
>
> (Bekoff and Pierce, 2009)

The same physiological mechanisms underlying attachment that exist in humans apply to higher animals as well; and disrupting them tends to produce similarly destructive effects on the individuals and communities involved. For example, Bekoff and Pierce describe the same effects in traumatised animal groups, such as elephant herds damaged by hunting, as are found in human communities where the natural bonding processes between infant and carer has been impaired – lack of empathy, and increases in violence and disruptive and disrupted behaviour being typical. And looking at the issue in another way – from the separated infants' point of view – Hrdy (2009) discusses experiments on separating animal babies from their mothers and the resulting "palpable suffering", distress and despair, concluding that: "given what we now know, it is no more ethical to experimentally separate baby monkeys from their mothers than to engage in other forms of animal torture." Is it taking things too far to say that separating human babies from mothers for any significant amount of time, especially in the early months, is also a form of animal abuse – the animal in this case being a still wordless but nevertheless fully sentient primate baby? "They have no legal right not to be tortured by longing for their mothers and left to scream their agony unheeded," as Liedloff (1975) unequivocally puts it, in making the case for the rights of the human infant.

It seems that there are many ways in which lack of in-arms nurturing and/or separation affect infants and adults biochemically or neurophysiologically. We will now look at two approaches to this topic, based firstly on Sue Gerhardt's work that considers the role of the stress response and cortisol in particular; and secondly on James Prescott's research linking somatosensory deprivation with violence-prone behaviour.

Separation, the Stress Response, and Cortisol

"The easiest way to induce depression and alienation in an infant or child is not to touch it, hold it, or carry it on your body."

(Prescott quoted in Young, 2009)

Babies expect to be unstressed. A crucial effect of non-continuum childhoods on babies is the way that it affects their stress response and the production of cortisol in their bodies. It is crucial because inappropriate amounts of cortisol cause many types of harm to the developing child. This very simple fact has a huge host of consequences which are discussed in detail with abundant corroborating evidence by Gerhardt in her *Why Love Matters* (2004).

Broadly speaking, human babies are born with low levels of cortisol for the first few months because, one can assume, they evolved with the expectation of being protected from stressful situations in infancy. As the previous chapter explained, a baby can cope with some stress as long as caring adults respond to it by holding, stroking, feeding, rocking or comforting it, or doing whatever else is appropriate to its needs. However, if no one responds properly to its needs, the baby's immature nervous system readily reacts to stressful situations with the 'fight or flight' response that floods its system with cortisol. Since a baby can neither fight nor flee, the most it can do is cry, freeze, or withdraw. Cortisol is therefore of little use to it, as it can't respond to this neurochemical in the appropriate way that an older organism would. Even more crucially, high cortisol is positively harmful to the child, having a directly toxic effect on its developing brain and organism generally. If it hasn't got sufficient cortisol receptors to absorb the hormone, harm will therefore result.

Separation = stress. A key point here is that *babies experience separation from loving carers – even for quite short times – as stress.* Their EEA or continuum expectations are of being in close contact with someone more or less all the time in the first two years of life. Not only is in-arms care directly soothing and nurturing; it also signals reassurance to the infant that a loving caregiver is pledged to protecting it and fulfilling its needs: "All infant primates are soothed by close bodily contact, but in humans the sharing of emotional cues becomes a more important part of the quest for continuing commitment," (Hrdy, 2009). Anything else arouses fear of abandonment – and abandonment is fatal for human babies, for we are all born in an immature state and are totally dependent upon others to look after us in infancy. This means that what is considered 'normal' treatment of babies in dominator society is experienced as abnormal (that is, non-continuum) and stressful – if not downright terrifying – by the infants subjected to this within Western-style cultures: "the agony of the baby left to weep in his cot, his terrible longing," as

Liedloff (1975) puts it. Being separated from mothers at birth or soon after; being made to sleep alone in a dark room – these are hugely frightening and painful experiences for this little creature who has literally been part of its mother till birth, and has continuum expectations of being closely connected to her for the months after birth. Fear and pain are stressful; and babies treated like this are therefore inevitably subjected to stress responses – that is, their bodies are flooded with cortisol – with which they're not designed to cope. The result of this, clearly, is that nearly all dominator-reared children are damaged to some extent by the harmful effects of excess cortisol on their immature bodies and brains.

Western culture ignores this source of stress. This very simple fact has a huge host of consequences, but it is definitely a truth by no means universally acknowledged. Indeed, many modern 'experts' on childrearing aren't willing to admit how harmful stress – even very small amounts of stress – with its accompanying unassimilable cortisol, is to young babies. So, incredibly, even in the relatively enlightened twenty-first century, we continue to think it's OK to part newborns from mothers, to let babies cry unattended, or to leave them alone all night. Yet such practices are quietly – and mostly irrevocably – harming the next generation to come, for the evidence is strong that the effects of stress and cortisol are key physiological factors underlying a wide spectrum of disorders in dominator culture:

> "The stress response is such an essential part of our organism's response to life that it appears to underlie an astonishing range of disorders. When it does not function well, we become vulnerable both physiologically and psychologically."
>
> (Gerhardt, 2004)

This disordering certainly begins in infancy: for example, can we really believe that it's normal for babies to need winding or to regurgitate milk or suffer gripe as a matter of course? Or for between 10 per cent and 30 per cent of babies cry to an extent defined as 'excessive' by doctors and researchers during their first five months? (Root, 2005). These events are common among Western babies, yet don't happen to any extent in simpler societies, so surely we can take them as clear signs of stress and of a young organism's systems gone awry? As Liedloff (1975) points out: "Vomiting, or 'spitting up', an everyday event in our infants' lives, is so rare that I can remember seeing it happen only once in my years with the Indians, and that baby had a high fever."

Emotional effects. On the emotional level, what babies *feel* as a result of separation and lack of nurturing care must surely be a toxic mixture of loss, fear, grief, rage, resentment, insecurity and unlovableness – the latter subsequently resulting in a deep-seated underlying lack of self-esteem or self-confidence in most of us. These emotions are amplified by the cortisol-related influences; and are – one can argue – the drivers of most of the negative behaviour that we call 'human nature' in dominator society. In addition, it seems likely that much of the bad behaviour we see in modern children stems from more or less unconscious resentment, and the child's desire to punish its parents, or adults generally, for the instinctively-felt mistreatment it's had in childhood. (And perhaps this also explains dominator society's obsession with revenge, seen in so many films: we seem to like to set things up in such a way as to legitimise, and provide opportunities to vent 'justifiable rage'.)

Physiological effects of cortisol. Experiencing excess cortisol in infancy tends to result in children and adults who subsequently have either abnormally high, or low, cortisol levels in their bodies. There are strong links between *high* cortisol and many emotional dysfunctions such as depression, anxiety and suicidal tendencies, as well as with eating disorders, obesity and alcoholism. There can be physical effects too, as high cortisol can compromise the immune system and wound healing, and plays a part in diabetes, hypertension and many other ailments.

Low cortisol also occurs in people stressed in infancy – probably because experiencing high cortisol for a prolonged period may cause the organism to close down cortisol receptors. It may also be a direct defence mechanism – the organism's attempt to disengage from painful feelings through avoidance, withdrawal, and denial of hurt: "better to feel nothing than to cope with relatively continuous painful experience," (Gerhardt, 2004). The result is emotional numbness or even dissociation: feelings are switched off, and there is a 'flattened' emotional life and reduced response to happy stimuli – what maverick psychologist Wilhelm Reich called *armouring*. This pattern is typical of children subjected to mistreatment which makes them angry, but whose family culture doesn't tolerate the expression of negative or critical feelings.

However, suppressed feelings don't go away: biochemical, muscular and autonomic responses have been aroused, and without some resolution have nowhere to go. These feelings therefore tend to burst out at some point, typically in outbursts of rage directed at a relatively 'safe' target such as a partner or child who is unlikely to retaliate (hence the paradox of the abuse of nearest and dearest, these being the easiest and safest targets on whom to vent suppressed anger). Low cortisol people are also likely to have what has been called a cancer- or disease-prone personality, and to be vulnerable to psychosomatic and auto-immune disorders such as asthma, allergies, arthritis, chronic fatigue, ME and cancer which are thought to have underlying roots in emotional suppression.

It is easy to see how these two modes – of high, and low, cortisol – can between them result in or enhance any or all of the negative feelings, behaviours and ailments which are typical of dominator people and societies. In the sections above we looked at the harmful effects that can arise even from what is considered 'normal' childrearing in dominator-style cultures. And, clearly, if a child's environment is worse than 'normal', then its correct development is likely get derailed even further. Most mental illness and antisocial or criminal behaviour can be linked back to non-nurturing or actively abusive or neglectful childhoods.

The body always tries to rectify harm done to it, and to re-establish some sort of working system when the indigenous one is disordered; but such attempts are always compromises – second-best to how our organisms are designed to function: "Nature will compensate as best she can – but compensation is always a poor substitute for natural, spontaneous mimetic growth," (Chilton Pearce, 2007). The emotional and the physiological impacts of dominator childrearing practices on children are also experienced as *shocks* to the system; and this is discussed further in Chapter 10.

Somatosensory Deprivation and Tendencies to Violence

American developmental psychologist James Prescott, working in the mid-twentieth century, was an early advocate of the need for physically tender loving care in childhood. He connected nurturing upbringings to the development of human beings who are *able to feel and enjoy physical pleasure*, while those deprived of what he terms somatosensory stimulation are *not* able to do so. Based on animal and human studies, Prescott became convinced that deprivation of physical sensory pleasure – "body touch, contact and movement", that is, holding, rocking, stroking, carrying and so on – *creates a neurophysiological predisposition for violence-seeking behaviour* (Prescott, 1975), and postulated a reciprocal link between pleasure-seeking and violence-seeking behaviour:

> "When the brain's pleasure circuits are 'on', the violence circuits are 'off'. Among human beings, a pleasure-prone

> personality rarely displays violence or aggressive behaviors, and a violent personality has little ability to tolerate, experience, or enjoy sensuously pleasing activities. As either violence or pleasure goes up, the other goes down."

The implications and ramifications of this concept are enormous; and Prescott, in the paper cited (*Body Pleasure and the Origins of Violence*) is arguing for his ideas to be used in understanding and mitigating the causes of violence in modern society. However, I feel that he didn't fully appreciate the deeper causes underlying dominator societies' love affair with violence, and the fact that they evidently *don't want* to end it, or to create a bunch of happy, pleasure-seeking citizens! (This aspect is discussed further at the end of this chapter.) And perhaps that is why Prescott's scientific work – important and relevant as it is – appears not to have been specifically pursued subsequently, although his concept of the importance of somatosensory stimulation for emotional health isn't an isolated finding (for example, it has a clear relationship to Wilhelm Reich's earlier ideas about armouring and the physically tense and psychosomatically defended body). Nevertheless, it is obvious that Prescott's ideas relate clearly and definitively to the basic thesis of this book. His work corroborates, and gives a further physiological basis to, this book's claim that nurturing childhoods create psychologically healthy people. It also helps to explain why unscrewed up peoples are happier than screwed up ones (because they are physiologically capable of experiencing pleasure); and why they tend to be more peaceful (because this capacity reduces the desire for or drive to violence).

Pleasure, violence and drugs. James Prescott and Terence McKenna both point out how a society's choice of 'acceptable' drugs is influenced by its underlying ethos. As Prescott (1975) says:

> "A society will support behaviors which are consistent with its

values and mores. US society is a competitive, aggressive, and violent society. Consequently it supports drugs that facilitate competitive, aggressive and violent behaviors and opposes drugs that counteract such behaviors. Alcohol is well-known to facilitate the expression of violent behaviors, and, although addicting and very harmful to chronic users, is acceptable to US society. Marijuana, on the other hand, is an active pleasure-inducing drug which enhances the pleasure of touch and actively inhibits violent-aggressive behaviors. It is for these reasons, I believe that marijuana is rejected by US society. For similar reasons, heroin is rejected and methadone (an addicting drug minus the pleasure) is accepted."

In other words, dominator societies tolerate drugs which stimulate dominator-encouraged feelings or behaviours, but fear and suppress drugs which stimulate partnership-style sensations, particularly pleasure.

Prescott also points out how dominator-style drugs come to be *preferred* to pleasure by those who are less capable of experiencing or tolerating pleasurable feelings: "Some people find alcohol more satisfying than sex... This is additional evidence for the hypothesis that drug 'pleasures' are a substitute for somatosensory pleasures," (Prescott, 1975). Liedloff (1975) also observes that many drugs produce the blissful in-arms feeling which so many of us lacked in childhood, and that this is the secret of their addictiveness. It also explains why screwed up, avoidant people may prefer drugs to pleasures such as love-making or socialising, as the drug gives them the in-arms bliss without having to engage with another human being.

Alienated from our bodies and real life. Childhood somatosensory deprivation results in a lessened ability to tolerate or fully experience pleasure: the physiological mechanisms tend to armour us; while the stress and cortisol effects discussed by Sue Gerhardt also lessen our ability to feel pleasure freely, and set us up to be depressed, angry and so on. People who have suffered hurtful experiences in childhood tend – as we have seen – to 'flee' their bodies somatically and psychologically – escaping into their heads in order to avoid unpleasant feelings and sensations, and becoming emotionally withdrawn or avoidant as a result. Indeed, wounding early experiences may have made them physiologically *unable* to tolerate any re-experiencing of those feelings; and most of us suffer from this sort of armouring to at least some extent. These factors therefore tend to result in people who aren't properly connected to their physical or emotional selves and who find it hard or impossible to 'be in the moment', to feel fully alive, to experience pleasure and enjoyment, or even, perhaps, to properly appreciate the aliveness of other creatures. This in turn rebounds on the next generation, with avoidant adults tending to become detached, unresponsive parents in turn (Root, 2005). And it rebounds on the environment and the rest of the world as well: armoured people readily and unheedingly inflict cruelties on animals, plants and the earth.

I believe that this point of view parallels John Zerzan's in his ongoing critiques of the ills of civilisation. Zerzan, too, discusses modern peoples' lack of connection to real feelings and real life – a mind-body split which is mediated by an increasing attachment to 'in-the-head' culture – including language, thought, virtual reality and so on: "Symbolic culture inhibits human communication by blocking and otherwise suppressing channels of sensory awareness... It is our fall from simplicity and fullness of life directly experienced," (Zerzan, 2002). Just to make a point of terminology clear: as I understand it, Zerzan is using 'symbolic culture' here in a different sense from Knight (1991), who sees the development of symbolic culture as the essential step associated with humankind's move away from primate despotism towards hominin cooperation.

Going back half a century, this is also the approach to life championed by D.H. Lawrence, and discussed at length by

Aldous Huxley through his Lawrentian character Rampion in *Point Counter Point* (1928). And Carl Jung, in 1963, also linked this 'living in the head' tendency to a muting of the feminine in women and the masculine in men in modern society: "The more rational the polity, the more blurred is the difference between the sexes."

Continuum infancies followed by dominator childhoods. Finally, in this section, we can speculate about the fact that *most* simpler peoples seem to be far more inherently cheerful and happy than Western ones. This seems to be the case even with those who live in very difficult conditions – conditions that most Westerners would find hard to bear, let alone bear with cheerfulness and good grace. And it also seems to be the case in cultures which are clearly quite dominator or patriarchal in style: rural Indian and African tribal societies come to mind. Here we can hypothesise that these simpler cultures treat their *infants and young children* in a nurturing, continuum way, so that even though older children come under increasing pressure to conform to the strictures of patriarchal norms, some of the benefits of kind childrearing persist into adulthood.

Compensatory Behaviours

> "*Loss of the essential condition of well-being which should have grown out of one's time in-arms leads to searches and substitutions for it.* Happiness ceases to be a normal condition of being alive, and becomes a goal."
>
> (Liedloff, 1975)

The first part of this chapter aimed to show the harmful effects of non-continuum upbringings. On the one hand, self-hate resulting from not having been given the sense of one's own loveableness in infancy is a major basis for *irrational hatred*, as Liedloff (1975) points out; and is one obvious driver for the anger and aggressiveness which we consider to be normal in dominator society. On the other hand, it seems that most of us are also driven by a tremendously strong compensatory need to be made to feel *right*, 'OK'. We may actually be addicted to always being in the right or having the last word, or just to getting the correct answers to puzzles, quizzes and so on. Or be neurotically oversensitive to slights and snubs, criticism and disapproval, which we're constantly trying to ward off or rebut. We're easily hurt, and want to get back at those who hurt us; feelings of frustration, jealousy and inadequacy spoil our days; or the even more toxic emotions listed above of loss, fear, grief, rage, resentment, insecurity and self-hate spill out into our lives, demanding to be vented somehow. The feeling of unloveableness which is ubiquitous among dominator citizens also tends to result in people who either lack confidence, neurotically seek approval and acceptance, need leaders or are susceptible to victimisation; or in those who overcompensate and wish to lord it over others – the ideal recipe for the constituents of a hierarchical society.

Escapist and compensatory behaviours; addictions. Damaged people may express their negative feelings directly, or try to avoid the pain or fill the hole left by unsatisfactory upbringings through a host of escapist and compensatory behaviours. A wide range of these are described with great insight by Liedloff in *The Continuum Concept* (Chapter 8, *Deprivation of the In-Arms Experience*); and we have mentioned some of them already in preceding chapters. As Liedloff puts it, looking at modern behaviour from the point of view of our non-continuum modern lives and what these have deprived us of helps to make it "increasingly clear why we do so many of the pointless things we do."!

Many of Liedloff's 'pointless things' are what we call addictions; and today we recognise a whole host of them – not just to illegal drugs, but to many socially sanctioned substances and activities too. Alcohol (discussed above) and nicotine are obvious examples; and it seems that – much as governments decry their use – the equilibrium of dominator societies is sustained to a significant extent by these harmful drugs, which act both to fill treasury coffers and as placebos for a dissatisfied populace. We also have flourishing addictions to food generally and to sugar in particular (to try to replace the sweetness in life that we've lost? See McKenna, 1992). Also to salt (and it's interesting that most addictive substances that are popular in dominator cultures are highly 'yin', acidify our bodies, and tend to stimulate negative states of mind and angry behaviour).

Certainly, all such substances are acceptable in moderation; and in traditional societies psychotropic substances such as tobacco, mescalin and magic mushrooms are used respectfully in rituals. It's also true that – given free access to products such as sugar, alcohol and tobacco – most hunter-gatherers overindulge or are drawn to partake addictively, so a physiological and psychological attraction to mood- and mind-altering substances seems to be innate in human beings. Nevertheless, I would still view modern society's tremendously excessive indulgence in both legitimate and illegitimate 'drugs' as being spurred on – at least partly – by unfilled inner cravings resulting from childhood deprivations or the desire to subdue unpleasant feelings, rather than from sheer opportunity or exposure to them.

Addiction to romantic love and sex is discussed in Chapter 12; but this is really just one aspect of the longing for manifest approval and love – for being made to feel 'OK' – caused by non-nurturing childhoods. People who have not experienced proper continuum love in infancy typically exhibit, as they grow up, "a state of longing for parental approval, for 'social reinforcement', love and belonging, whilst having little confidence in being able to obtain these things," (Gerhardt, 2004). Our society's love of pets probably also belongs in this category, with many people undoubtedly keeping them in order to gain the unconditional love and tactile affection that they missed in childhood.

Addiction to fame is very similar, seeking as it does to obtain attention and unconditional love. Even much petty crime and anti-social behaviour can be seen as a form of attention-seeking.

Workaholicism is a well-known addiction. Other behaviours not always thought of as addictions include our craving for material things and 'stuff' generally; and for power. Addiction to excitement and adrenalin – perhaps partly stemming from what Zerzan calls the 'domestication' of modern life – is also widespread, ranging from the illegal thrills of antisocial behaviour and crime to the legitimate (but pointless? And risky and expensive) excesses of mountain-conquering, extreme expeditions and so on.

We Don't Notice the Screwing-Up Because We Need Damaged Citizens

We now need to return to the line of argument with which this chapter began, and stress again the point that – unconsciously or deliberately – we appear to be screwing up our population from birth, without actually seeming to notice this much. We may be dimly aware of how much is wrong with our childrearing and our children, but strong invisible forces seem to prevent us from being too conscious of this, questioning why it is so, or doing much to prevent it. And if we don't notice it, then we can't take preventative action against the screwing-up process – and so we automatically go on creating the next generation of screwed up citizens. And we do this despite all the harm which non-continuum childhoods wreak on other people and society generally – both directly and indirectly. Yet if we *really* wanted to do all the things we say we do in order to improve society – reduce crime, drug addiction, overeating, pornography, paedophilia, and so on – we could actually help immensely by simply providing children with nurturing, continuum-style childhoods for the first two years of their lives.

All this seems to support the argument that dominator

societies *need* damaged citizens in order to perpetuate themselves, and therefore have to somehow accommodate the ancillary harm which damaged people inflict on those societies without noticing this too much. David Smail (1993) corroborates this point of view in *The Nature of Unhappiness*:

> "A society which, even if inadvertently, creates distress in its members is highly likely to develop institutional systems for distracting attention from the more unfortunate consequences of its organisation and absorbing the worst effects. It seems obvious that preventing the level of critical analysis from extending beyond the individual to the nature of society itself would be greatly to its advantage. In circumstances such as these, rational evidence is likely to be the last thing anyone takes any notice of."

This does indeed seem to be what's going on in current society: we have abundant evidence to show that things are going badly wrong in Western life, and we seem willing to throw money endlessly at treating the *symptoms* of our malaise, but remain resolutely unwilling to address the *causes* of those symptoms. As Thoreau (1854) said: "There are a thousand hacking at the branches of evil to one who is striking at the root."

Conclusion. In order to survive and thrive, dominator culture needs citizens who will perpetuate its hierarchies, are psychologically pre-set to be top dogs or under dogs and whose hunger for acceptance and approval can be manipulated to exploit them as wage slaves or consumers; who are insecure, and can be reassured through adopting the roles which dominator society requires; who are afraid, and can be kept in their place through the dogmas of religion; who have stores of unvented rage which can be harnessed to fight wars. So the last thing dominator culture really wants to do is to start producing emotionally healthy and psychologically free people – the sort of individualistic and egalitarian humans which continuum-style childrearing practices create.

In 1975 Jean Liedloff believed that "Once we fully recognise the consequences of our treatment of babies, children, one another and ourselves... we cannot fail to act more suitably." But alas, this belief has proved naïve; for dominator culture has shown us through its own continuing harmful actions and lack of preventative measures that *it definitely doesn't want or intend to* improve life for its population, *if that process of improvement threatens its own survival*. If we want to change dominator culture in any radical way, therefore, we shouldn't expect to get significant help from its institutions, however many rational arguments or pleas for fair play we employ. As Eisler said in 1987:

> "Much of the ideological confusion, as well as the one-step-forward, two-steps-back cultural movement of modern times can be traced to the failure of those working for progress to perceive the logical impossibility of creating a just and equal society as long as a dominator-dominated model of human relations remains in place."

Instead, a fundamental critique of our whole dominator *zeitgeist* will need to be taken on board; and quite different routes to change will probably be required. These are discussed further in Chapter 14.

Chapter 8

'Burying' Partnership Cultures

'Things Have Always Been This Way'

So far, we have explored some of the key characteristics of partnership-type societies – ancient and modern; and shown what sane, happy people they produce. We have then gone on to consider how dominator societies might have arisen initially; and the mechanisms involved in creating dominator citizens and perpetuating dominator society. It is now time to look at why we are so unaware of partnership societies and our egalitarian, cooperative past. This chapter therefore discusses why and how dominator societies suppress the truth about partnership cultures. This carries on the discussion about conspiracies which we began in Chapter 1.

It is clearly in the interests of dominator cultures to uphold the impression that life could not be fundamentally different from what it is now, and apparently has been for most people for thousands of years. As Eisler put it in 1987:

> "it is precisely because... new knowledge about the original direction of our cultural evolution casts such a different light on our past – and our potential future – that it is so difficult for us to deal with. And because it represents such a threat to the prevailing system, there are massive efforts to suppress it."

So, in spite of periodic attempts to show that a dominator-style approach to society *isn't* the only one possible, and that in fact cooperative, partnership-style societies pre-dated it and were the norm for hundreds of thousands of years across the globe, the prevailing dominator world view persists that 'things have always been like this', and that misery, conflict and competition are inevitable.

Egregious examples of this process over the last two centuries are the deliberate suppression of Lewis Henry Morgan's work on primitive communism among Native Americans and of Engels' work on the origins of the family (mentioned earlier, and discussed by Knight, 1991); and the virtual disappearance of Kropotkin's *Mutual Aid* and of Briffault's *The Mothers*. The sidelining of these works illustrates the struggle between partnership and dominator ideologies which was already being fought in the Western world from the mid nineteenth century on (far earlier than most people realise); and the way that authoritative and valid works of scholarship can nearly vanish through the effects of mainstream indifference, neglect or scorn.

Modern authors with pro-dominator agenda. As we've already seen in earlier chapters, many orthodox pro-dominator views are now being challenged by evidence from a variety of disciplines, and by scholars who see things in a different and less dominator way. And this book, of course, is part of this challenging process, and seeks to remind us that dominator societies – in order to maintain their ascendancy – continue to have strong vested interests in forgetting, denying or suppressing what partnership cultures have to teach us in terms of creating healthy societies. Nevertheless, in spite of these pro-nice trends, many popular modern books which purport to be scientific and objective about human nature or what it is to be human still present highly dominator-style views of our prehistoric forebears, human nature, and the drives behind their behaviour.

One example of this genre is Stephen Pinker's 1998 popular science best-seller *How the Mind Works*. A more recent example is well-known neuroscientist Michael Gazzaniga's 2008 book *Human: The Science Behind What Makes Your Brain Unique*. For example, Gazzaniga uses Richard Wrangham's book *Demonic Males* as a major source in his discussion of human violence and whether it is innate, ignoring abundant counter-evidence proffered by experts such as Bekoff, (2007, 2009), Boehm (1999) or Hrdy (2008). He goes on to 'prove' that humans are innately patriarchal and prone to violence, asserting that "Wrangham reviews the ethnographic records, studies of modern-day primitive peoples, and archaeological finds to show that humans are, and always have been, a patrilineal society, regardless of what some feminist organisations assert." This claim by a well-known scientist seems extraordinary when one considers the long-standing, authoritative and far-reaching evidence to the contrary (for example Briffault, 1927; Knight, 2008; Alton, 2011) – including the existence of matrilineal communities at the present time.

Pinker, Gazzaniga, Wrangham and their ilk clearly have a definite vested interest in portraying *all* human – and most animal – behaviour as being uncompromisingly dominator in nature; and show great ingenuity in twisting interpretations of even the most obviously partnership behaviour round so that it can be taken to have a dominator motive. Readers who have got this far in *Do We Need to Be So Screwed Up?!* can decide for themselves whether such pro-dominator views are justified or not. Nevertheless, the fact that prominent scientists still promulgate them is disturbing just because these authors *aren't* overtly fringe fanatics or extremists but, rather, are influential scholars and authors, writing best-selling books, and teaching and broadcasting internationally. They are therefore highly visible to lay people, which is why I've gone into some detail about them here; but they are, in fact, just current, high-profile examples of the aforementioned trend which has existed since the early days of anthropology, Darwinism and Marxism, and which seeks to 'rubbish' the evidence for primitive communism, matriliny, classificatory kinship, egalitarianism and so on.

The bottom line is that authors purveying these pro-dominator views seem unable or unwilling to comprehend – or perhaps bear? – the idea that, for example, people might be happy to follow someone's lead purely out of a respectful acknowledgement of their bravery, knowledge, wisdom or healing abilities rather than from fear, coercion or because they've been manipulated. Or that altruistic behaviour can stem solely from innate lovingness, kindness or a group sharing ethos – from partnership motives, in fact. They certainly don't acknowledge that there *could* be a category of human beings such as hunter-gatherers who seem to be quite unscrewed up and aren't motivated in life by selfishness, fear or other negative drives. And if they don't acknowledge this for pristine hunter-gatherer peoples, they're certainly not going to acknowledge what has been suggested earlier in this book – which is that at least some significant proportion of human behaviour – even today, in strongly dominator societies – is naturally cooperative rather than competitive.

Skewed views from sociobiology and evolutionary psychology. The same fervently pro-dominator point of view is also the norm for much of sociobiology and evolutionary psychology, which is particularly unfortunate as it is material from these fields which tends to enter the public's consciousness via pop psychology, self-help books and so on. These disciplines have, for example, stressed the inevitability of conflict between female and male gene-replicating strategies, so that we got the stereotypes of roving Palaeo-man restlessly trying to spread his seed as widely possible while Palaeo-woman was stuck by the fire trying to coerce him to look after her and the kids! Or again we get dominator-style, patriarchally-oriented depictions of prehistoric life, such as Wrangham's in *Catching Fire* (2009), which – despite all the evidence to the contrary – persists in presenting early human life as consisting of nuclear-type families. Here is Wrangham's idea of life round the prehistoric home fire after a hard day's foraging:

> "Having a husband ensures that a woman's gathered foods will not be taken by others; having a wife ensures the man will have an evening meal. According to this idea, cooking created a simple marriage system; or perhaps it solidified a pre-existing version of married life that could have been prompted by hunting or sexual competition. Either way, the result was a primitive protection racket in which husbands used their bonds with other men in the community to protect their wives from being robbed, and women returned the favour by preparing their husbands meals."

"Protection racket" egad! How different this picture is from the relaxed, friendly, hospitable, sharing, teasing, fun-loving reality of hunter-gatherer life as described by sympathetic participants in their lives, or imaginatively reconstructed about our prehistoric forebears by Chris Knight in *Blood Relations*!

Boehm (1999) sums up the contrary view well:

> "In my opinion, traditional approaches in social biology have been seriously out of touch with common sense when traits such as human cooperativeness and one-way helping behaviour are explained wholly in terms of selfish desire for self-aggrandizement, innate nepotism, exact reciprocation, or third-party coercion."

He suggests that such approaches stem from "a set of deep biases" as well as from some technical misunderstandings, and that they call for a substantial paradigm shift.

Dominator Stereotypes Continue to be Promulgated

"Misery's the River of the World. Everybody Row! Everybody Row"
(Tom Waits, Misery is the River of the World, *Blood Money*, 2000)

"Miserable savages". In light of the previous section, it is obviously thoroughly galling for anyone who has studied the widespread and ancient nature of mutual aid in humans, as well as in many animals, plants and microorganisms, to observe how dominator-style stereotypes continue to be trotted out whenever an opportunity arises. We seem to project our own dominator-style fears and aggressive drives onto primitive peoples now or in the past, despite all the evidence to the contrary – assuming that they would feel or behave as *we* would if we were dropped in the wilderness and had to fend for ourselves. So we are presented with the 'miserable savage' shivering in fear around the campfire; the Hobbesian image of primitive life as "solitary, poor, brutish and short" (Hobbes, 1651); the 'drag his woman to the cave by her hair' caricature. Whereas – as we have seen – studies of actual forager or tribal societies shows people who are cheerful, fun-loving and merry; sanguine and confident; at home in their environment; alert rather than fearful; and peace-loving rather than bloodthirsty or warlike.

Sarah Hrdy (2009), too, notes our "tendency to project onto early Paleolithic ancestors patriarchal attributes from later time periods", and discusses the issue of endemic pro-patriarchal biases in archaeology and related fields at length – for example in relation to matrilocal versus patrilocal residence patterns, which are key to questions about cooperative breeding and alloparenting, as well as to scenarios about early human families, society and kinship. So, for example, she shows how evolutionists developed a pro-patrilineal, pro-androcratic, pro-nuclear family model for our early ancestors (typified by the sort of Australopithecine 'mum, dad and the kids' dioramas beloved of museums), based on faulty analyses of ethnographic information: "Patrilocal residence became an integral feature of hominin family life as reconstructed by physical anthropologists in the twentieth century. The resulting assumptions were subsequently incorporated wholesale into early sociobiology and evolutionary psychology." But they are not supported by the evidence: "Rather than being naturally patrilocal, most hunter-gatherer societies have remarkably flexible and opportunistic residence patterns as couples move between the women's natal group and the man's."

Briffault's *The Mothers* (1927) illustrates this sort of disinformation or suppressive process perfectly, as we explained in Chapter 2. Elements of his argument were found to be incorrect, and science took the opportunity to debunk his entire *oeuvre* in the cause of promoting the fallacy of the nuclear family and monogamy. Nevertheless, Briffault was mainly right; and we are now turning to his encyclopaedic work again in order to debunk the debunkers.

Schools don't tell us about our partnership past either. It's alarming how little Western-style schooling or further education does to dispel pro-dominator or anti-partnership myths either. To give a personal example: when I first looked at Marija Gimbutas' books on Old Europe around 2005, I was amazed by the beauty, skilfulness and sophistication of the prehistoric artefacts shown in the illustrations, particularly the ceramics. Most potters today would be proud to create such lovely, imaginative forms and decorations, I thought. And I was shocked, because I hadn't been taught anything about these works or the civilisation that produced them when I was a schoolgirl in the 1950s. The impression given by my teachers then – and by everything I had read since until Gimbutas – was that the inhabitants of that part of Eastern Europe in those prehistoric days were 'Beaker folk' who produced rather rough, dull, rudimentary 'Beaker ware' pottery. What a difference from these marvellous products of Old Europe! Why weren't we shown photos of these artefacts at my school – artefacts which clearly implied that their makers were people of great skill, aesthetic sensitivity and *joie de vivre*? Why weren't we given at least some inkling that highly civilised societies existed in prehistoric Eastern Europe – not just humble 'Beaker folk'? And has anything changed now? Are school children today taught any differently? Do people travel to Eastern Europe agog to view the treasures of Old Europe which await them in museums there? No, not as far as I'm aware, as I've never heard anyone talk about the existence of these wonderful works of craftsmanship or seen a TV programme about them or a travel article recommending going to see them. Is it just me, or does there seem to be a conspiracy to draw a veil over this whole subject – that is, the true, civilised, highly advanced (and evidently partnership) nature of our prehistoric European roots?

Equally worrying is the fact that most children and adults today are largely ignorant of many basic points which are taken as read in this book. To sum a few of these up, there's abundant evidence to show that: prehistoric peoples were far more technologically, socially, artistically and spiritually advanced than the cave man stereotype allows (Rudgley, 1998). And that all societies were originally matrilineal, and that matrilineal societies have persisted well into the historic era too, and even into the twenty-first century (Briffault, 1927; Knight, 2008; Alton, 2011). And that all humans were originally primitive communists or anarchists (in the original sense of that word, which means 'without rulers'); and that democracy – far from being invented by the Greeks – is a feature of all hunter-gatherer and most tribal cultures; and persisted as a strong component of most societies' governance throughout history to the present day (Boehm, 1999; Lee, 1998; Kropotkin, 1902). For example, Weatherford (1988) speaks of the influence of Native Americans on the American founding fathers and others like this:

> "Although today the notion of the noble savage usually reaps only scorn and historical footnotes as a quaint idea of a less-informed era, the idea had ramifications of great width and magnitude. The noble savage represented a new ideal of human political relations that mutated into the hundreds of political theories that have swept the world in the past five hundred years. The discovery of new forms of political life in America freed the imaginations of Old World thinkers to envision utopias, socialism, communism, anarchism, and dozens of other social forms. Scarcely any political theory or movement of the last three centuries has not shown the impact of this great political awakening that the Indians provoked among the Europeans."

Yet the fact that this is now taught in US schools is cited by Edward Stourton in his *It's A PC World* (2008) as an example of political correctness gone mad!

We urgently need to try to get at least the gist of these truths taught properly in schools, as – for most people – the only easily-accessed or prominent information about anthropology comes from a few TV programmes which tend to focus mainly on eye-catching aspects of tribal life such as rituals and hunting. But they rarely, if ever, for example, mention the classificatory kinship systems that underlie these societies and prove that an alternative to the nuclear family – with all its inherent problems – is possible and worked well for thousands of years.

And how about history taught from a Kropotkin point of view? He presents the sweep of history from a mutual aid perspective – redressing the current dominator bias towards studying "the quarrels of popes and kings... wars and pestilences"! Instead, Kropotkin focuses on the 'good news' of history – everyday life and what holds it together and makes it bearable or enjoyable, rather than on the 'bad news' – the powermongering, fighting, cruelties and injustices perpetrated by rulers and inflicted on communities:

> "most historians... exaggerate the part of human life given to struggles and... underrate its peaceful moods... The bright and sunny days are lost sight of in the gales and storms... They hand down to posterity the most minute descriptions of every war, every battle and skirmish, every contest and act of violence, every kind of individual suffering; but they hardly bear any trace of the countless acts of mutual support and devotion which every one of us knows of from his own experience; they hardly take notice of what makes the very essence of our daily life – our social instincts and manners."

History taught from this point of view would be far more accurate; and would, I should think, definitely be of much more interest to most girls.

Nasty, brutish and *short*. Another particularly irritating and widespread misunderstanding bruited about in regard to 'primitive' peoples is the cliché about their average length of life: "Nasty, brutish, and *short*" is the received wisdom. If only one could dispel this misconception once and for all! But again, it seems to persist, perhaps because of modern society's subconscious desire to subtly denigrate non-modern peoples. The mistake arises partly from the fact that most mortality in less developed cultures is among babies and young children; once past childhood, however, many people live into old age. (Even rough and ready measures, like the impression gained by reading novels written during the last four centuries, shows that they're well populated by the elderly. In fact, European men in previous centuries were considered 'in their prime' and women as 'merry widows' in their fifties...)

This misapprehension also perhaps stems from a misunderstanding of the demographer's term '*median age*'. This is, in fact, the age that divides a population into two numerically equal groups; that is, half the people are younger than this age and half are older; and it is useful because it's a single figure that summarises the *age distribution* of a population. For example, currently, the median age ranges from a low of about 15 in Uganda and the Gaza Strip to 40 or more in several European countries and Japan. But people tend to take it to mean the average *lifespan* of individuals in a population. In reality, a significant proportion of hunter-gatherers live into their sixties and seventies. Hrdy states that: "Careful demographic analysis revealed that a forager who survived to age 15 had about a 60 percent chance of living to 45. And those who made it to 45 had a good chance of surviving into old age." Among the !Kung, for example, about eight per cent of the population live on to 60 or older; and Hrdy goes on to say that there is now a remarkable convergence among demographic anthropologists, evolutionary-minded historians, and human biologists who study life history patterns across primates, that the bodies of *Homo sapiens* are "designed" to last about 72 years. In earlier times, among hunter-gatherers living in reasonably productive environments, more people even than this would probably have reached a fit, healthy and active old age; and this is still the case for some tribal peoples living traditional healthy lifestyles in unpolluted areas, such as the Ladakh of the Himalayas (Norberg-Hodge, 1991). And remember McDougall's Tarahumara people: "They didn't get diabetes or depressed, or even old: fifty-year-olds could outrun teenagers, and eighty-year-old grandfathers could hike marathon distances up mountainsides."!

We go on forgetting... So, to recap: in spite of feminism and modern liberal or left-wing thought which has challenged many accepted wisdoms about dominator-written history, we seem to have a huge mental block about accepting our partnership past. And though a sequence of partnership-oriented authors and unbiased scholars keep trying to bring the facts back to light again, we seem to constantly regress and forget them. How successful our society is, indeed, at sidelining, ridiculing or suppressing uncomfortable truths! What Eisler wrote in 1987 about new discoveries concerning our prehistoric goddess-centred past holds as true as ever today:

> "even when confronted with the authority of new research, with new archaeology, and the corroboration from social science, this truly huge block of new knowledge about millennia of human history so contradicts all we have been taught that its hold on our minds is like a message written in sand. The new knowledge may linger there for a day, or even a week. But relentlessly the force of the teaching of centuries works to undermine it... Only through reinforcement from other sources – both familiar and unfamiliar – can we hope to retain this knowledge long enough to make it our own."

Indeed, it may be that immersion in the memes, stories and narratives with which a culture surrounds us may have an actual, literally *hypnotic* effect upon us all (Griffin and Tyrell, 2004); and that modern dominator culture, which bombards us with dominator stories day and night, may be achieving part of its self-perpetuation through this hypnotic 'normalizing the craziness' process. But obviously I hope that *Do We Need To Be So Screwed Up?!* will be part of Eisler's reinforcement process; and that, in future, school education and the culture generally will make countervailing knowledge normal and everyday.

So far in this book we've looked at how human beings used to be in their innate, natural, unscrewed up state. We've seen that they were evidently saner and happier than we are now; and we've put forward the view that this is therefore how all human beings *could* be. We've also examined the forces that have moved humanity away from its happy roots. In the next chapter we examine human happiness and its roots further.

Chapter 9

Creating Happiness: What is It? What is Its Source?

"The Pirahãs are an unusually happy and contented people. I would go so far as to suggest that the Pirahãs are happier, fitter and better adjusted to their environment than any Christian or other religious person I have ever known."

Everett, 2008

Current Mainstream Ideas on Happiness

So far in this book we've looked at human origins, at what early humans were likely to have been like, at how partnership-type societies have been overtaken by dominator ones, and at the effects which this has had on our species. Now it's time to return to our original line of thought, and pull together some of the ideas we've developed about being 'unscrewed up' and 'screwed up', happy or not so happy.

Happiness is a big topic these days. Governments discuss it, it's become a respectable academic subject, and happiness experts work on national policies which might help to increase it. This book is also inevitably involved with the issue of happiness because it's suggesting that increased happiness results from being less screwed up and more closely aligned with our evolutionary roots. I therefore hoped and expected that the new sciences of happiness studies, positive psychology and social intelligence would be illuminating; and that leading authors such as Jonathan Haidt, Richard Layard, Paul Martin and Martin Seligman would have helpful things to say upon the subject. However, I was very disappointed by what I read, largely because these leading experts don't seem able or willing to step outside a dominator-world view of things. Their vision of what's possible is therefore sadly constrained, and is based largely on dominator presumptions about what is natural to human beings. This in turn makes their conclusions and recommendations pretty unadventurous and uninspiring. The same applies to David Smail's detailed examination of current human *unhappiness* (Smail, 1993), which also seems unable to see beyond a basically pessimistic, power-based (that is, dominator) view of society. Oliver James, too, in his popular *Affluenza* (2007), rightly lays current social ills at the door of wider social factors (childhood abuses, materialistic capitalism and so on) without really challenging the dominator values which in turn underlie these factors.

Here, for example, are some of Layard's conclusions regarding public policy-making from his 2005 *Happiness: Lessons from a New Science*. "What should we do differently if we shifted our goal towards achieving a happier way of life?" he asks, and goes on to list ideas such as: monitor the development of happiness as closely as we do income; spend more on helping the poor, and on tackling the problems of mental illness; introduce more family-friendly practices at work; subsidise activities that promote community life; eliminate high unemployment; fight the constant escalation of wants eg by limiting advertising to children; teach morality and citizenship in schools. Laudable as these recommendations are, they are hardly revolutionary; and most of them are basically hard to implement in any life-changing way in a fundamentally capitalistic, 'affluenzal' society such as Britain's or the USA's. The same applies to Daniel Goleman's discussion of the conclusions arising from his concept of Social Intelligence (in *Emotional Intelligence*, Goleman, 2006).

So it looks as if we need to look for much more revolutionary, ground-breaking, or fundamental ideas about the roots of happiness.

A Somatic View of Happiness

> *"the intense, uninhibited enjoyment of life, the irrepressible sense of well-being..."*
>
> (Finnegan, 2009/10, on Yaka women dancing)

Undamaged physiology. My own views are in line with Jean Liedloff's as outlined in Chapter 6, and are that *happiness arises principally from undamaged – that is, natural – physiology*. A human being whose organism is functioning as it should, as it was designed to do by evolution, feels good both physically and psychologically. These feelings of well-being are rooted in, and inseparable from, a healthy soma – from a physical body that is working optimally on every level from the sub-microscopic quantum realm and microbiological cellular level up to the macro level. Indeed, everything in the body that manifests on a macro scale has been produced by processes working (or not working) correctly at the micro level. And at the deepest micro levels, these processes are operating in the mysterious quantum world where psyche and soma affect each other – where repressed anger or grief cause stress, headaches, back pain or cancer; sedentary lifestyles or junk food diets cause depression, and so on. This is a realm of pure energy – and one which is mostly disregarded or pooh-poohed by mainstream science and medicine. Nevertheless, it is at this level that we are affected most by physical energies such as electromagnetic radiation and polarity, as well as by other forms of energy not recognised directly by science, including those which constitute emotional interactions (Goleman, 2006).

Real good health. However, the point needs to be made that most of us in the twenty-first century Westernised world have never experienced a genuinely undamaged body-and-mind state – either in ourselves or in anybody else. This is obviously because – as we've discussed in Chapter 7 – dominator-style childrearing damages our psyche and our soma right from the start (sometimes even in the womb). Dominator life then continues to harm us as adults. Most of us therefore don't actually know what a properly functioning, undamaged human being looks like, how it would feel to be with one, or how it would feel to *be* one. As Liedloff says: "We do not look upon happiness as a birthright, nor do we expect it to be more than peace or contentment. Real joy, the state in which the Yequana spend much of their lives, is exceedingly rare among us," (Liedloff, 1975).

The nearest we are likely to get to experiencing pure healthiness is from being around kindly-reared babies, children and animals, or unspoilt hunter-gatherers. The innate happiness, joyfulness and zest for life that spring from an undamaged soma is indeed a rare and strange quality in the modern world. So, for example, when Western doctors use the term 'healthy' about someone, what they really mean is 'without obvious signs of disease'. Most doctors have probably never encountered a truly healthy person – not just in the negative sense of 'not unhealthy' but in the positive sense of actually glowing with health from a properly functioning body and mind, filled with vitality and happiness. And yet this is how I believe humans are designed to be – this is what 'normal' *should* be.

Natural happiness. I also believe that the sort of happiness, contentedness and embracing attitude to life found among most unspoilt traditional peoples stems at least partly from this source. For example, Norberg-Hodge (1991), writing about the tribal Ladakh of the Himalayas, stresses their contented, relaxed, cheerful, non-grasping nature, and attributes it to factors such as their Buddhist beliefs and their close-knit, supportive, stable community. And yes, these must indeed play an important part in the Ladakhis' happiness. But they also bring up their children in a highly nurturing, continuum way, and it seems likely that much of their inner repose and ability to be contented arises from this source:

"The Ladakhis enjoy a feast more than everyday food, and they would rather be comfortable than uncomfortable, healthy rather than ill. But, finally, their contentedness and peace of mind do not seem dependent on outside circumstances; these qualities seem to come from within... Contentment comes from feeling and understanding yourself to be part of the flow of life, relaxing and moving with it. If it starts to pour with rain just as you set out on a long journey, why be miserable? Maybe you would not have preferred it, but the Ladakhis' attitude is 'Why be unhappy?'."

Joie de Vivre

"And the most joyful sound of all, to me, is the sound of the voices of the forest people as they sing a lusty chorus of praise to this wonderful world of theirs – a world that gives them everything they want – a cascade of sound that echoes among the giant trees until it seems to come at you from all sides in sheer beauty and truth and goodness, full of the joy of living." (Turnbull, 1961)

People who aren't screwed up somatically naturally approach life playfully and easily. Their bodies and feelings aren't in a distressed, screwed up state. They can enjoy the moment; and aren't armoured, or driven internally by the sort of motives that impel most dominator-encultured people. These drivers, such as the Protestant work-ethic, the desire to impress or please a parent, or to outdo a competitor, stem from damaged psyches and self-esteem, and result in many actions being forced and willed, or impelled by negative feelings, rather than flowing healthily and enjoyably. Everett (2008) describes how a group of visiting US psychologists commented that:

"the Pirahãs appeared to be the happiest people they had ever seen. I asked them how they could test such a statement. They replied that one way might be to measure the time the average Pirahã spends smiling and laughing and then to compare this with the number of minutes members of other societies, such as Americans, spent smiling and laughing. They suggested that the Pirahãs would win hands down."

"Life is very sweet, brother". Real health and wholeness don't just manifest in physical health and vitality, but in how one behaves, in *joie de vivre*, and positive attitudes and beliefs. A good Western example of this can be found in the famous 'wind on the heath' passage in George Borrow's autobiographical book *Lavengro* (1851). Much of this book is about his life with the gypsies in the early nineteenth century; and in this section Borrow, in one of his depressed periods, asks his Romany friend Jasper what his opinion of death is. Jasper replies:

"When a man dies, he is cast into the earth… and there is an end of the matter."

"And do you think that is the end of a man?"

"There's an end of him, brother, more's the pity."

"Why do you say so?"

"Life is sweet, brother."

"Do you think so?"

"Think so! There's night and day, brother, both sweet things; sun, moon and stars, brother, all sweet things; there's likewise the wind on the heath. Life is very sweet, brother; who would wish to die?"

"I would wish to die – "

"You talk like a gorgio [non-Romany] – which is the same as talking like a fool – were you a Rommany Chal you would talk wiser. Wish to die, indeed! A Rommany Chal would wish to live for ever!"

"In sickness, Jasper?"

"There's the sun and stars, brother."

"In blindness, Jasper?"

"There's the wind on the heath, brother; if I could only feel that, I would gladly live for ever. Dosta, we'll go now to the tents and put on the gloves; and I'll try to make you feel what a sweet thing it is to be alive, brother!"

'He ain't heavy'. Some other fine examples of the crucial difference in attitude between dominator-conditioned Westerners and partnership peoples can be found in Liedloff's *Continuum Concept* (1975). In the introductory chapter, *How My Ideas Were So Radically Changed,* Liedloff describes her first encounters and sojourns with the Tauripan and Yequana tribes in South America. It is full of marvellous descriptions of the difference in mindset and behaviour between these partnership people and their Western visitors, particularly in relation to the concept of 'work' (for which the Yequana don't actually have a word). One story is particularly telling. Here Liedloff describes how her party, helped by a group of Tauripan, need to portage a heavy dugout canoe over rough terrain. The European party have been dreading this task in advance, and "were primed to suffer and started off, grim-faced and hating every moment." Things go 'wrong', as expected by the Europeans, who are tense, swearing and losing their tempers. But the rest of the group – the Indians – "were having a fine time. They were laughing at the unwieldiness of the canoe, making a game of the battle, were relaxed between pushes, laughing at their own scrapes... All were doing the same work, all were experiencing strain and pain," but the difference in attitude and belief between the two groups meant that one experienced the portage as hardship, hurt and aggravation, the other as a merry opportunity to enjoy camaraderie and team effort. It is a delightful illustration of the radical and fundamental difference between hunter-gatherer and Western approaches to life.

'R and R': Play, Fun, and Lazing About

When I was a university lecturer in the early 1990s, I used to teach postgraduate students about designing and managing landscapes for play. I was attracted by the whole subject of play – sensing that there was something inherently important in it; but found the literature on it dismal because it dwelt solely on the educational or developmental aspects of play. Not once was the word *fun* mentioned as a worthy aim in its own right! I understand that the same has applied to animal studies until recently – the emphasis again being on play's functional role in practising for real life, strengthening muscles and neural pathways and so on. I'm therefore delighted to see that the enjoyable, sheer fun side of play is now being looked at too; and once again it's salutary to return to our animal roots on the subject. Bekoff and Pierce in *Wild Justice* (2009) devote a considerable amount of time to animal play:

> "Play is not only serious business, but also fun. Animals get deep joy and pleasure from playing alone or with friends. Rats emit a high-frequency chirp when they play wrestle and when they get tickled, a sound that some rat researchers describe as a laugh. Dogs laugh too. They make a kind of breathy, forced exhalation that is recognized by other dogs as an invitation to play. It feels good to laugh because it triggers the brain to release dopamine. The rhythm, dance, and spirit of animals at play is also incredibly contagious, and spread like an epidemic; just seeing animals playing can stimulate play in others."
>
> (Bekoff and Pierce, 2009)

Nor are these claims about joy and pleasure speculative, but are based upon neurobiological research that demonstrates that a wide range of play behaviour does indeed cause the release of opioids like dopamine into the brain. Moreover, play is evidently ancient – one expert claiming that its evolutionary roots go back a billion years! (Bekoff and Pierce, 2009). Placental mammals, birds, and even crustaceans show evidence of play behaviour; with non-human primates, rodents, canids, felids, ungulates, pachyderms and cetaceans tending to be the most playful groups. All this confirms my view that play and laughter are important in their own right; and that there don't have to be functional reasons to play.

Dolce far niente. Anthropologist-neuroscientist Charles Whitehead sees our culture's apparent fear of, or aversion to, play for its own sake as a manifestation of the Protestant work ethic (which is itself, of course – from this book's point of view – a manifestation of the dominator world view). Clearly, one aspect of play is that it's 'a waste of time', doesn't achieve anything and isn't productive; and the same applies even more so to *dolce far niente* – that charming Italian term meaning 'sweet doing nothing'. Moreover, *not* working in itself leads us into temptation and worse: "The Devil makes work for idle hands to do" and so on. Lazing about, doing sweet nothing, playing and having fun therefore all tend to be seen as threatening in our work-is-good-oriented culture. However, the biological reality is that most animals spend the majority of their time sleeping or resting. And, as we saw in Chapter 3, hunter-gatherers ('the original affluent society') don't have a work ethic either, and are happy to spend the majority of their time on *dolce far niente* if they can and wish to. Good for them, I say, and let's have more of it! (*The Idler* magazine, edited by Tom Hodgkinson, is the main vehicle which promotes this ethos in Britain.)

Bonding. A further way of looking at play and lazing about, as well as other 'non-productive' activities such as ceremonies, rituals, feasting, making music, dancing and so on, is that they contribute to community spirit and help to bond individuals and societies together. This point of view seems to have considerable truth in it; and we can see this 'special occasion' bonding aspect expressed in all societies and eras down to our own. Even today, in recession-bound Britain for example, we seem to seize upon opportunities to celebrate together, and even create new occasions when we can. Music festivals proliferate and grow enormous, and every town and city has its cultural, arts, food or other special festival. From Canela log-carrying and social sex (see Chapter 13) to the Olympics and the World Cup, games, fun and feasting – far from being trivial or immoral things – actually play a vital role in local, national and international social cohesion. From this perspective, the fact that simpler cultures view celebrating together as a very important part of life seems perfectly sensible: in societies which aren't materialistic, and which value harmony and the strengthening of social ties far more than they do working or earning money for its own sake, socialising, feasting and so on have a higher priority than being busy for busyness's sake.

Why shouldn't enjoying life be seen as directly adaptive in its own right? Another interesting aspect of the happiness issue is the fact that mainstream science seems to have such difficulty in accepting fun and enjoyment as valid elements of evolutionary adaptedness. Instead, as has been discussed earlier in this book, the relevant disciplines such as anthropology, genetics, and socio-biology have, until very recently, tended to interpret both animal and human behaviour in a highly 'dominator' way – seeing every behaviour as a manifestation of some dark drive such as Machiavellian intelligence or strategising to dominate or intim-idate (think of Wrangham's 'primitive protection racket' hypothesis quoted in Chapter 8!). Or, as we've discussed at several points in the book so far, they have consistently overem-phasised the role that conflict, violence and so on plays in animal and human societies. So I'm inclined to put the counter-argument even more strongly, and ask: why shouldn't enjoying life, playing, lazing about and so on be directly adaptive in their own right? Doesn't it make sense that all creatures have got a better chance of surviving if they positively enjoy life and want to continue living for this reason as well as for more primitive survival reasons? Why shouldn't animals as well as humans actively enjoy their leisure hours?! Or prefer to spend their time feeling happy, rather than in scheming and plotting, threatening and coercing? I leave the question with you, dear reader.

We have already seen in previous chapters that the relaxed, cheerful state which is normal to simpler peoples is spoilt by dominator-style upbringings; and that most Western people today are – to a greater or lesser extent – uptight, anxious, unhappy, fearful and functioning sub-optimally. The next four chapters look in more detail at the lasting impact of non-nurturing childhoods and other toxic influences on modern people; and the knock-on effects that these have on our whole life – physical, emotional, spiritual and sexual.

Chapter 10

Hindering Happiness and Well-being

"We are living lives for which our evolution did not equip us, and we are also handicapped, in our attempts to cope, by faculties crippled by personal deprivation." Liedloff, 1975

'Insults' to Our Systems and Unresolved Shocks

"A time of ever-mounting everyday horrors, of which any newspaper is full, accompanies a spreading environmental apocalypse. Alienation and the more literal contaminants compete for the leading role in the deadly dialectic of life in divided, technology-ridden society. Cancer, unknown before civilization, now seems epidemic in a society increasingly barren and literally malignant."
(*We Have to Dismantle All This* in Zerzan, 2002)

"Naturalizing the craziness" in relation to children. In addition to the damage inflicted on dominator-bred people simply by their upbringings, there is also a host of other factors – many of which result from dominator-caused influences on our environment – that adversely affect our well-being even further, and children's well-being in particular. For example, modern life subjects us all to a host of new unnatural and stressful factors compared to our Stone Age forebears – so many stressors, indeed, that it would be impossible to list them all (but see Table 2 for an attempt.) It is also remarkable – as we said in Chapter 7 – how little mainstream culture seems to *notice* the unnaturalness of modern Western childrearing compared to more Stone Age, continuum ways.

Furthermore, we seem to constantly normalise, minimise, and treat as inevitable all sorts of crimes against the child. On the one hand, these include acts which society treats as formal crimes such as various sorts of abuse and neglect; and also behaviours which are not legal crimes, but which hunter-gatherers would find absolutely unthinkable such as preventing or discouraging in-arms nurturing of babies; allowing children to live in homes where they are subjected to significant physical or psychological cruelty; or forcing children to attend schools where they are bullied. In addition, a host of damaging acts are also inflicted willy-nilly upon children, and are treated as acceptable or inevitable parts of childhood today. These include causing harm to children through medical insults to their systems such as vaccinations or allopathic medicines; or through environmental toxins, too much TV and computer exposure, junk food, lack of exercise and so on. Overprotectiveness, and the 'imprisoning' of children in order to keep them safe from the perceived dangers of modern life also come into this category (Palmer, 2006).

On the other hand, we also normalise the difficulties of modern childrearing for *caregivers*, and accept as standard more and more trials and tribulations that parents, teachers, and others have to deal with – many or most of which are surely caused by the factors above. These include learning difficulties, tantrums, ADHD, and disrespect, disobedience and even violence against caregivers.

We ignore the link between causes and effects. Again, let us stress that these are behaviours that are quite alien to hunter-gatherer communities, and would probably be viewed by them with horror and shock. Yet we now treat them as normal in developed cultures; and – rather than addressing basic questions like "Why is this happening?", or "What's causing these behav-iours?" – put most of our time and effort into merely trying to *cope* with them. Perhaps even more tellingly, we don't make the connection between the likely cause-and-effect relationship between the two sides of the coin described above – that is, between modern dominator societies' harmful effects on children on the one hand; and all the problems and costs that damaged children bring to society, sooner or later, on the other. The expense to modern society of special needs children alone is enormous in its own right; while the more extreme effects that many damaged children inflict on society as they grow older, such as binge drinking, addiction, antisocial behaviour generally, crime, and violence, is an even heavier burden whose costs we all bear.

Specialist in this field Sue Gerhardt makes this disconnect plain in *Why Love Matters*:

> "What we do know is that aggression and antisocial behaviour which start in childhood are the most damaging to society. It is very costly to society. Yet although crime is always high on the political agenda and increasingly the behaviour of antisocial boys and young men is seen as a prime target of various initiatives, there has been little attempt to link this problem behaviour with early maltreatment. Instead of recognising its roots in infancy and early childhood, the focus is on the management of current problem behaviour."
>
> (Gerhardt, 2004)

There is definitely real resistance to accepting the role that upbringing and childhood experiences play in modern society's problems: damaged people don't want to acknowledge either the harm that was done to them or the harm that they in turn may be letting happen to others.

Diseases of civilisation. In addition to mental and behavioural problems, an increasing percentage of modern populations – including children – suffers from heart disease, diabetes, depression, autism, addictions, allergies, auto-immune disorders and a cascade of other ills not found in traditional peoples. Clearly it is not just the everyday problems, dangers and strains of life that cause stress and illness in modern people, as indigenous peoples have always had many of these difficulties in their lives too. (In fact, compared to modern people, they have always had far more real and direct hardships and threats in their lives, as was mentioned in Chapter 3 – ranging from dangerous wild animals, heat, and cold, to the realities of drought and starvation.) It seems, therefore, that we suffer from so many health problems for three reasons. First of all, we have already discussed the directly harmful effect of stress and cortisol arising from non-nurturing childhoods. Secondly, this makes it hard for us to process and shake off the current stresses and strains of life. And thirdly, we're increasingly being subjected to a myriad of new and unnatural harmful physical and psychological influences in our lives (which one can also view, as Zerzan does, as further manifestations of the dominator approach to life). Together, these three factors make us prey to an ever-growing range of ailments.

Table 2

Stressful Influences in Modern Life

- Babies in the womb exposed to cortisol, residues of drugs, toxins, the contraceptive pill, anti-depressants, etc
- Unnatural birth and early childrearing practices especially separation of mothers from babies resulting in stress and excess cortisol
- Little or no breastfeeding
- Abusive, neglectful, cold, over-controlling parenting
- Broken homes
- Imprisoned-in-the-home syndrome; overprotective parenting
- Increasing addiction to computer-based activity
- Lack of exercise
- Lack of natural light, sunlight, fresh air
- Lack of contact with the natural world; hyper-hygienic syndrome
- Stressful schooling; bullying

- Isolated adults; reduced strength of extended families and communities
- Stressful or excessive work
- Junk food diets – over-processed, 'dead' food; food contaminated with pesticides, antibiotics, hormones, trans fats, etc; food depleted in essential vitamins and minerals; excessive consumption of empty calories, refined carbohydrates, sugar and fats
- Widespread use of recreational drugs/self-medication with alcohol, nicotine, cannabis, sugar – as well as the harder cocaine, heroin, etc
- Inadvertent exposure to a cocktail of myriad synthetic chemicals and unnatural influences in every aspect of the environment: 'sick building' chemicals and traffic pollutants in the air; pesticides, hormones, fluoride, etc in water; mercury fillings in teeth; synthetic ingredients in cosmetics, cleaning products, etc; fluorescent lighting in buildings, sodium lighting in streets
- Man-made radiation, ranging from multiple electric/electronic devices at home and work to the wavelengths transmitted to feed those devices (think what they seem to be doing to the bees) to radiation from nuclear power stations
- Deliberate/intentional exposure to a cocktail of synthetic/unnatural medical chemicals – inoculations, antibiotics, allopathic drugs
- Medical interventions and insults to our bodies: inoculations again; biopsies, mammograms, and other tests; unnecessary surgery (so much of it is…)
- General negative effects of living in a dominator culture: being immersed from birth in an anti-woman, anti-feelings culture; being drip-fed fear and hatred via the media, etc
- Lack of spirituality in people's lives

The effect of many if not all these harmful influences is to *shock* us physiologically and energetically: that is, organisms experience these influences, which our bodies aren't designed to tolerate, as shocks to our system. Things are made worse by the fact that there are so *many* of these unnatural influences these days; and that they tend to behave synergistically, so that a cocktail of them is much more damaging than one toxic effect alone. In addition, we need to note again that our cortisol-influenced childhoods are likely to have made us unable to process any subsequent shocks well. The overall effect, therefore, is that our bodies – which are still in essence Stone Age affairs, adapted to a pre-chemical-and-electronic era – can't process and shake off these many and complex assaults. Most people today are therefore carrying a significant burden of unresolved shock; and I believe that it is this which – along with the cortisol effects discussed earlier – is at the root of most ills of mind, body and spirit today. Our organism tries to deal with this state of affairs, and adapt as best it can, utilising emergency physiological systems in order to cope; but is inevitably functioning sub-optimally.

The Spectrum of Damage

The basic view of well-being put forward in this book is that real well-being and happiness isn't possible unless these cortisol, toxicity and shock states are either avoided at source, or resolved and the body brought back to its proper, natural functioning. Clearly, this is a tall order if nearly everybody in dominator cultures is damaged to a greater or lesser extent by these harmful influences. Ideally, in order to achieve it, we would need to alter society so that it didn't inflict any significant damage on its members in childhood or thereafter, and hence that no one suffered from anything deep-seated that needed curing. However, as this isn't currently the case, and is unlikely to be so for a considerable time, I think it is important to realistically tackle the issue of trying to cure (unscrew-up) ourselves as much as possible now.

What chance have we got of doing this? Clearly, it depends on the extent of the damage we've experienced; and one can hypothesise about a *spectrum of damage* within the population. We also need to speculate about how much of the damage within the different categories of harm can be successfully treated, cured or ameliorated; and what sort of treatments might work on different levels and types of damage. Table 3 attempts to roughly estimate this.

Table 3

The Spectrum of Somatic and Psychological Damage To Be Found in a Typical Western Population, and What Treatments May be Helpful

Negligible Damage: people brought up with much emotional and physical love, and subjected to as little as is feasible of the toxic influences shown in Table 2, or to other traumas. Maybe 0.5% of the population or less? A range of complementary therapies work well here and can probably cure most ailments that arise. Spiritual practices such as meditation and healing are likely to be very effective and beneficial.

Moderate Damage: the majority of the population, probably, say over 85%. They probably suffer from at least some unresolved shocks from childhood, and are performing sub-optimally both physically and psychologically. Society would consider them normal; doctors would consider them averagely healthy. Mainstream medicine will be fully at work on any health problems here, and may be causing more problems than it cures (even if the cause-and-effect influences aren't immediately obvious) because it treats symptoms and not causes, and because it is often so inherently damaging. Ordinary complementary and mind-body-spirit/self-help therapies will be of use, but will probably not be able to get at the core shock state, and so not be able to restore full wellness. Ditto for spiritual practices. Only exceptional techniques, such as quantum homoeopathy, may be able to actually help such states; and there are currently nothing like enough practitioners to go round. It may also be the case that many 'Highly Sensitive People' (Aron, 1999) are in this category, and might actually not be highly sensitive if their shock states were resolved.

Serious Damage: probably a significant proportion of people, say 10%. This would include people who have been traumatised by abusive or seriously neglectful childhoods; by traumatic events like a criminal attack or house fire; been seriously damaged by well-meant interventions such as inoculations or medical treatments that have gone badly wrong; or been badly hurt in 'everyday' events such as traffic accidents. Mainstream medicine will again be heavily involved here, and will be excellent for treating mechanical injuries such as from traffic accidents or burns, but again may create more problems than it solves in the short or long term. Complementary therapies, etc may help a little, but will probably be even less able to get at core shock states. Ditto for spiritual practices.

Extreme damage: would include those who have suffered typically dominator-caused PTSD-type traumas from war, torture, genocide, very serious crime; the more extreme sorts of abusive childhoods; and from natural disasters such as earthquakes, fires, tsunamis; maybe around 5%? Treatments are likely to be even less successful than for the Serious Damage category.

We can't cure most of the damage at present. What Table 2 implies is that we may be able to *ameliorate* some of the more serious damage found in a typical modern dominator society, but that at present we aren't in a position to cure most of it – either because we don't have enough (any?) successful techniques to do so, or not enough practitioners, or both. Some schools of thought do claim that it is possible to undo even very deep-seated damage through purely spiritual practices such as spiritual healing or meditation; through psychological methods like cognitive behavioural therapy (CBT), or part-physical techniques like hypnosis, neurolinguistic programming (NLP), emotional freedom technique (EFT), or psychological kinesiology (Psych-K). Most of these methods claim to be able to directly affect our unconscious and its belief systems, or even our very soma itself; but my experience is that they may still not be able to free badly – or even moderately – harmed people from the prison of their damaged soma, as many of us who have been on personal growth paths have already found out to our disappointment and chagrin. Certainly, some spiritual practices can have notable effects on both psyche and soma; but unless they also undo cortisol and shock states and the associated harm in the body, they can only help us so far. So attempting to release ourselves from deep-seated, long-standing fear, anxiety, depression, resentment, grief and so on, or from physical/ psychosomatic disorders, through such methods may help us a bit, but usually only works to a certain extent, and does not reach the deepest levels of malfunctioning.

Overall, the conclusion seems to be that the only really effective way to address all these ills is to *do our best to prevent them at source.* In other words, in order to restore well-being and health to our world, we need to move away completely from forms of society which inevitably cause harm to children and adults, and towards a world where the Hippocratic oath "Above all, do no harm" has real meaning!

We *are* damaged. I would also like to take this opportunity to disagree strongly with the school of New Age thought which keeps trying to impress on us that we're 'perfect just as we are'; and that it's just our perceptions about ourselves that are at fault. This point of view is put across, as far as I can see (maybe I'm missing the point) in works like *A Course in Miracles* and *There Is Nothing Wrong With You: Going Beyond Self-Hate* by Cheri Huber. The whole premise underlying such claims seems faulty to me. First of all, as this book has set out to show, we mostly *are* damaged people – physiologically as well as emotionally; and all the reconfiguring of our beliefs in the world isn't actually going to change that much. Tell someone who is in physical pain with, say, a broken bone that they're 'actually really perfect', that it's just their belief system that's at fault, and that what they need is to develop unconditional self-acceptance! Surely it makes more sense to acknowledge that we really *are* damaged by our upbringing and conditioning, and use that as a kicking-off point for trying to improve things? First we need to fix the broken bones; then we need to try to make sure we don't keep breaking any more of them!

We're *unable* to follow the spiritual teachings we want to. The same applies, to a large extent, to teachings such as Eckhart Tolle's in *The Power of Now*. Again, the author's intentions are laudable and the book's exhortations are unarguable, yet most of us are utterly unable to achieve them because – in our damaged state – we are constitutionally *unable* to 'be in the now' for more than a snatched second or so. We can read the books, and understand what's required, but we can't actually *do* it – we *can't* walk the talk until we ourselves have changed constitutionally, physiologically. The image I always have in my mind when thinking about this sort of unfollowable spiritual teaching is of one of those automatic door closers. For most of us, our 'doors of perception' are fitted with one of these closers; and it doesn't matter how often we push the door open with meditation or other practices – that door closer will *always* push the door shut again as soon as we stop making an effort. I know people who've sincerely struggled to meditate for an hour or two a day in order to follow the spiritual path and Master they believe in; and still, decades later, are unable to do so. On and on they struggle, achieving very little at the cost of enormous amounts of effort. Exhorting them to carry on with such practices seems to me to be quite futile and cruelly misleading. Surely what is needed for such people (most of us, probably) is to *remove the door closer*! And this, I believe, can usually only be done by addressing damage done to us at a somatic level. This issue is considered again in Chapter 11.

Then there's another school of New Age thought which seems to covertly try to justify or excuse the harm inflicted by dominator life by saying that we 'need' the harsh lessons of the earthly plane in order to grow, learn, develop compassion and so on. Again, I personally don't believe that we 'need' these harmful experiences, simply because – it seems plain to see – unharmed people are happier, and find it much easier to be good and kind, than damaged people.

Chapter 11

Spirituality – Screwed up and Unscrewed up

Natural Spirituality is Our Birthright

> *"It is suggested that the infant state is innately more 'spiritual' than the adult in two senses: firstly, children have fundamentally 'spiritual' characteristics as a stable structure of being; and secondly, they appear to have easy access to higher intensity spiritual experiences."*
>
> (Taylor, 2009)

I agree with Taylor that inherent spiritual sensitivity and awareness, and access to other levels of reality, *are* our birthright; and that children who have had unscrewed up upbringings usually have these abilities to a notable extent. It therefore seems likely that most of us would have quite high levels of spiritual awareness, without having to do anything deliberate to achieve them, if we grew up in partnership-style communities. We wouldn't need to seek out spiritual practices or therapies in order to develop basic levels of spiritual perception, nor would we have to do anything special at all in order to be happy. Moreover, any spiritual practices we *did* undertake would be likely to have a very strong effect, as Liedloff (1975, already cited in Chapter 3) describes for the Sanema, giving them "a huge head start over us on the road to serenity… The proportion of Sanema who have attained truly impressive states of joy and harmony with their surroundings is remarkable, and would be impossible to match anywhere in the West or East."

Intravertive and extravertive spirituality. The subject of human spirituality and its different forms – natural, and less natural – is discussed in an enlightening way by Taylor in *The Fall* (2005, Chapter 15). He links 'fallen peoples' damaged state to the development of the human Ego – a term which he uses as many Eastern spiritual teachings use the word 'Mind' (and with the same rather pejorative connotations.) And he introduces the very helpful concepts of *intravertive* and *extravertive* mystical states and paths – that is, spiritual ways which see the physical world as either a snare to be fled from into the inner spiritual realms; or as part of a divine whole to be embraced in the physical world.

Taylor describes extravertive spiritual paths such as Vedanta, Taoism and, in particular, Tantra as ways which "saw all reality as the manifestation of Spirit, and treated the human body and the whole of the gross physical world as divine." Shamanism, which is a spiritual approach that is characteristic of tribal peoples, is similar; and its extravertive perspective fits in well with a hunter-gatherer, partnership or continuum view of life, since it holds that true spirituality is absolutely compatible with the physical world and the down-to-earth life of ordinary (unfallen) people.

From this extravertive point of view, there is no need to flee the world, condemn everything to do with the body as unholy, or spend years meditating in a dark cave in order to experience spiritual realities: those are intravertive ways, typical of patri-archal religions. In contrast, within extravertive spiritual world views, God/Spirit can be found naturally – particularly within his own primordial creation, nature – by opening and expanding our senses into our surroundings, and by embracing 'all that is'. As Colin Turnbull says of the Mbuti pygmies:

> "They were a people who had found something in the forest that made their life more than just worth living, something that made it, with its full complement of hardships and problems and tragedies, a wonderful thing full of joy and

happiness and free of care."
(Turnbull, 1961)

My own personal view is that God or a Higher Power would surely prefer us to have this sort of approach to life rather than see us spending our precious lives meditating in a cave or monastic cell!

Extravertive Spirituality

In the extravertive way of life, everything in life is embraced; and those who live like this are far less inclined than intravertives to fall into the patriarchal trap of dualism – of dividing the world into good and bad, light and dark, mind and body. So, while Christianity (as Jung pointed out) has shunned nature, the feminine and the dark side of life, extravertive peoples tend to embrace the whole shebang – a far healthier thing to do psychologically (as Jung again avers). So extravertively-inclined cultures are, typically, tolerant of differences in people, and can accept a wide range of individualistic behaviour (Brody, 2001; Liedloff, 1987; Woodburn, 2005). They tend to have a healthily accepting attitude to bodily functions such as defecation and menstruation (see Chapter 13); and can enjoy the good things of the physical world such as food and sex without seeing them as sinful. Taylor points out that Tantra went further than any other tradition in emphasising the sacredness of the human body. "It's often seen as being all about sex, but its main insight is the same as Mahayana Buddhism: all the world, and all its living things, are infused with Spirit, including the human body. All parts of the body and all physical processes are sacred." But maybe even the concept of 'sacredness' in relation to sex and the body shows some level of body-spirit split? Perhaps hunter-gatherers have always had it right in treating sex as something that is desirable, enjoyable and also magical – but definitely a natural part of mainstream life. (This is also discussed further in Chapter 13.)

Fun and anti-fun. Extravertive cultures also usually have a big fun-loving side, as we've seen in several previous chapters, They love to laugh and joke, and don't see this as being incompatible with more sacred sides of life. In contrast to this, authoritarian, patriarchal religions such as Christianity, Judaism and Islam are not only notoriously repressive about 'sins of the flesh', but also tend to have a big 'downer' on fun in general (as we touched upon in Chapter 9). Music, singing and dancing are often frowned upon, as are wearing bright colours and jewellery, and playing even very harmless games (Hutton, 2001). It is evident that this pattern – which identifies fun, laughter, playfulness and levity with sin – exists wherever heavily dominator cultures prevail (as we've already touched upon in Chapter 9); and is clear to see today in, for example, places under Taliban rule or strict Christian influence. As Ian Suttie aptly said in 1935: "The indulgences we have been forced to renounce ourselves, we will certainly not permit to other people," (quoted in Gerhardt, 2004).

Surely Jesus enjoyed a good laugh? I agree with the unconventional spiritual teacher Osho in feeling sure that the originator of Christianity, Jesus, not only didn't disapprove of fun and laughter but also enjoyed plenty of it himself!

> "Christians have been trying to efface all traces of his humanity; so he is born out of the Virgin Mary, a virgin mother, which is absolutely absurd. Then he lives a life in which all human traits are removed. Christians only talk about his miracles, not about his ordinary life. They are afraid. Christians say that Jesus never laughed! Now this seems to be the ultimate in stupidity. Jesus... and never laughed? Then who else can laugh? But laughter seems too human, too mundane: they cannot allow Jesus to laugh. But Jesus' life is such that he must have been really laughing... because he says again and again, 'Rejoice! Be merry! Celebrate!' These words

> cannot come from a man who has never laughed... And he was a mixer. Every day, every night, he was moving with people. He was not secluded. He must have been really laughing, enjoying."
>
> (Osho, 2008)

Repression or elision of the fun-loving side of humanity isn't just the prerogative of dominator religions, but seems to go hand-in-hand with our contemporary secular 'religions' such as political correctness, 'health and safety gone mad', and officialdom generally. These seem to take particular pleasure in constraining or eradicating relatively harmless pleasures – live music in pubs, November the Fifth bonfires, village fetes (all a bit pagan when one comes to think about it) via excessively restrictive legislation. It is interesting that left-of-centre regimes seem to be as bad – if not worse – about this fun suppression as more right-wing governments – the Protestant work ethic at work again, no doubt.

Ahriman rules. One possible perspective on this sort of restrictive bureaucracy is to view it as an expression of the fallen angel *Ahriman* who, with Lucifer, holds particular sway over the world in these fallen days, according to visionary teacher Rudolph Steiner (Wilkinson, 1993). Steiner describes Ahriman as the force in the world that leads humankind away from spirituality through the allure of the material world and materialism. This includes officialdom and bureaucracy (whereas Lucifer does his tempting through pride, hubris, desire for power and so on – through the Ego or Mind, as some would see it). Ahriman is particularly associated with the currents in life which increase dogmatic party politics, subjugation of cultural life, Philistinism, tedium, alienation, mechanistic science and medicine, and reductionist, scoffing belief systems generally. He seems the perfect figurehead for our unbelieving, materialistic, institution-ridden, anti-fun world today! One associates dominator culture particularly with the more Luciferian forces of warfare, violence, coercion and so on; but the Ahrimanic influence seems to represent another, less obvious, but perhaps even more insidious side of dominator life?

Magic, mystery, excitement. A perhaps parallel aspect of patriarchal religions is the way that they stress the *tamer* aspects of spiritual life – particularly peace (in the sense of peace and quiet), quiet contentment, or – at most – bliss, as the goal of religious practice. Whereas I believe that many developed-world people want to experience, at least part of the time, something far more exhilarating – something that's to be found in the freedom and excitement of wild nature or good sex, or in the magic and mystery of a night under the full moon. What is "the wind on the heath" if not wild and free? And what are hunter-gatherer erotic rituals if not wildly exciting as well as sacred? So personally I don't think that a desire for these things by modern, first-world peoples is necessarily unhealthy, neurotic or unspiritual. The fact that dominator religions play down such qualities or actively disapprove of them again seems to be a manifestation of the deadly taming of natural instincts and of the magic of real, natural 'felt' life which Zerzan and D.H. Lawrence decry. Surely thrills, mystery and excitement are to be found in paradise as well as peace and contentment?

Being and Doing

Another aspect of spirituality in dominator cultures (which we touched on already in Chapter 9) is that the screwed-upness caused by dominator life makes it hard – if not impossible – to *be* a properly spiritual person. For example, in order to follow Jesus' teachings and *be* a Christian, it is necessary to be *able* to be loving, unselfish, charitable, compassionate, patient, humble, brave and so on. But this is exactly what being screwed up prevents one from being. Most of us in dominator societies have a residue of inner fear, anger, resentment, jealousy and so on which is always present, and just needs some trigger to be activated and manifest in our behaviour. Screwed up people literally *can't* be as Christian or spiritual as we might wish, because our being, or essence, (as Gurdjieff uses these terms) is full of negative emotions. Inevitably, therefore, our 'doing' will express this – however hard we try to hide or repress that negativity. As Gurdjieff said in his typically forthright, pull-no-punches way:

> "… religion is doing: a man does not merely *think* his religion or feel it, he 'lives' his religion as much as he is able, otherwise it is not religion but fantasy or philosophy. Whether he likes it or not, he shows his attitude towards religion by his actions and he can show his attitude *only by his actions*. Therefore if his actions are opposed to those which are demanded by a given religion he cannot assert that he belongs to that religion. The vast majority of people who call themselves Christians have no right whatsoever to do so, because they not only fail to carry out the demands of their religion but they do not even think these demands ought to be carried out [Gurdjieff was referring particularly to wars and legalised killing here]… People call themselves Christians but they do not realise that not only do they not want, but they are unable, to be Christians, because in order to be a Christian it is necessary not only to desire, but *to be able*, to be one."
>
> (Ouspensky, 1950)

So, unless we change our 'being' into one which means that we *can* act in a spiritual way, or are already in a state of being which makes this possible (an unscrewed up one, that is), we *can't* actually be the spiritually-oriented people we might want to be. This is clearly another incentive for not screwing people up in childhood – for not screwing up our population at source.

Not 'sinful'. A further point I'd like to make on the subject of screwed-upness and spirituality is that, from this book's point of view, people don't behave negatively because they are 'sinful' or 'evil' or full of naughty 'desires', but because of dominator society's effects on them. From this point of view, it is not just unkind, but futile to use pejorative, judgmental terms like lust or greed about people's behaviour, as this just judges symptoms rather than tackling causes. It is no better than smacking a hungry baby for crying. What we need is to address, and redress, the causes of such symptoms; and, as we have seen (Chapter 7), most 'sinful' behaviour is caused by the deep hurt and want resulting from dominator upbringing. This is not to exonerate people for *acting out* their negative impulses, or hypocritically calling themselves servants of God when their actions belie this. But we will not get very far in addressing our problems if we don't recognise what actually causes them at root.

Spiritual Leaders Are Silent About Dominator Effects on Spirituality: Why?

Finally, on the subject of screwed up and unscrewed up spirituality, I would like to raise an issue that I haven't seen addressed anywhere else. This issue is the complete silence that seems to reign in the spiritual field about *the role of dominator culture in separating us from our spiritual roots* and our natural, birthright, spirituality. It seems that not a single spiritual leader of any creed or path throughout recorded history has pointed out that our lamentable unspiritual state *isn't* fundamentally due to original sin, or the Mind or Ego, or lack of self-remembering (as Gurdjieff puts it), and so on; but *is* due to our being screwed up by dominator childhoods and dominator culture. This seems extraordinary to me. Most, if not all true spiritual leaders are fearless visionaries and revolutionaries in the sphere of human spirituality. With their mystical insight they surely must have known that the move away from partnership life is where things began to go wrong?

So why haven't Jesus, Buddha, Mohammed, the Sufis,

Gurdjieff, Steiner, Krishnamurti, Osho, the Dalai Lama, The Maharishi, Guru Maharaji, Neale Donald Walsch, Eckhart Tolle and others told us this? Why go on making us feel that it's all or partly our fault?! And teaching us methods for restoring our spirituality and wholeness that are unlikely to work properly except maybe for a tiny handful of (probably unscrewed up) people? Why don't even the most esoteric and 'secret' teachings state what it seems – from the evidence presented in this book – that they should? Which is that *Homo sapiens* apparently evolved as a naturally happy, kind, trusting, peaceful species, and that for hundreds of thousands of years this is the way that human beings lived on earth. Isn't The Tao – The Way, for example, describing exactly this state and way of being? If it is indeed our birthright and our natural state to live harmoniously, cooperatively and joyfully, then we need to know that human beings *can* be like that – that this is how we are designed by God and evolution to be – even if most of us who have grown up in a dominator world aren't like that at this point in time. I eagerly await a spiritual teacher who will make this point! Or a reader who can put me straight if I've somehow missed the point completely… ?

Chapter 12

Screwed up Sexuality: The Effects of Dominator Society on Our Love Lives

The 'Sexual Revolution': Has It Lived Up To Its Name?

Dominator cultures have a negative affect on human love and sexuality in a host of different ways, despite the twentieth century's much-vaunted sexual revolution, movement away from Victorian repressiveness, and apparent sexual freedoms. In fact, it seems – perhaps not unexpectedly – that it is actually impossible to have really healthy sexuality within a dominator society.

Prurient attitudes to the body. For example, we would like to believe that we have a reasonably liberated and relaxed approach to our bodies and bodily functions these days, and we probably do compared to the Victorians. But in many ways we have actually gone backwards compared to pre-Victorian times, and have no reason at all to feel complacent about our liberatedness in this area. For example, think how inhibited we are about seeing or talking about breastfeeding or bowel movements compared to the eighteenth century or before. And it was only the last few generations that got rid of the 'Gropecunt Alley' and 'Harlot's Lane' type of place names that used to abound. (We might not like the robust language these names employ, but at least we can admire their refreshing directness.) And compared to hunter-gatherers, our relationship with sexual and bodily matters today is definitely prurient and inhibited. In fact it is more or less impossible to bring children up in our purportedly liberated society without them being affected by the guilt, shame, 'dirtiness' and general unnaturalness that tends to taint the way we treat sex and our bodies. And this is despite a sincere drive throughout most of the last century to shed shame and guilt and to feel more at home with our physical selves. There is certainly *less* shame and guilt these days, about some things; but this definitely hasn't removed problems around sex and bodily affairs in our society. In some ways it seems to have made them worse. For example, think of the plague of depilitation that's affecting women, with men finding more and more types of natural female bodily hair unacceptable.

Puerile or negative language. This uneasiness about our physical selves is highlighted in the language we use about our bodies these days. For example, what does it say about us that even doctors and scientists now routinely use infantilisms instead of grown-up or scientific terms in referring to bodily parts: 'poo' instead of shit or faeces; 'bottom' for behind, bum or arse; 'tummy' for stomach or belly; 'willy' for cock or penis. And what does it say about us that we *still* don't have a kind, warm, friendly, respectful and sexy term for female genitals in English?! No 'yoni' or 'zsu zsu' for us – just a list of clinical (vagina), ashamed (front bottom), derogatory (the famous c-word, rarely used in the loving or admiring way of D.H. Lawrence's Mellors) or downright hateful words (box, slit, hole, etc). 'Pussy' is about as good as it gets... The same applies to breasts: for example, the commonly used slang terms 'tits' and 'boobs' denote fools or mistakes in other contexts. What does that say about us and how we feel about these purportedly adored parts of women's bodies?

Uneasy attitude towards sex. Western society's persistently uneasy attitude towards sex and the body is demonstrated every day on the front pages of tabloid newspapers. These pander overtly to our population's evidently relentless appetite for sexual scandal and titillation; and the 'sexual revolution' certainly hasn't done anything to reduce this phenomenon. If anything, our prurient interest in sex seems to have got worse over the decades, which definitely doesn't indicate a culture whose citizens enjoy satisfying natural love lives. US psychotherapist and popular commentator Esther Perel (2006) has this to say about attitudes to sex in contemporary North American society:

> "While we recognize the importance of sex, we nonetheless vacillate between extremes of excessive license and repressive tactics... Porn sites proliferate on the Internet, yet we continue to debate whether or not to provide sex education in our schools... Despite living in times of unprecedented sexual freedom in America, the practice of policing sexuality has continued unabated since the days of the Puritans... Never before has sex been so publicly displayed, an incessant barrage of explicit images wherever we rest our eyes [yet] Let's not be fooled into thinking that this saturation reflects enlightened sexual attitudes... the central idea that sex is dirty remains unchallenged... Taboo-ridden sexuality and excess-driven sexuality converge in a troubling way. Both lead us to want to dissociate psychically from the physical act of sex. A society that sees sex as soiled does not make sex go away. Instead, this kind of anxious atmosphere breeds guilt and shame in its more extreme version, or a generalised discomfort in its more ubiquitous expression. Sex is divorced from emotional and social continuity. What is missing is a sexuality that is integrated, in which pleasure flourishes in a context of relatedness. I'm not talking only about deep love; I'm also talking about basic care and appreciation for another person."

What's Gone Wrong With The 'Sexual Revolution'?

So why is our culture still so sexually screwed up, when most books and media tell us that we are thoroughly sexually liberated and capable of all the multiple orgasms that magazine covers promote?

Inability to experience pleasure. One can see some of this uneasy and divided attitude towards sex discussed above as stemming from the inability to fully experience pleasure which is discussed by Prescott (1975), and is outlined in Chapter 7. Most people's sexuality has been damaged to at least some extent from the direct psychological and somatic effects of dominator childrearing on children which produces armouring of our feelings and bodies – even when there has been no actual sexual abuse or overt repressiveness in the upbringing. And it seems likely that this is one of the main drivers contributing to our culture's restless and insatiable approach to sex: "body pleasure is very different from promiscuity, which reflects a basic inability to experience pleasure. If a sexual relationship is not pleasurable, the individual looks for another partner."

Sex as a release of tension or frustration; sex as excitement. Liedloff (1975, Chapter 7) and Gerhardt both discuss the way in which non-nurturing childhoods create states of undischarged energy and chronic tension in people's bodies – tension which dominator life goes on to exacerbate. In addition, modern life provides fewer and fewer opportunities for everyday tensions to be released in natural ways, as they would be in simpler societies through hunting, gathering, walking, climbing, running, swimming, dancing, riding, herding, field work and so on, as well as through making love. Sex in dominator life has therefore tended to become a channel into which all sorts of inappropriate and sometimes unhealthy energies are poured in order to express/expel them somehow.

Modern life is also desperately *tame* compared to hunter-gatherer or much tribal life, with few natural or healthy opportunities for excitement. Most developed-world peoples don't take part in exciting rituals or thrilling hunts; don't dance until they reach a trance state; don't have the varied, guilt-free sexual life which many hunter-gatherers enjoy (see Chapter 13); don't live cheek by jowl with the vivid realities of wild animals, wild weather and so on. Sex in modern society has therefore probably tended to become a substitute for the natural excitement which these things occasion in simpler cultures.

Longing for attention and validation. Our approach to sex and love in dominator cultures is also distorted by our longing for *attention, validation and approval* – for the undivided love and interest of another, or others. As we also saw in Chapter 7, this longing and seeking for the unconditional love we didn't get enough of in childhood underlies much love or sex addiction – and even what we would consider normal behaviour in the field of love, romance, mate-seeking, marriage or partnership. In strictly patriarchal cultures, having a husband is required if a woman is to be acceptable within the society: but even in less strict dominator-predicated communities, most women feel that having a committed partner is essential to their well-being and stature within a community. It makes them feel psychologically validated: 'Look! I must be OK because someone wants me and loves me!'; and a loved one also provides emotional nourishment via their commitment, attention and devotion. This is the same basic idea that James Redfield expresses in *The Celestine Prophecy*'s Fourth Insight, 'The Struggle for Power': "To gain energy we tend to manipulate or force others to give us attention and thus energy," (Redfield, 1993). Without these, modern women all too often feel bereft.

And conversely, losing a lover has a disproportionately negative effect on women in modern society (one that simply doesn't exist in classificatory kinship cultures.) This is the stuff of so much of chick lit: "That was what being dumped did to you, sapped your confidence as if you were walking around with a huge notice saying: this person is unloved and unwanted," (Duncan, 2008).

Exclusivity. Perel believes that the longing for attention also underlies our Western culture's insistence on exclusivity within serious relationships:

"The isolating conditions of modern life only amplify the

> rumbling insecurity that hides in the background of our romantic possessiveness. Fear of loss and fear of abandonment tighten our grip on fidelity. In a culture where everything is disposable and downsizing confirms just how replaceable we really are, our need to feel secure in our primary relationship is all the greater. The smaller we feel in the world, the more we need to shine in the eyes of our partner. We want to know that we matter, and that, for at least one person, we are irreplaceable. We long to feel whole, to rise above the prison of our solitude... Monogamy, it follows, is the sacred cow of the romantic ideal, for it is the marker of our specialness: I have been chosen and others renounced. When you turn your back on other loves, you confirm my uniqueness; when your hand or mind wanders, my importance is shattered."
>
> (Perel, 2007)

But this brings its own problems, as popular writer and social commentator Andrew Trees suggests:

> "Perhaps the biggest single problem for many married couples today is the enormous expectations that are routinely loaded onto marriage by both the culture at large and the couples themselves. Just think of the various social roles that have been conflated into the marital relationship – best friend, closest kin relationship, sexual playmate, and economic partner to name just a few... Traditionally, though, this was not the case. Your wife or husband was just that, and people did not expect their partners to perform numerous other roles, such as best friend."
>
> (Trees, 2009)

This last is a good point; and it is clear from classificatory kinship societies, or interwoven tribal communities of the

Ladakh type, that this issue of enormous expectations loaded on to one person simply doesn't exist in such cultures. One could say that "it takes a whole village" to support rational love relationships, as well as to bring up a child...

Anger and Even Hatred Underlying Desire

Jealousy. If the "enormous expectations" are dashed, and something goes wrong in Western monogamous relationships, anger and jealousy as well as pain and grieving, are considered to be normal reactions. This at least partly because jealousy is validated by patriarchal culture, which views partners as possessions to which one has a 'right'. Jealousy is also a good vehicle or outlet for 'justified rage', and is therefore something which those with suppressed anger may actually actively seek (Chapter 7). In addition, jealousy is an emotion to which dominator-damaged people are particularly prone because the lack of unconditional love and security that they experienced in childhood pre-conditions them to feel it. But again, this isn't the case in matrilineal or classificatory kinship-type societies, for jealousy features very little in such cultures, and is usually derided or frowned upon. This fact is discussed further in the next chapter.

Animosity towards women. Typically, dominator childhoods make boys avoidant of emotions. Underlying most men's mistreatment of women, it can be argued, is a hatred of the fact that women *do* attract them. Avoidant men dislike the weakness which this brings; and their emotional lives typically swing between giving in to their (natural) desire for closeness, love and sex; and revolting away from that into a detached, emotionally-avoidant state – and a desire to punish the woman for making them give in to this weakness. Often, love-seeking women are drawn into this scenario – resulting in a very common type of co-dependency of damaged couples, with insecurely attached women pursuing avoidant men.

Taylor (2005) puts this in a historical and religious context:

> "The sexual power that women have over men was probably a factor too [in men's inhumanity to women]. Since men felt that sex was sinful, and that sexual desires were base, they were bound to feel animosity towards the women who produced those desires. In addition, women's sexual power must have affronted men's need for control. It meant that they couldn't have complete domination over women – and over their own bodies – that they craved. They might be able to force women to cover their bodies and faces and make them live like slaves, but any women was capable of arousing powerful and uncontrollable sexual impulses inside them at any moment. The last 6,000 years of man's inhumanity to woman can partly be seen as a revenge for this."

Sex and violence. The worrying way in which sex and violence are linked together in dominator cultures no doubt springs partly from the dynamics described above. However, there are other drivers for this syndrome. We have already described James Prescott's work on the relationship between non-nurturing childhoods, the inability to experience pleasure, and a tendency to violence-seeking. Prescott goes on to discuss the "special relationship" between sexuality and violence in modern society, observing that "there is... evidence that points to preference for sexual violence over sexual pleasure in the United States." Though the exact physiological mechanisms are complex, it nevertheless seems highly likely that if an organism is unable to experience bodily pleasure fully, and also has a level of suppressed anger, the result will be that it seeks (or is only to be able to find) satisfaction in sex which is linked to hurting the sexual object. It must also be significant that there appears to be very little up-to-date research on what exactly is going on here physiologically and neurologically, despite sex n' violence playing such an enormous role in modern life. It's as if we don't *want* to understand the mechanisms at work...

We can also quote Suttie again: "The indulgences we have been forced to renounce ourselves, we will certainly not permit to other people." So if men have been forced to hide, suppress or renounce their softer, gentler side, they will tend to hate this in other people – including women – and to try to 'kill' it or hurt it in them, as it was killed or hurt in themselves. And because sex normally elicits warm, loving feelings, when it brings these up in a man who doesn't want to feel them, he is likely to punish the woman who 'caused' them – behaving cruelly rather than kindly.

A 'culture of hard'. The factors above are particularly toxic in the way that they affect the overall relations between girls and boys, and young women and men. These are inevitably distorted by the effects of dominator, by the power imbalances in dominator societies, and by the warped values and behaviours that these cause. So, despite the sexual revolution, girls in our society can't avoid growing up in a misogynistic, macho, 'culture of hard' – one where boys and men are encouraged by laddish norms to act as if they despise and want to mistreat girls. Rap and hip-hop lyrics are notorious for expressing this. Or one has only to look at the type of sexist jokes which seem to be considered quite acceptable on the Internet to realise the extent of men's negative feelings about women (and vice versa, alas).

In fact, the sexual revolution seems to have made girls' journey through adolescence more fraught than it has ever been, with apparently ever-growing peer pressure for them to get involved with sex, while the feeling, emotional side which should make sex feel special and even magical is sidelined or ignored. Even basic kindnesses, courtesies or gentlemanliness from boys appears to be steadily reducing – and this is particularly harmful for adolescent girls who are just beginning to explore love, sex and relationships, and need at least some reasonable level of kindness and tenderness at this vulnerable time. Perel (2006) describes a growing acceptance among young people in the USA – girls as well as boys – of what she terms "hit-and-run sex" –

booty calls; 'hooking up' rather than going on proper dates and so on: "They get drunk, have sex, then *pretend it never happened*." And it is sad to see that this trend towards the type of heartless, uncommitted sex formerly associated mainly with men is now increasingly seen in women too - in laddettism, woman deliberately seeking one night stands, female sex tourism, use of himbos or male escorts, and other manifestations of sex divorced from feelings.

Unreal Sex

> *"Not only do Cyberspace and Virtual Reality express avoidance and denial in terms of what was and is being obliterated of nature and direct experience. They also represent new realms for domination itself. A growing misogyny is perhaps the ugliest, worsening aspect of a society that is becoming increasingly separated from the authenticity of direct accountability."*
>
> (Zerzan, 2002)

A huge increase in the amount of unhealthily 'unreal' sexuality in modern life – particularly via the medium of Internet porn – is also a major feature of dominator society today. One can surmise that this is caused by the distortions that dominator life inflicts on our soma and psyche, combined with new factors like media-warped views of reality (sexualised; airbrushed), and the limitless opportunities provided by the Internet. This situation encourages people to escape proper human emotional intimacy, and real, soma-rooted experience, into unreal virtual worlds of sensation detached from tenderness or love.

Misuse of sex energy. Gurdjieff talked about the misuse of sex chakra energy by other chakras nearly a hundred years ago, and what he had to say on the subject is still illuminating today:

> "It is necessary to know the human machine very well in order to grasp what abuse of sex in the real meaning of these

> words is. It means the wrong work of centers [chakras] in relation to sex, that is, the action of the sex center through other centers, and the action of other centers through the sex center; or, to be still more precise, the functioning of the sex center with energy borrowed from the other centers and the functioning of other centers with energy borrowed from the sex center... The energy of the sex center in the work of the thinking, emotional, and moving centers can be recognised by a particular 'taste', by a particular fervor, by a vehemence which the nature of the affair does not call for... together with the *uselessness* of the work in question."
>
> (Ouspensky, 1950)

Gurdjieff cites political disputation, hell-fire preaching, unnecessary abstinence, intolerance, persecution, revolution, and pointless physical feats, sports and record-setting as examples of the emotional, thinking, and moving centres robbing the sex centre of and working with its energy.

Sex in the head. What is of even more concern is the reverse situation – of the sex chakra being fuelled inappropriately by other chakras' energies – notably those of the 'thinking centre'. It is notable how our culture, these days, seems to be moving more and more towards a left-brain, abstract, conceptualising way of relating to the world: that is, how it is becoming increasingly 'mental' or mind-centred. It therefore seems to be the case that it is this energy of the thinking centre which is fuelling many peoples' sex chakras nowadays, with all sorts of harmful results, including high levels of addiction to pornography:

> "When the sex center works with energy that is not its own... it ceases to play the role in the organism which it could play. At the same time union with, and use of its energy by, the thinking center creates far too great an imagination on the subject of sex, and in addition *a tendency*

to be satisfied with this imagination."
(Ouspensky, 1950)

Gurdjieff said this around 1915, drawing on Sufi and other esoteric sources of knowledge, but it hits the nail on the head more than ever now in respect to our salacious, porn-addicted society. Indeed, this sex-in-the-head plague seems to be scaling new heights in twenty-first century society, with more and more people (mainly men) apparently finding it easier to evade proper human relationships by spending time on their computers having sex with themselves in mental fantasy lands instead. Tantric and similar schools also point out that real sex or sensuality involves an *interchange* of energies between two organisms – an interchange that brings new energy to each partner. 'Solitary sex', on the other hand, doesn't do this; and esoteric sources say that it is therefore relatively sterile and unrefreshing, or even depleting, to the organism if practised to excess.

It is also interesting to note that traditional peoples like the Amazonian Canela (Crocker and Crocker, 2004) who practice group sequential sex (see next chapter) frown on masturbation largely, it seems, because this involves sex without *sharing* or social bonding. It is therefore seen as an activity which can encourage antisocial attitudes in young people – something much to be avoided in such closely interconnected and bonded communities.

Conclusion. To conclude this chapter: if we measured all the sexual activity that went on in a year in the world, and estimated how much is actually done with another, grown-up human being, and with both real joyful physical desire, and with love and kindness, it probably wouldn't be a big percentage. I feel that this is a great indictment of our so-called liberated society and the 'sexual revolution'. There is definitely a lot of room for improvement. Let us give D.H. Lawrence the last word through his own inimitable Oliver Mellors:

"I believe in being warm-hearted. I believe especially in being warm-hearted in love, in fucking with a warm heart. I believe if men could fuck with warm hearts, and the women take it warm-heartedly, everything would come all right. It's all this cold-hearted fucking that is death and idiocy."

(Lawrence, 1928)

Chapter 13

Unscrewed up Sexuality: Matrilineal Love Lives

Sex Can Be a Beneficial Force in Communities

Hunter-gatherer societies generally, and some tribal societies too, have a great deal to teach us about how sex can be a genuinely beneficial force in communities, rather than a difficult, disruptive or damaging one, if practiced within the context of a classificatory kinship system. It needs to be emphasised again that one can't cherry-pick features that one likes and would wish to emulate in simpler cultures and apply them in isolation to our own modern lives; and this certainly applies to indigenous sexual customs, for the classificatory kinship framework is crucial to the way these work in simpler cultures. All the same, it is surely salutary to realise how differently sex lives can be lived in other societies; and how sex can be a socially bonding rather than a divisive, jealousy-breeding power in communities. For example, in most hunter-gatherer cultures, sex before marriage is normal; sex at puberty or even before (as with the Canela: see Crocker and Crocker, 2004) is usual; and though some form of marriage usually does exist, it is mostly less binding and more easily dissolved (if either partner proves unsatisfactory) than in Western societies. Tradition also usually allows for sex with non-partners or actively encourages this – at feast times and celebrations; or with visitors as part of normal hospitality; or as the main type of sexual life, as with the Na. As a result of these customs, nearly all the problems associated with sex in patriarchal or Western societies, and which are such seemingly insoluble dilemmas (failed monogamy, unfaithfulness, divorce, broken homes, teenage pregnancies and so on), don't even exist within the context of communities structured on classificatory kinship lines.

Sex within such cultures also tends to exemplify some of the broader characteristics of egalitarian society, notably the right to individual freedom and the duty to share. So, many societies with a classificatory kinship structure regard sex with partners other than husbands or wives as a right and often as a duty too – and usually one which is uncontroversial because it contributes to community well-being. Shared sex does this through increasing individual happiness; and such peoples believe that the happier everyone is, the better society functions. The right to a fairly free sex life is also part of wider rights to individual freedom in such cultures – to using your body as you see fit, or to choosing a sexual partner freely within the constraints of any more general rules or customs relating to sexual pairing. These points are considered below.

Sexual Freedom

> *"Fidelity as a social restriction does not exist, and virginity has no importance."*
>
> (Hua, 2001, on the Na)

Freedom to choose partners. One key aspect of sex lives in strongly matrilineal societies is that there is either complete freedom to pick one's own sexual partners as and when one wants to, or a great deal of freedom. We have already discussed the importance of matriliny to 'women-power' and to egalitarianism in Chapters 2 and 4. In matrilineal societies, women are relatively or completely free to choose their husbands or partners without the pressure, coercion or fear that prevail in patriarchal societies. In addition, they only need to keep him as long as he's a good partner. In many cultures he won't even have taken up residence in the matrilineal home; and if he has, but doesn't come up to scratch, the women can demand that he leave it as a matter of right. The following well-known quotation, based on information from Asher Wright – for many years a missionary with the Iroquois Senecas – expresses this pithily:

> "… woe to the luckless husband or lover who was too shiftless to do his share of the providing. No matter how many children or whatever goods he might have in the house, he might at any time be ordered to pick up his blanket and budge; and after such orders it would not be healthful for him to attempt to disobey. The house would be too hot for him; and, unless saved by the intercession of some aunt or grandmother, he must retreat to his own clan; or, as was often done, go and start a new matrimonial alliance in some other. The women were the great power among the clans, as everywhere else."
>
> (Morgan, 1877; and quoted in part in Engels, 1884)

Writers from former centuries who described the Na of China said much the same thing:

> "In Yung-ning it is the woman who remains in the home, and she takes unto herself a man as husband whom she keeps as long as he works, and as long as she enjoys his presence. She can send him away at any time, and take unto herself another husband. Her brother, if she has one, may remain with her and he takes the place of the father… "
>
> (Rock, quoted in Hua, 2001)

Partners just for pleasure. Partners are not just utilitarian – chosen for their good-householder qualities: sexual partners can be chosen for other reasons too. For example, among the Na, the main form of sexual life is *acia,* which involves nearly complete freedom for both sexes to have liaisons with whomever they please, for as short or long a time as both parties are willing.

These are affairs, dalliances, flings – usually not long-term matters. Anthropologist Cai Hua says of *acia,* and also of some more long-standing arrangements:

> "All of my sources confirmed: 'we do not arrange or propose sexual partners for a person. No one can force anyone to do something against his wishes. To each his own. I go with the one I love. No one can stop me.'… Breaking off an *acia* relationship is a matter of personal freedom; a person wishing to do so has no need to explain why… a vow of fidelity is shameful because it is considered a negotiation, an exchange, which goes against their customs. We can find in this attitude a key concept: no sexual relationship can lead the lovers to promise each other a monopoly on their sexuality nor bring them to give, trade or sell themselves. Sexuality is not a piece of merchandise but a purely sentimental and amorous matter that implies no mutual constraints… An attempt to monopolize one's partner is always considered shameful and stupid, and the villagers will mock it for a long time."
>
> (Hua, 2001)

Even though the Na are an agricultural tribal, rather than a foraging, society, one can see a clear link between such attitudes and the requirement for personal autonomy unconstrained by others which exists in hunter-gatherer societies.

Mutual good treatment; lack of jealousy. In sexually free societies, there is a clear onus on both parties in a sexual partnership to behave nicely to each other, for if they don't, each side has complete freedom to seek a more pleasant partner elsewhere – a good recipe for mutual kind treatment. As one of Hua's male Na sources put it: "It's enough that my partner be nice to me and not see other men in front of me." Hua investigated jealousy among the Na, and found that – although there are cases of jealous outbursts, and, very occasionally, attacks – these are rare and are strongly disapproved of. Daniel Everett (2008) also reported upon responses to unfaithful partners among the South American Pirahã, and found that a relatively mild, ritualised form of 'punishment' of short duration (a day, say) might be all that a transgression elicited. Observations of classificatory kinship societies therefore indicate that strong jealousy is *not* necessarily normal, or an inevitable reaction to 'infidelity' (which is how it is usually viewed within patriarchal societies). Rather, it is a cultural artefact to at least some extent – one that is sanctioned by dominator norms. Aggressive jealous behaviour can therefore be viewed as something that dominator people 'allow' themselves to indulge in, rather than as an inevitable human reaction to perceived unfaithfulness.

Sex and Social Bonding

Shared sex. This seems to be an aspect of hunter-gatherer/tribal sex lives about which not much has been written, but which has evidently been very important in many communities. One of the best descriptions of group and extra-marital sex customs can be found in William and Jean Crocker's book (2004) on the Amazonian Canela, which chronicles their customs before these quite disappeared during the twenty-first century. It describes how sex was used in various circumstances – formal and informal; in semi-public group sequential situations or in private trysts; in the context of special occasions, feasts and dances or informally and *ad hoc* – largely as a pleasurable social bonding device. Sharing oneself sexually demonstrated generosity and lack of stinginess: "Generosity and sharing was the ideal, while withholding was a social evil. Sharing possessions brought esteem. Sharing one's body was a direct corollary." Shared sex tended to equalise relative advantages particularly between men, contributing to male bonding and tribal morale; or was a reward for those working on communal tasks for the common good. Men and women had a more or less equal say in things; and different age classes were involved with each other. If women couldn't contribute children to the tribe, they could contribute sex.

Some researchers do still report on contemporary shared sex. For example Hrdy (2009), in a modern-day illustration of Knight's sex-strike scenario, describes current traditions in South American tribes like the Canela and Kulina which involve shared sex:

> "When they find themselves 'hungry for meat', Kulina women order men to go hunting. On their return, each woman selects a hunter other than her own husband as a partner... After cooking the meat and eating, each woman retires with the man whom she selected as her partner for the sexual tryst."

Canela contributors to the Crockers' book had the following to say about the group sex that had been part of their former way of life:

> "Group sequential sex was very good because it brought a great deal of value to the older people during past times and gave much joy to groups in general. Besides serving one particular group on one occasion, it served all the four age classes at other times, giving them strength, a lot of courage, great joy and much animation... The age classes... went singing in the boulevard because they had just had sequential sex, and they passed on this animation to the entire population. This is what group sequential sex provided." (His Water, male)

Yontam (female) also regretted the loss of these customs:

> "I loved all the men. They were so handsome, in their wristlets and other decorations. They were so beautiful and there were

so many of them... I wanted to go with the group of men. I like the other men... Yes, it's been lost. The custom has been lost. I miss it, but what can be done about it?"

Many partners/many fathers. In cultures where it is acceptable or normal for a woman to have many sexual partners, this practice can actually be directly beneficial for both women and children – in great contrast to patriarchal societies where it is more likely to be at least disreputable, if not illegal or even punishable by death. Hrdy (2009) discusses such arrangements in matrilineal cultures up to the present day; and sees them as adaptive for women because they help recruit men who just may be fathers to cooperate in childcare:

> "Contrary to the widely held dogma that only men who are certain of their paternity provide for young, in many widely separated corners of the world there exist customs and beliefs that help mothers elicit tolerance, protection or assistance from men who are only possibly, rather than certainly, related." Among a wide range of tribal peoples from several continents, "women are permitted or even encouraged to have sex with real or fictive [classificatory] brothers of their husbands."

Indeed 'father' is a concept that isn't even recognised in many such societies. For example, the most that the Na acknowledge is that the 'seed' in the women must be 'watered' by a man or men: who, or how many, have watered it is immaterial. Some peoples also believe in what scientists term *partible paternity*, holding that:

> "... semen from every man a woman has sex with in the months her infant is born supposedly contributes to the growth of her fetus, resulting in a chimera-like composite

young sired by multiple men... Belief in partible paternity and other customs that facilitate maternal manipulation of information about paternity tend to be more feasible in groups with long-standing matrilineal traditions where sexual attitudes and childcare options are already tilted in favor of maternal interests. Such mindsets are very different from those in Western society, where a long history of patrilineally transmitted resources leaves men preoccupied with genetic paternity and puts children where paternity is in doubt at a serious disadvantage... Through regularly enacted rituals where sex is used to forge bonds with multiple partners, virtually every Kulina child is guaranteed more than one father. Through ritual sex, a mother lines up extra provisions for both herself and the child while at the same time taking out insurance lest her current husband default or die."

(Hrdy, 2009)

Sex and the Spiritual or Magical

In many hunter-gather (and other 'pagan') societies, sex or eroticism is thought to energise nature, stimulate natural growth, bring luck in hunting, create links with the world of spirits and so on. It is therefore considered to have a magical or sacred role in life. Here Morna Finnegan describes Central African Yaka women dancing: "They link arms, work up erotic frenzies, sing and dance choreographies the beauty of which is believed to summon forest spirits and captivate game animals," (2009/10). Other researchers such as Lewis (2002) and Turnbull (1961) describe the *trancelike* state arrived at during erotic dances performed by Central African pygmies. So sex and eroticism are understood to have a transcendent purpose and a primal connection to the success of nature, to fertility, to luck and good fortune – beliefs which underlie myriad traditions down the ages: European May Day customs of making love out of doors on the morn of May the first spring to mind as examples from Western culture. But sex and eroticism of this pagan or animist sort is also very human and down-to-earth: it isn't much separated from everyday life and love. In cultures such as that of the Canela, sex also has a sacred role in bonding community members together.

Is natural sexuality disempowered by mysticism? As early humans became more sophisticated, it appears that lovemaking and sexual energy were increasingly used deliberately for sacred purposes. This was certainly the case in ancient India – the home of Tantra – and no doubt in other cultures too: "Ancient Tantra is a spiritual system in which sexual love is a sacrament," say Charles and Caroline Muir (1989), authors of *Tantra: the Art of Conscious Loving*. And Taylor (2005) believes that Tantra went further than any other tradition in emphasising the sacredness of the human body, as we saw in Chapter 11.

But was the elevation of sex away from its natural roots altogether a good thing? We can speculate that the earthy unscrewed up sexiness of hunter-gatherers is close to what would have prevailed in our original prehistoric state. And Knight (1991) actually views any development away from this original natural sexuality towards something more 'elevated' or 'refined' as indicating the malign influences of encroaching patriarchy:

> "Mysticism and convoluted theologism emerged only when masculinist institutions began reasserting themselves as the first step in an immensely drawn out process which was eventually to result in class society and so-called 'civilisation'. Constructs of 'the feminine' became deified only in proportion as real women, in the flesh and blood, were deprived of their power. Goddesses, gods and other miraculous powers could enrich themselves only in proportion as ordinary humans were impoverished – robbed of the magic of their own lives."

This is an interesting point of view which has much to recommend it; and makes the priestesses of Old Europe – and perhaps even shamans – appear to be a step or two away from humanity's original pre-Eden condition of down-to-earth sexuality. Reading Briffault on the subject certainly gives that impression.

Unscrewed up Attitudes to the Body and Bodily Functions

A society's attitudes towards sex tend to go hand-in-hand with its attitudes towards the body and bodily functions generally. And patriarchal societies tend to treat affairs of the body as shameful or disgusting in a way that matrilineal cultures don't (as we said at the start of Chapter 12.) The difference in attitudes between these two types of culture is illustrated well by Turnbull (1961) in his description of girls' first-menstruation coming-of-age rites in 1950s Central Africa. In *The Forest People*, Turnbull contrasts the difference in approach between the hunter-gatherer forest pygmies, and the more patriarchal, superstitious, neighbouring villagers. To the pygmies, their girls' first menstrual blood means life:

> "So when a young pygmy girl begins to flower into maturity, and blood comes to her for the first time, it comes to her as a gift, received with gratitude and rejoicing; rejoicing that the girl is now a potential mother, that she can now proudly and rightfully take a husband. There is not a word of fear or superstition, and everyone is told the good news."

But the villagers treat the same occurrence of first menstruation "as a calamity – an evil omen. The girl who is defiled by it for the first time is herself in danger, and even more important, she has placed the whole family and clan in danger." She then has to be secluded, cleansed and purified, so that "at the best, the unfortunate girl is considered a considerable nuisance and expense." It is assumed that the natural occurrence of menstruation was brought about "by some kind of illicit intercourse"; a boy is "accused"; and the entire event is turned from something natural and happy into something involving evil, guilt, accusations, propitiation and so on. What a contrast between two world views!

Conclusion. So, to conclude: what might we learn from matrilineal cultures generally, or from more sophisticated spiritual approaches to love such as Tantra, and bring forward into a new partnership world? My own belief is that – to reinforce what was said at the beginning of Chapter 12 – it is difficult to have really healthy, happy love and sex lives within a dominator culture because so many obstacles stand in the way. To create any really radical changes in this situation we therefore need to steer our whole culture towards one where more partnership values prevail, and where physical and psychological unscrewed-upness is the norm. What is needed is not just the *wish* for love, kindness, friendliness, equality and freedom between the sexes, but also the actual *ability* to create a society in which these things are possible. Is that feasible outside of matrilineal societies? What could we do in order to approach the conditions of more partnership-style cultures – to be less screwed up generally? This 'million dollar question' is discussed in the final chapter of this book.

Chapter 14

Towards a New Partnership World

"In the practice of mutual aid, which we can retrace to the earliest beginnings of evolution, we thus find the positive and undoubted origin of our ethical conceptions: and we can affirm that in the ethical progress of man, mutual support – not mutual struggle – has had the leading part. In its wide extension, even in the present time, we also see the best guarantee of a still loftier evolution of our race."
Kropotkin, 1902

Can We Recreate New Forms of Partnership Society?

"Perhaps the future of the world would be better if we forgot about discovering something new and concentrated on recovering our past." (Morgan, 1991)

Is it possible to bring back or recreate the beneficial aspects of hunter-gatherer or partnership-style life today? This is the million-dollar question. Partnership ways evolved when there were only a few thousand humans in the world: could they survive or thrive on our immensely crowded earth today? And though it seems that true partnership societies did exist in prehistoric towns (that is, in settled, urban societies – see Chapter 4), what chance would they have in our incredibly technologically-complex industrial and post-industrial societies today? It is also difficult to separate out the individual components of life in partnership-type societies which hold the key to their ability to create unscrewed up people. This is because it is clearly the *whole package* – childrearing practices, world view, belief systems, accepted behaviours and so on – including Woodburn's (2005) "coherent interlocked and mutually reinforcing institutional procedures" (Chapters 2 and 3) – which forms the people brought up in these cultures. This is also why it is nearly impossible for us, who have grown up in our own modern *zeitgeist*, to be able to imagine what life could be like – and what we could be like – in such cultures, without dominator conditioning.

Obviously, this million dollar question has been wrestled with by many thinkers, and some who are particularly relevant here are John Zerzan, Richard Lee, Bruce Trigger, and Chris Knight and Camilla Powers and their colleagues. Zerzan thinks that a wholesale return to prehistoric-style life is the only answer. Lee envisions a more Marxist-style future, in which "everyone will have a car but nobody will have a Bentley or a Rolls Royce," (Lee, 1988).

Trigger deals with the issue in some depth in his paper *All People Are (Not) Good* (in Solway, 2006) – stating his belief that "Hunter-gatherer societies do not provide a model for the future; they merely demonstrate that social and political egalitarianism was possible in societies that were small enough to be controlled by public opinion." He then goes on to challenge "progressive anthropologists" to:

> "shift from merely criticizing the more deplorable features of contemporary societies to using what they and other social scientists, as well as psychologists and neuroscientists, know or can learn about human beings to formulate practical and attractive alternatives."

Trigger's paper goes on to pose a number of interesting questions about how, and to what extent, large-scale, enduring egalitarian societies could be fashioned artificially, and therefore takes the discussion well beyond the limits usually found in mainstream debates about happiness, for example; but doesn't suggest anything very concrete. Nor does he factor in the difference between partnership and dominator humans, which in my opinion is crucial to discussions of this kind. Nor do any of these authors bring in a spiritual dimension, which I also think is crucial, and which is examined later in this chapter.

The latter criticisms can also be applied to Knight, Powers *et al*, who suggest a return to a lunar-based way of life and to a new 'lunar economics' (www.lunarchy.org). Here, the overworked employed and the underfunded unemployed would even out their unequal share of resources (time and money) by the former working only half as much, and only during the waning/dark moon time (the old 'sex-strike' hours); and 'donating' the rest of their work load to the unemployed. The waxing/full moon period would be, as in classic hunter-gatherer times, only for play, feasting and so on. This is a nice – though seemingly logistically challenging – idea; and one very much in tune with Tom Hodgkinson's *Idler* magazine ethos.

What about feminism? We've already, through Zerzan and Trigger, criticised anthropologists for not taking a lead in critiques of current civilisation or promoting non-dominator ways of leading our lives. I would also criticise modern feminism for similar shortfalls. For example, to my knowledge, it hasn't incorporated crucial ideas such as Eisler's concepts of partnership and dominator life, or Liedloff's thoughts about continuum versus non-continuum upbringings, into its discussions, even though these ideas have been around for twenty-five years or more. Nor, it seems, has it really been effective in helping mainstream society (or even just modern women) properly understand what matriliny and classificatory kinship are all about, and the advantages that these ancient, original forms of social organisation had – and could have – for modern women and society as a whole. Yet it seems to me that these, or equivalent, concepts provide the absolutely essential underpinning to any fruitful understanding of or advancement of feminism.

Does democracy equate with partnership? Some people may argue that we already have appropriate forms of government in the shape of democracies through which we could develop partnership ways. It isn't unreasonable to think this; and maybe it is possible. However, it is interesting that Boehm (1999), in his discussion of various types of human political societies down the ages, groups modern nation states along with primitive kingdoms and ancient civilisations, classifying them both as "highly despotic" because their leaders can govern strongly with abundant coercive power: "Ancient and modern democracies may temper individual power with checks and balances, but centralised power still exists and is backed by the coercive force supplied by professional policemen or soldiers." The iron fist of despotism therefore isn't far behind the velvet glove of democracy even in mild and peaceful Britain. Nevertheless, most modern democracies are certainly greatly preferable to malign dictatorships; so perhaps it would be fair to call them the 'acceptable face' of dominator culture. But they are still formed from, and are expressions of, dominator life and dominator people.

Could partnership ways come out of such democracies? If they do, I personally believe it will be because of some mass change of consciousness among *individuals*, causing a bottom-up alteration in the way we think, live our lives and fashion our politics (see below).

Are Communes an Answer?

In Chapter 4, we briefly examined modern state communism and socialism, and also modern communes and other attempts at more communal or partnership ways of living. We saw there how poorly the former have performed in terms of providing partnership-type lives for ordinary people; and quoted Boehm as he concluded that "the social engineering was inept" and was based on a lack of understanding and naïve concepts of human nature. In this book, we have argued against the idea that human hierarchical tendencies are inevitable, and have maintained that they are caused more by conditioning than by genes. Nevertheless, as the world stands at present, Boehm's views are realistic, and a different sort of social engineering or social change would indeed be needed to make communism work. Nor were the communes, imposed on the Russian, Chinese and other peoples under state communism in the twentieth century, what most of us would have in mind when envisioning a return to hunter-gatherer-type egalitarian communities: I would see them rather as 'dominator wolves in partnership sheep's clothing'! Partnership ways and forms of living, by their very nature, can't be forced or imposed upon people, as communes largely were under communism. They need to be mutually-agreed movements arising from the grass roots in order to work properly – to be bottom-up rather than top-down. In Chapter 4 we also looked at how poorly modern communes and other attempts at more communal or partnership-oriented living have fared in terms of creating a growing, thriving contemporary movement.

Individualism and 'me time'. Another factor that stands in the way of creating modern communes is contemporary people's increasing trend towards individualism. Most of us haven't grown up with a strong network of extended family nearby, let alone lived in households shared with extended kin: single life or nuclear family homes are what we are used to. We may have had brief student-life experiences of sharing flats or houses with people other than family or partners; but, these days, sharing homes before marriage or cohabitation is more likely to be with one's parents than with other extended kin, friends or peers. Our society mourns the loss of the 'extended family', but in truth, most of us wouldn't relish the thought of living in continuous close contact with our relatives if we could help it. And most modern women, for example, would hate to have their freedoms curtailed by the restrictions which traditional patriarchal extended families tend to impose. As we said in Chapter 4, our individualistic desire to manage our own home lives unhindered, to *not* share our belongings, to make our own rules, and to not have to take others' desires into account, have made most of us give up on trying to live communally. Even the less challenging co-housing movement seems to have had only limited success in the developed world, perhaps for similar reasons.

Another factor that also militates against the successful development of communes is people's apparent increasing need or desire for privacy and 'me time', plus a tolerance of, or active desire for, solitude compared to traditional cultures. This may be a natural desire in those urban dwellers who are crowd-averse, and who therefore wish to swap heavily populated surroundings for unspoilt rural peace. However, in light of Chapter 7, it seems likely that this desire for aloneness is at least in part a result of harm done to us by dominator upbringings, rather than a natural or innate quality.

Toxic families. Alas, another aspect of this issue is that some family relationships within patriarchal societies can be quite toxic; and most tend to be marred to at least some extent by the psychological harm wrought on us by our dominator upbringings and environment. At their most extreme, Hrdy (2009), for example, discusses the potentially malevolent or even lethal influences of mothers-in-law in some traditional patrilineal societies, as opposed to the benign and helpful equivalent relationships usually found in classificatory kinship cultures. And it is a sad but true fact that crimes against family members – particularly women, girls and children – is a feature of patriarchal society. Even in the developed West, significant proportions of all crimes are committed within families by close relatives or connections. This inevitably makes the idea of living in close quarters with one's extended family unpalatable to some people.

A Spiritual Evolution Point of View

To go back to the million dollar question posed at the beginning of this chapter – *is it possible to bring back or recreate the beneficial aspects of partnership life today?* – I believe that we need to look beyond physical forms of organisation such as communes; and beyond political systems or movements too, for I personally don't think that these will provide adequate solutions to our problems. I myself feel that it we need to examine the query from a different point of view altogether – from a spiritual, and specifically a spiritual *evolution* – perspective. In the context of this book, I am taking spiritual evolution to mean a spiritual point of view which considers human beings within the wider context of the solar system, the earth, and its inhabitants; and which believes that there is some element of higher wisdom and guidance involved in the overall development of the world. Obviously this sort of perspective won't be acceptable to all readers, and will be anathema to some (please feel free to skip this section if you dislike this type of non-scientific discussion). However, for those who are comfortable with the concept, it provides some different approaches our million dollar question – even if it doesn't provide any very clear answers.

A need for individuation? Many spiritual paths and teachings have a view on the spiritual development of the earth and its creatures; and there is a degree of concordance between a number of these. For example, visionary Rudolph Steiner taught that:

> "The human being has achieved his present constitution through a series of developments… first the physical… then the etheric, the astral and the ego, until… all were finally fused together in the being of man. After long periods of development a new age begins in which man is to come into consciousness of his ego and to take over his further development himself. This is man's present stage of evolution."

(Wilkinson, 1993. NB The word *ego* was used by Steiner to mean "an individualised portion of the divine substance" rather than in the sense of the self-centred, egocentric self, as Taylor, for example, employs it.)

As I understand it, Steiner's view was that the human psyche had evolved through a long period in which it was relatively immersed in and identified with the community or group to which it was closest, and with the values of that group. Then, more recently, a period began in which the task of individual humans (incarnated souls) was to develop their own direct relationship with the universe or God – independently of society's requirements and expectations – this being the stage that we're in now.

One can surely equate this idea of the ancient community or group to classificatory kinship, partnership-type communities; but here we come up against the problem that such communities – certainly in their pristine or original state – seem to have been (or still are) 'pretty damn good', as we discussed at length in Chapter 3. Moreover, such hunter-gatherer-style cultures also seem to allow a lot of scope both for spiritual development and for the individualistic expression of this, as Liedloff and others point out, and as *Mutant Message Down Under* illustrates well. So what higher or cosmic purpose can have been served in changing or trying to improve on our original partnership communities, which seemed to be so successful? I don't know the answer to this question, which is related to the one posed at the end of Chapter 11.

A 'need' for suffering? In Hindu cosmology, the understanding is that the universe changes cyclically throughout enormous spans of time, and is now considered to be going through one of its regularly recurring Kali Yuga or 'Dark Times' periods before a new Golden Age emerges. During these dark times, human morality is thought to decline drastically, so from this Eastern point of view our current bleak state of affairs on earth is only to be expected. Some related schools of spiritual thought also take the view that the evolving human spirit must have *needed* to go through a prolonged period in which dominator-style values prevailed; and that the developing human psyche has had to explore great depths of selfishness, cruelty and greed in order to recoil against them – as we are doing now – and evolve to new levels of cooperation and kindness.

This view is quite widespread in New Age thinking, but I struggle with it, as I struggle with the idea of 'needing' negative personal experiences which was mentioned in Chapter 11. Indeed, the scale of the horrors, cruelties and injustices which have been experienced on earth during the last 10,000 years are so enormous that I think most of us struggle with this Theology 101 issue of 'why does God allow suffering in the world?' I likewise struggle with the Hindu idea that this cycle from Golden to Dark Age and back is just a game played by the creator: what divine being could enjoy such a cruel 'game'?

Higher powers make mistakes too? A more cynical view suggested by certain spiritual adepts such as Gurdjieff is that something went badly *wrong* with the higher powers' plans for the Earth's development, so that what we're seeing now is a cosmic experiment gone awry! Not a comforting thought, but who knows? Doris Lessing suggests something similar in *Briefing for a Descent into Hell*; and over the years I have heard several psychics say that "them upstairs" underestimate how tough things are for a soul incarnating on earth, and that if they "tried it themselves" they might make an effort to improve things down here a bit quicker!

Society is Diverging Along Two Different Paths

My own personal view on all this is that I *do* believe that the world is being guided in some way; that there *is* some reason and purpose in what's going on (even if we can't see it clearly); and that we *are* heading for better things. I suppose that this point of view comes from the same source as my 'pro-nice' perspective on human beings; and obviously, it has been backed up by the evidence I've found to support that perspective and which is set out in this book.

I also believe that we are seeing a major and growing *divergence* in society between a basically hopeful, positive, New Age, partnership-oriented group (who comprise part of what Taylor calls the Second Wave) on the one hand; and a fundamentally more dominator-inclined or dominator-influenced tranche on the other. Again, the concepts of partnership and dominator come in useful here, as they make it easy to assign trends, news events and other currents in society to either group. So, if one pays attention solely to mainstream – that is, mainly dominator – news and media, then the impression one gets of our world's direction is largely a bleak and frightening one which is worsening in many ways (as described in Chapter 1). But those of us who are part of Taylor's Second Wave, or have sympathies with it, can also see more and more *hopeful* trends running counter to this mainstream, pessimistic, world view. And, whether one has a spiritual perspective on these matters or not, many people in this more optimistic group do feel that human society is evolving in some way, away from our despotic past and towards a more equal and cooperative future.

Positive signs. Significant changes in society and its attitudes have certainly occurred even during the last fifty years or so. Indeed, despite the many old and new horrors of modern life on earth, it is clear that there *is* a gradual overall movement towards a recognition of the need for more justice, tolerance, equality and so on – even if these aren't equally distributed throughout the globe. For example, it is easy to forget the achievements of feminism, which are now largely embedded in the laws and norms of Western society, and aspired to by women throughout much of the rest of the world; and the same applies to minority rights in many spheres. Barriers between cultures have thinned;

and though wars still rage, and prejudice and intolerance are rife in some quarters, increasing numbers of us do now feel that we inhabit a Global Village and are linked to people from other cultures. Nor do we accept the validity of war as readily as we used to. Many of us also sense that there's some truth in the Gaia hypothesis – or at least feel an increasing protectiveness towards the earth and its creatures and sympathy for environmental movements worldwide.

The fact that so many complementary therapies and practices have crept inside the mainstream pale is another striking change. And the move away from established religions and towards freer spiritual beliefs, with increasingly widespread acceptance of spiritual events such as intuitive or psychic experiences, is heartening too. These are all movements which run largely counter to traditional dominator values and beliefs.

So, as Eisler put it in 1987:

> "In sum, under the new view of cultural evolution, male dominance, male violence, and authoritarianism are not inevitable, eternal givens. And rather than just being a 'utopian dream', a more peaceful and equalitarian world is a real possibility for our future."

Finally, while on this subject, it's worth making the point again about how *costly* the harm created by dominator life is. Even if nothing else motivated us to strive for a more peaceful and equalitarian world, just think how much of our earth's Gross National Income currently goes on combating these ills; and of all the money we'd save if we lived in a world without war, violence, crime, the diseases of civilisation, or self-destructive behaviour. No need for a defence budget, police forces, social services, mental health institutions (or most of the NHS, perhaps?), rehab clinics, foreign aid… the list goes on. This has ultimately got to be an incentive, surely?

Better to light a candle than rail against the dark. Overall, I'm definitely not as gloomy as Zerzan (2002) who feels that: "Daily existence is increasingly that of despair, depression and derangement, punctuated by news of the latest serial murder spree or global eco-disaster, consumed as horrible entertainments in the emptiness."! My own view is rather that – while we do all need to be aware of the factors that are driving or underpinning mainstream modern life (dominator ways being the key factor, this book is claiming) – it is nevertheless 'better to light a candle than rail against the dark'. Personally, I do have hope and faith that the world can improve, and even that we can build Jerusalem on earth. But I also believe that – as suggested above – this change will come about as the result of a *groundswell of new consciousness,* rather than because of any secular external effort, movement or activism. In fact, my own belief is that politics, activism and so on reflect or are produced *by* unconscious changes in the world's *zeitgeist,* rather than the other way around.

Positivity is an essential foundation. I also definitely believe that a good future can only be built upon *positive* thoughts and actions; and absolutely disagree with any 'ends justifies the means' approach to creating change. I certainly believe that we need to fully face up to the things that are wrong with our dominator-damaged world – and outrage or anger may be suitable reactions to this facing-up process, for a while, at least. But a time comes when we need to move beyond anger, for we can't build a positive future from a stance of ongoing negativity – we need to light and carry that candle.

Moreover, from the perspective of spiritual laws and the concept that we all help create reality through what we think, believe and wish for as well as through what we do, any positive changes that we make individually will also help to improve the whole world. As Taylor (2005) puts it: "If we make a conscious effort to move towards a trans-Fall psyche, it will become easier for other people to do the same, as the 'morphic resonance' for the psyche builds up."

Creating a New Partnership World: What We Can Do

So what *can* we do to help move the world towards this possible future? How can we steer our whole culture towards one where more partnership values prevail, and where physical and psychological unscrewed-upness is the norm? I reiterate my belief that, in order to do this, there needs to be a mass, grassroots change of consciousness towards one that accepts the need for partnership ways of living and wants to actively work towards bringing this change about. We can all do our bit to help the process along, and here are some suggestions.

Action List

- Let's never forget that we evolved as species which, for maybe two million years, lived in an **egalitarian**, **cooperative**, kind, trusting, peaceful way. The more we **aim for and emulate those good qualities** now, the more of that prosocial positivity we will put out into our modern world, which needs it so much.
- **Happiness** is our natural state: it's a valid aim to want to be happy, so let's have as much fun as we can, and lots of laughs.
- We may not be able to **undo** all the **harm** that dominator life has inflicted on us, but let's do our best to unpick what we can.
- I can't help thinking that one key to our dilemma lies in attempting to regain the hunter-gatherer's ability to **wholeheartedly trust** that the world is *literally* a magical place that is designed to provide us with all we need if we treat it right and are good (unscrewed up) people ourselves. Let's try to regain that trust and unscrewed-upness.
- **Bring up children in as continuum a way** as we can, with

abundant love and physical affection.

- Try to **avoid toxic influences** (emotional and psychological as well as physical), and work to make our life and the world as wholesome and natural as possible.
- **Don't subscribe to dominator views of the world!** We don't need to listen to the news, with its constant hypnotic message that things *have* to be this bad because humans are innately aggressive and competitive. Turn it off!
- **Spread the word** about our partnership past. Challenge the dominator world view; refuse to forget or disbelieve that an alternative is possible. We probably can't go back to prehistoric-style partnership societies, or create artificial hunter-gatherer societies, so we need to create something new. But the first step is surely to remind the world that an alternative existed and worked well for hundreds of thousands of years in the past.
- Let's therefore strive to get these facts **taught** properly **in schools**. We need school-level anthropology, and history taught from a Kropotkin point of view. And let's get the partnership story made into documentaries on television, movies for the big screen, a best-seller of *Celestine Prophecy* proportions…

Overall, then, let's have faith that the New Jerusalem or Heaven on Earth is possible, and work towards achieving that. Or – to use Steve Taylor's words which close his Introduction to *The Fall*: "If there's just one thing that you, the reader, take away from these chapters I hope it's the idea that *it doesn't have to be like this.*" Amen to that! So let's misappropriate Sky TV's slogan and encourage each other to **'Believe in better'**!

References

Alton, Hilary, 1984. *Alternatives to Adoption*. hilaryalton@ntlworld.com

Alton, Hilary, 2011. *Matriarchy Really Did Exist*. Radical Anthropology Group Booklet, London. www.radicalanthropologygroup.org

Aron, Elaine N., 1999. *The Highly Sensitive Person*. Thorsons, New York

Bekoff, Marc, 2007. *The Emotional Lives of Animals: A Leading Scientist Explores Animal Joy, Sorrow, and Empathy – and Why They Matter*. New World Library, California

Bekoff, Marc and Pierce, Jessica, 2009. *Wild Justice: The Moral Lives of Animals*. The University of Chicago Press, Chicago

Boehm, Christopher, 1999. *Hierarchy in the Forest: The Evolution of Egalitarian Behavior*. Harvard University Press, Massachusetts

Borrow, George, 1851. *Lavengro*. John Murray, London

Briffault, Robert, 1927. *The Mothers*, Vol 1. Allen and Unwin, London

Brody, Hugh, 2001. *The Other Side of Eden*. Faber and Faber Ltd, London

Chilton Pearce, Joseph, 2007. "Birth and Bonding" *in* Robinson, Veronika Sophia, 2007. *The Drinks Are On Me*. Starflower Press, Penrith, Cumbria

Conrad, Jack, 2011. "When all the crap began". *Weekly Worker* 854, Feb 24 2011, Supplement Parts 1 and 2

Cremo, Michael A. and Thompson, Richard L., 1993. *Forbidden Archaeology*. Govardhan Hill Publishing, San Diego, California, USA

Crocker,William H. and Crocker, Jean G., 2004. *The Canela: Kinship, Ritual and Sex in an Amazonian Tribe*. Wadsworth/Thomson Learning, California

Dashu, Max, 2000. *Knocking Down Straw Dolls*. Beacon Press,

Boston. Republished 2005 in *Feminist Theology 13.2*, Sage Publications, UK

Douglas, Kate, 2001. "Painted ladies". *New Scientist*. 13 October

Duncan, Sarah, 2008. *A Single To Rome*. Headline Publishing Group, London

Eisler, Riane, 1987. *The Chalice and the Blade*. Harper & Row, San Francisco

Engels, Friedrich, 1884. *The Origin of the Family, Private Property and the State*. Published with a new introduction by Penguin Classics, London, 2010

Everett, Daniel, 2008. *Don't Sleep, There Are Snakes*. Profile Books Ltd, London

Finnegan, Morna, 2008/9. "Political bodies: some thoughts on women's power among Central African hunter-gatherers". *Radical Anthropology 3*

Gazzaniga, Michael, 2008. *Human: The Science Behind What Makes Your Brain Unique*. HarperCollins Publishers, New York

Gerhardt, Sue, 2004. *Why Love Matters: How Affection Shapes a Baby's Brain*. Routledge, Hove

Gimbutas, Marija, 1991. *The Civilisation of the Goddess: The World of Old Europe*. Thames and Hudson, London

Goleman, Daniel, 2006. *Social Intelligence*. Arrow Books, London

Gow, Peter, 2001. *An Amazonian Myth and Its History*. Oxford University Press, Oxford

Grandin, Temple and Johnson, Catherine, 2005. *Animals in Translation – The Woman Who Thinks Like a Cow*. Bloomsbury Publishing Plc, London

Griffin, Joe and Tyrrell, Ivan, 2004. *Dreaming Reality*. Human Givens Publishing Ltd, Chalvington, East Sussex

Haidt, Jonathan, 2006. *The Happiness Hypothesis: Putting Ancient Wisdom and Philosophy to the Test of Modern Science*. Arrow Books, London

Hamilton, Annette, 1981. *Nature and Nurture: Aboriginal child-rearing in north-central Arnhem Land*. Australian Institute of

Aboriginal Studies, Canberra
Hays-Gilpin, Kelley, and Whitley, David S. (eds.), 1998. *Reader in Gender Archaeology*. Routledge, London
Hewetson, John, 1946. *Mutual Aid and Social Evolution: Mutual Aid and the Social Significance of Darwinism*. Reproduced as introductory essay to the 1987 Freedom Press edition of Kropotkin's *Mutual Aid*
Hobbes, Thomas, 1651. *Leviathan*. 1996 Edition. Tuck, R. (ed.), Cambridge University Press, Cambridge
Hrdy, Sarah Blaffer, 1999. *Mother Nature: Natural Selection and the Female of the Species*. Chatto and Windus, London
Hrdy, Sarah Blaffer, 2009. *Mothers and Others: The Evolutionary Origins of Mutual Understanding*. The Belknap Press of Harvard University Press, Massachusetts
Hua, Cai, 2001. *A Society Without Fathers or Husbands: The Na of China*. Urzone Inc, NY, USA
Hutton, Ronald, 2001. *The Rise and Fall of Merry England: The Ritual Year 1400–1700*. Oxford Paperbacks, Oxford
Huxley, Aldous, 1928. *Point Counter Point*. Vintage, London
Isaacson, Rupert, 2009. *The Horse Boy*. Little, Brown and Company
James, Oliver, 2007. *Affluenza: How to be Successful and Stay Sane*. Vermilion, London
Jones, Terry, and Ereira, Alan, 2006. *Barbarians*. BBC Books, London
Jung, Carl G., 1963. *Memories, Dreams, Reflections*. Fontana Press, London
Knight, Chris, 1991. *Blood Relations*. Yale University Press, New Haven and London
Knight, Chris, 2008. "Early Human Kinship Was Matrilineal" *in* Allen, N. and Jones, W. (eds.), *Early Human Kinship*, Blackwell, Oxford
Kropotkin, Peter, *Mutual Aid: A Factor of Evolution*. First published 1902, William Heinemann, London. Unabridged

republication 2006, Dover Publications, Mineola, NY, USA

Lafitau, Robert Francois, 1724. "Moeurs Des Sauvages Ameriquaines Comparees

Aux Moeurs Des Premiers Temps", 2 vols. Paris. In Briffault, Robert, 1927. *The Mothers*, Vol 1. Macmillan, NY

Lawrence, D.H., 1960 [1928]. *Lady Chatterley's Lover*. Penguin Books, London

Layard, Richard, 2005. *Happiness: Lessons from a New Science*. Penguin Books, London

Lee, Richard B. and DeVore, Irven (eds.), 1968. *Man the Hunter*. Aldine Publishing Company, Chicago

Lee, Richard B., 1968. "What Hunters Do for a Living, or, How to Make Out on Scarce Resources". In Lee, Richard B. and DeVore, Irven (eds.), 1968. *Man the Hunter*. Aldine Publishing Company, Chicago

Lee, Richard B., 1988. "Reflections on Primitive Communism" in *Hunters and*

Gatherers: Vol 1. Ingold, Tim; Riches, David and Woodburn, James (eds.). Berg Publishers Ltd, New York/Oxford

Lewis, Jerome, 2002. *Forest Hunter-Gatherers and Their World: A Study of the Mbendjele Yaka Pygmies of Congo-Brazzaville and Their Secular and Religious Activities and Representations*. PhD Thesis for Department of Social Anthropology, London School of Economics and Political Science

Lewis, Jerome, 2008/9. "Managing abundance, not chasing scarcity: the real challenge for the 21st century". *Radical Anthropology, 2*

Liedloff, Jean, 1975. *The Continuum Concept*. Duckworth, London

McKenna, Terence, 1992. *Food of the Gods*. Random Century Group Ltd, London

Martin, Paul, 2005. *Making Happy People*. Harper Perennial, London

McDougall, Christopher, 2009. *Born to Run*. Profile Books Ltd, London

Morgan, Lewis Henry, 2000 [1877]. *Ancient Society*. With a new introduction by Robin Fox. Transaction Publishers, New Jersey

Morgan, Marlo, 1991. *Mutant Message Down Under*. HarperCollins Publishers, Inc, NY

Muir, Charles and Caroline, 1989. *Tantra: The Art of Conscious Loving*. Mercury House, San Francisco, USA

Norberg-Hodge, Helena, 1991. *Ancient Futures: Learning from Ladakh*. Sierra Club Books, USA

O'Callaghan, Chris, 2004. *Newgrange: Temple to Life*. Mercier Press, Cork, Ireland

Osho, 2008. *Meetings with Remarkable People*. Watkins Publishing, London

Ouspensky, P.D., 1950. *In Search of the Miraculous*. Routledge and Kegan Paul, London

Palmer, Sue, 2006. *Toxic Childhood: How the Modern World is Damaging Our Children and What We Can Do About It*. Orion, London

Parry, Bruce, 2007. *Tribe: Adventures in a Changing World*. Penguin Group, London

Perel, Esther, 2006. *Mating in Captivity*. HarperCollins Publishing, USA

Pinker, Stephen, 1998. *How the Mind Works*. Duckworth, London

Redfield, James, 1993. *The Celestine Prophecy*. Bantam, London

Roberts, Alice, 2010. *Digging for Britain*. BBC2 TV, UK, 26 August 2010

Root, Tim, 2005. *Love, Empowerment and Social Justice*. Open Gate Press, London

Rudgley, Richard, 1998. *Lost Civilisations of the Stone Age*. Arrow Books Limited, London

Sahlins, Marshall, 1968. "The Original Affluent Society" in Lee, Richard B. and DeVore, Irven (eds.) *Man the Hunter*. Aldine Publishing Company, Chicago

Seligman, Martin, 2003. *Authentic Happiness*. Nicholas Brealey,

London
Shuttle, Penelope and Redgrove, Peter, 1978. *The Wise Wound*. Victor Gollancz, London
Sims, Lionel, 2006. "The 'Solarization' of the moon: Manipulated Knowledge at Stonehenge". *Cambridge Archaeological Journal* 16:2
Smail, David, 1993. *The Nature of Unhappiness*. Constable Publishers, London
Solway, Jacqueline (ed.), 2006. *The Politics of Egalitarianism*. Bergahn Books, New York and Oxford
Stone, Merlin, 1976. *The Paradise Papers: The Suppression of Women's Rites*. Virago Ltd, London
Stourton, Edward, 2008. *It's a PC World: What it Means to Live in a World Gone Politically Correct*. Hodder and Stoughton, London
Taylor, Steve, 2005. *The Fall*. O Books, Ropley, Hants, UK
Taylor, Steve, 2009. "Beyond the Pre/Trans Fallacy: The Validity of Pre-Egoic Spiritual Experience". *The Journal of Transpersonal Psychology*, 41, 1
Thoreau, Henry D., 1960 [1854]. *Walden or Life in the Woods*. Dolphin Books, NY
Tolle, Eckhart, 1997. *The Power of Now*. New World Library, Canada
Trees, Andrew, 2009. *Decoding Love*. Hay House UK Ltd, London
Turnbull, Colin, 1961. *The Forest People*. Chatto and Windus, London
Turnbull, Colin, 1968. "The Importance of Flux in Two Hunting Systems". In Lee, Richard B. and DeVore, Irven (eds.) *Man the Hunter*. Aldine Publishing Company, Chicago
Weatherford, Jack, 1988. *Indian Givers*. Ballantine Books, NY
Wilkinson, Roy, 1993. *Rudolf Steiner: Aspects of his Spiritual World-View, Volume 1*. Temple Lodge Publishing, London
Woodburn, James, 1981. *Egalitarian Societies*. Malinowski Memorial Lecture, London School of Economics and Political

Science

Woodburn, James, 2005. "Egalitarian Societies Revisited" in Widlok, Thomas and Tadesse, Wolde Gossa (eds.) *Property and Equality, Vol 1: Ritualisation, Sharing, Egalitarianism*. Berghahn Books, Oxford/New York

Wrangham, Richard, 2009. *Catching Fire*. Profile Books Ltd, London

Wright, Rita P. (ed.), 1996. *Gender and Archaeology*. University of Pennsylvania Press, Philadelphia, USA

Young, Cori, 2009. *The Science of Mother Love*. In www.touchthe-future.com, newsletter of James W. Prescott

Zerzan, John, 2002. *Running on Emptiness: The Pathology of Civilization*. Feral House, Los Angeles

About the Author

Suki Pryce is a former university lecturer with a lifelong interest in hunter-gatherers, mind-body-spirit matters, and what simpler cultures have to teach us today. She has been carrying out research on this book since 2003. She lives in north Norfolk, UK.

Acknowledgements

My main thanks go to Chris Knight, and Hilary Alton. Chris read the first and last draft of this book, introduced me to a host of essential sources, and gave me the continuing guidance needed to change it from a well-meaning but naïve submission into something far more substantial. Hilary has been my most sympathetic and encouraging reader, and also a wonderful source of unusual and hard-to-obtain references which have added immeasurably to the book's strength. Many, many thanks to both of you.

Thanks also to Iain Manson who kindly commented on an early draft; to Sue Curran for invaluable advice on electronic copy-editing; and to Veronika Sophia Robinson, whose enthusiasm about a 2008 article I wrote for *The Mother* magazine on this book's topic encouraged me to take the subject further. My gratitude also to the authors of the sources I've used, whose works have led me along a fascinating path of discovery and have opened my eyes to new ways of seeing the world. Finally, heartfelt thanks to O-Books for taking me on as an author.